I.A.M.

I.A.M.*

A COMMON SENSE GUIDE TO COPING WITH ANGER

MELVYN L. FEIN

*INTEGRATED ANGER MANAGEMENT

PRAEGER

Westport, Connecticut
London

Library of Congress Cataloging-in-Publication Data

Fein, Melvyn L.
    I.A.M. : a common sense guide to coping with anger / Melvyn L.
Fein.
      p. cm.
    Includes bibliographical references and index.
    ISBN 0–275–94773–4 (alk. paper).—ISBN 0–275–94244–9 (pbk. :
alk. paper)
    1. Anger. I. Title. II. Title: IAM. III. Title: Integrated
anger management.
    BF575.A5F45 1993
    152.4′7—dc20   92–46556

British Library Cataloguing in Publication Data is available.

Library of Congress Catalog Card Number: 92–46556
ISBN: 0–275–94773–4
      0–275–94244–9 (pbk.)

First published in 1993

Praeger Publishers, 88 Post Road West, Westport, CT 06881
An imprint of Greenwood Publishing Group, Inc.

Printed in the United States of America

The paper used in this book complies with the
Permanent Paper Standard issued by the National
Information Standards Organization (Z39.48–1984).

10 9 8 7 6 5 4 3 2 1

To my father,
for the good,
and the bad.

Contents

Preface

Although it may not be written in a very personal style, this is a very personal book. It chronicles decades of discovery and disillusionment. Anger has long been a problem for me, as it was for my father before me. It is an emotion that I have both experienced and hated. Over the years it has cost me a great deal of pain and denied me much happiness. What follows is a distillation of what I have learned, and I proffer it in the hope that it may save others from some of the grief I have had to endure.

Perhaps I had best begin by explaining that my father was a very angry man. Even on his death bed, his teeth were clenched in rage and fury gurgled up through his throat. He hated the agony of dying, but his anger was so constant that he could not peaceably loosen his grip on life. Not long before he died, I sat by his side while he grasped my arm with all his remaining strength. I felt then, and I feel now, that he was imploring me to finish work that he had left undone. And as I looked into his eyes, I promised him that I would. Part of what I had in mind was solving the riddle of his anger. How could it have been controlled? What might he have done differently?

Despite the intensity and pervasiveness of his rage, my father was deeply troubled by his anger. It was always with him, but he detested the fact that sometimes he could not control it. I remember him chasing me about when I was a small boy and trapping me under his bed or in the corner by the front hallway. His eyes seemed to bulge out of their sockets, and his temples rhythmically throbbed, as he vowed he would kill me unless I immediately did his bidding. I could also see that his fists were clenched, not in preparation to beat me, but in an effort to regain his composure. He did not want to hit his first-born son, and his body trembled as he fought with himself not to lash out. In fact, he rarely did; and though when he beat me I knew he meant business, he never inflicted real physical damage. My derriere might pulsate in pain, but he never came close to breaking a bone or puncturing my skin.

Nevertheless, I was terrified. I could see in his eyes what he thought himself on the verge of doing. I also knew that I was motivated to confront him. Inside my heart I ached to resist. When I was very young, I did throw tantrums in which I rolled around on the floor and screamed out my defiance; but as I grew older and his blows grew heavier, I learned to suppress the impulse. I knew, or I thought I knew, that if I pushed him too far, he would do something both of us would regret. Instead I sought to quash my feelings and desire nothing. My strategy was to avoid a confrontation by not challenging him. The hope was that if I did not openly refuse or visibly contradict him, his explosiveness might subside.

Here I must interject a word about my mother's attitude toward anger. In contrast to my father, she never felt there was a suitable occasion to express anger. A confirmed "peace-maker," she believed in being "nice." Two of her favorite admonitions were: "It takes two to fight" and "Someone has to be reasonable." As her favorite child, I knew that these were meant to be especially applicable to me. What my mother never told me—and probably never allowed herself to realize—is that reasonableness is not always reciprocated and that it only takes one to commit a massacre. Rather, she sought to reinforce my guilt about wanting to resist my father. After all, he only reacted as he did for my "own good."

As the years passed, many people came to think of me as a very mild-mannered person. My voice was soft and my requests few. Rather, I buried myself in books and had fantasies about being a warrior on horseback. I could visualize myself sweeping out of the Russian steppe, sword in hand, conquering vast swathes of territory through my audacity and clever planning. In the eyes of others, I might be a negligible commodity, but I was biding my time, waiting for adulthood, so that I could march forth to reform the world. About the only kind of external passion I allowed myself was of the intellectual variety, for it was relatively simple to control.

When I arrived at my majority, I was in for a rude awakening. Whether in college or in the world of work, I found that people were often neither fair nor rational. Nor were they were awaiting my leadership to shepherd them into the utopias of which I had dreamt. What was worse, I was no more comfortable confronting them than I had been in confronting my father. I was still sitting in my reading chair fantasizing about some distant and fabled future. Indeed, my experimentation with intimate relationships convinced me that I was vulnerable to manipulation in just the area where I might have hoped for support. If I could not stand up to the anger of a woman, what likelihood was there that could I manage the long-term consequences of marriage or children?

It was at this juncture that I realized I needed help and sought the intervention of a psychotherapist. The woman with whom I worked was very gentle and very supportive, but was also sufficiently confrontive to make me aware of the rage buried in my chest. She encouraged me to express my feelings and urged me to be more assertive. Naturally I found it difficult to do either. It still seemed to me that the full fury of my anger was too powerful for anyone to withstand, including a professional helper.

As the years passed and I became a clinician myself, anger remained a conundrum. Periodically I returned to it to investigate new modes of expression or new forms of self-assertion. I listened to and read about practitioners of every stripe. But psychoanalysts, cognitive therapists, and rational-emotive therapists all advocated different strategies. At their behest I lashed out at punching bags, screamed my rage from the window of my automobile, and directly (and I thought persuasively) challenged my superiors at work. Somehow, none of this seemed to work. The world did not change, and I did not feel better. Instead, I found myself alternatively engaged in interminable battles, fearing utter defeat, or lying exhausted on my couch, condemning myself for cowardice and/or laziness. Moreover, much of what I was trying to do made me feel obnoxious. The words I was urged to intone sounded simplistic and impolite. Something was definitely wrong.

Because reputable professionals were assuring me of the efficacy of their techniques, I assumed that what was wrong somehow had to do with me. Evidently I was so flawed as a human being that methods that were valid for others were not useful for me. It was not until I had a great deal of practice working with angry clients at a methadone program, a mental hospital, and a community mental health center that I realized the prescribed methods were not working for them either. Perhaps, just perhaps, it was the methods that were flawed.

I also had the advantage of being a clinical sociologist. This discipline made it possible for me to look at anger from other than the standard psychological or medical perspectives. In particular, it made it possible to perceive that the emotion had social consequences and to realize that it was functional, not merely expressive. Once I noticed that overcoming frustration was what made anger dissipate, a whole new universe opened up. It became evident that interpersonal influence was key and that using this influence effectively was dependent on social variables. As a sociologist, I could not dismiss such factors as social class, which turned out to make an enormous difference.

Slowly, over a period of a decade and a half, I experimented with myself and my clients. I engaged in providing therapy, held workshops, and gave talks both to professionals and to laymen. Gradually the outlines of integrated anger management emerged. I could see that others had not been wrong, but merely incomplete. What was most gratifying was that my new ideas were helping people. With myself and with my clients, they made things happen that hadn't happened before. These new techniques—or, more properly, clarified techniques—were converting a negative into something very positive by treating it for what it really was. As a high school student, I had learned that science was supposed to work by measuring its hunches against the real world, and here was the world telling me my hypotheses were correct. This was very comforting. It meant that I wasn't crazy and, as important, that my father hadn't been crazy either.

Also enormously gratifying was the reaction of laymen when I described integrated anger management to them. Almost universally the reaction was, "But, of course." My ideas did not seem exotic, but more like an explication of what people already knew. Once enunciated, these ideas seemed no more than common sense; and if, in fact, we are all socialized to use anger, that reaction is understandable. The way anger works should seem obvious because on a certain level we are all experts at using anger. If we were not, we would suffer dramatically at the hands of others. The difficulty is that in using anger we learn to fool ourselves and our role partners. We are not consciously aware of what we are doing. We just do it.

The reader is now invited to judge whether or not the following system accords with his or her personal experience. The validity of any method is to be found in whether it achieves what it says it can. Can anger actually be used to make the world better for the individual or society? Does anger dissipate when its underlying goals are achieved? Does interpersonal influence help accomplish this end?

Before I conclude this preface I must briefly acknowledge some of the many people who have helped me learn about anger. Of these I must begin with my father, to whom this book is dedicated. He taught me not only through his negative example but also through his tenacity and his fierce devotion to honesty and morality. I deeply regret that he is unable to read this book. Next come the hundreds of clients with whom I have worked over the years. Although none of them is personally acknowledged in the text, the omission reflects only my desire to avoid intruding upon their privacy, not their lack of input. Had they not been generous enough to open their lives to me, I could never have learned much of what appears on these pages.

On a more specific level, I wish to thank Dr. Louise Bill of Kennesaw State College. Her patient review of my manuscript, though not always in agreement with it, has provided me with invaluable insights. I must also personally recognize the contributions of Margaret Balconi of Rochester ARC and Jean Kaidy, formerly of Rochester Psychiatric Center. Had Margaret not encouraged me to pursue my ideas about anger and provided me some initial opportunities for committing them to paper, I might never have started this project. Had Jean not participated as a co-counselor in my first workshops on anger, I might never have had the courage to persevere. Finally, I must mention my other colleagues and students at Kennesaw State college. They—which includes Dr. Barbara Karcher, Dr. Vassili Economopoulous, Dr. Lana Wachniak, Dr. Willoughby Jarrell and Martha Boyd—have had the patience to endure being used as sounding-boards and have provided me with feedback that has, I hope, kept me in touch with reality.

I.A.M.

1

A Difficult Emotion

DANGEROUS, BUT UNAVOIDABLE

Roger was acknowledged by all to be an angry young man. In the substance abuse program he attended, he stood out as more violent and quick tempered than his pugnacious peers. If approached by others from an unexpected quarter, he would whirl around brandishing a huge walking-staff as a weapon. His eyes would flash out his hatred, and his muscles tense for action. If caught totally off guard, he had been known to pummel an innocent friend. In consequence, most people gave him a wide berth; certainly, they did not approach him from the rear. Nor was he much in demand as a friend. Even staff members dealt with him reluctantly, for they knew they were not immune to his wrath.

Although Roger hardly ever spoke about himself, he did reveal to his counselor that his had not been a happy childhood. According to him, his parents were not very supportive, if not abusive. His major complaint was that they were never there when he needed them. Now that he was nearing thirty years of age and thinking of establishing a family, he found himself still wishing for their advice and comfort. One day Roger came in and announced that he had a plan. He would visit his parents, who were living across the country, and attempt a reconciliation with them. His hope was that, if he could solidify a relationship with them, he might become less angry and more capable of being a loving husband and father.

When Roger returned from his trip, he immediately went to see his counselor. He related how the visit had degenerated into a series of acrimonious arguments, which were terminated only by his leaving ahead of schedule. Now he didn't know what to do. He was beside himself with anger, and there seemed to be no outlet for it. When his counselor questioned him about his feelings, Roger declined to say anymore, indicating that doing so might make him feel worse. He then thanked the counselor and agreed to return the next day. The following day, however, he did not return; nor the next, or the next. Three days later the counselor read in the newspaper that Roger had gone home and calmly shot his pregnant girlfriend to death, before turning his shotgun on himself. Now it was the counselor's turn to be distraught. What could he have done to preclude so horrible an outcome? Was Roger's anger controllable, or was it a force of nature to be endured and lamented, but not deterred?

Jenny was trying to be a good wife and mother. Yet everything she touched seemed to turn out badly. The hours she spent preparing meals for her family went unappreciated, as did her efforts to help her children with their homework or her husband with his job. Instead of thanking her, everyone seemed to take her for granted.

As a child, it had been Jenny's responsibility to care for her invalid mother. Although at times she suspected that her mother's constant calls for attention were more the product of a desire to be special than a result of her illness, she dared not express this thought aloud. To do so would have vexed her father considerably. He was a high government official whose duties during World War II required him to spend much of his time away from home. The last thing he wanted was an unhappy wife or an eldest daughter who couldn't keep the household running without detailed instructions.

When she contemplated her own marriage, Jenny had fantasized a loving husband who would honor her as her mother had been honored and children who would be close to her in a way that had not been possible with her own parents. But now that she was a wife and mother, everyone spurned her attentions. Her husband and daughters seemed to have no use for her except as a servant. In times of crisis they might reach out, but ordinarily they didn't even want to sit down and speak to her. Though this seemed incredibly unfair, she choked down her bitterness and tried to persevere. As far as she was concerned, she was not angry. Yes, she had complaints; yes, she sometimes felt empty and sad; but anger was a mean-spirited emotion felt only by unloving people. It was simply not in her lexicon. Even when she discovered that her husband had been cheating on her, she was angry more at herself than at him.

Some people seem to explode very easily, while others have a fuse that never gets lit. Some say and do too much, while others apparently react too little. The first sort of person often makes others suffer grievously; the second typically casts himself in the role of victim. Either way terrible things can happen. Anger is a dangerous and difficult emotion, one that can be uncomfortable to feel and a challenge to manage. Most of us hate to experience it. We find it both frightening and confusing; and we fear that should it go out of control, it will cause serious repercussions. Even helping professionals find it a conundrum. They know they must assist clients to deal with anger; but because it is so unpredictable and difficult, their techniques often fail to work.

Yet we all know that we will and must get angry. The world gives none of us a special dispensation to live free of conflict. So what are we to do? What is the best way to be angry? Are there methods for managing the emotion that can serve our purposes without causing further distress?

Anger can be a problem in its own right and an impediment to the achievement of other ends. Whether it is under-controlled or over-controlled, it can be oppressively painful to experience or to endure. It is a violent emotion that can set our teeth to gnashing and pound upon our heads or those of our victims. As all of us are aware, people in its grip do things they would otherwise abhor. Sometimes they behave in a fashion ordinarily considered crazy. In their own eyes and those of their targets, they become red-eyed monsters, unfit for civilized society.

Excessive anger likewise interferes with the achievement of crucial goals. In addition to its churlish instability, it often prevents vital circumstances from unfolding. First, when anger goes out of control, it can block others from cooperating with us. Instead of sympathizing they become furious at our barbarous stupidity and attempt to deny us important satisfactions. Because our irrational outbursts and sullen intransigence undermine mutual trust, productive interactions become virtually impossible. Second, intemperate anger can impair our competence in pursuing success. It can render us inept, preventing a full utilization of our talents. Furious people are often so full of rage that they see little else and stumble along until they run into a barrier. They fail to understand what is in their interest, and they neglect to use their energies in ways calculated to effect desirable results. Should a dangerously angry person command a position of authority, he can seriously interfere with the happiness of others. If sufficiently influential, he can destroy the effectiveness of a whole organization. Third, rage forms an obstacle to personal change. When someone is trapped in a losing situation, his anger can keep him there. Ferociously angry people are motivated to keep fighting for lost causes and don't make the adjustments necessary to overcome their abiding difficulties. In consequence, they remain miserable, perpetually sabotaging themselves.

As must be clear, anger is not "nice." In the best of circumstances it hurts people, and it feels atrocious. It is, however, necessary. Although it may be unfair and frightening, anger is unavoidable. Those who elect to ignore their anger will pay a horrific penalty. In fact, people must accept both its not-niceness and its necessity. All of us must understand that anger is not namby-pamby. Partly it works by scaring people, and partly by manipulating them. Implementing the emotion with only a forthright smile can rob it of its clout. As we shall see, anger is a hammer, and sometimes hammers smash things. Sometimes that's their job.

No one can abstain from anger. If it is not used by us, it will surely be used against us. If allowed to, others will use it to beat us into submission, thereby forcing us to become perpetual losers. Unless we are willing to accept such a fate, we must be able to resist. This means that we must sometimes be prepared to meet force with a counterforce. Doing so will inform potential adversaries that they face a fight and perhaps should reconsider their demands. Anger also enables us to fight for what we need. It energizes our efforts to obtain necessities. Without it, we would be exposed to the vicissitudes of an often unmerciful Providence. Getting what we need would then depend on luck. In contrast, anger allows us to take charge of our destinies and to make things happen in accord with our wishes. It helps us give the world a push in directions of our choosing. Lacking anger, we would be the ones getting pushed.

Still, anger can go wrong. It becomes problematic when it (1) gets out of control and inflicts injury on others, (2) is turned inward and inflicts damage on ourselves, or (3) is so ineffectual that it does not achieve the goals it is intended to serve. These three possibilities, namely, out-of-control anger, over-controlled anger, and ineffectual anger, form a troika of infamy.

Out-of-control anger feasts on fantasy. It is juvenile, besotted with delusions of grandeur. Such anger is so intoxicated with its own intensity that, when it tries to break down walls, it fails to notice that they may fall on people. Being totally fixated on a particular goal, it is utterly unconcerned with the collateral damage it causes and can literally be fatal. When completely out of control, anger becomes rage. It turns violent and stupid and must be disciplined before being permitted to roam free. We are all familiar with this sort of anger. Its fury perpetually tries to shout others down; it has a knife in its hand ready to slash out at the slightest provocation.

Over-controlled anger specializes in prohibitions and guilt. Rather than allowing those who experience it to encroach on the territory of others, it places them in a private prison. Over-controlled anger is intent on *not* doing things. If, in order to achieve this end, it must berate and punish a person, it will. Self-injury is discounted or even considered a virtue and may be carried to disquieting lengths. Over-controlled people are tight-lipped and apparently passive, but on the inside they ache with unfulfilled wishes. Coolness and indifference mask an often violent internal struggle.

Ineffectual anger trips over its own feet. Though it has no desire to injure anyone, it just can't seem to get out of its own way. With the best of intentions, it acts in an uncoordinated fashion and collides with the aspirations of others. Most likely it winds up sputtering in impotence, unable to understand what has gone wrong. Ineffectively angry people don't know which buttons to push. Where they should be assertive, they whine; where they need to be modest, they boast. This sort of anger tries and fails, then tries again, only to subside in a soggy pile of frustration and self-pity. It is more sad than dangerous.

Whether manifested in outbursts, bitterness, resentment, conflict, or misery, problem anger is an emotion that has not been mastered. It can literally pick people up, toss them around, and fling them to the ground. It engulfs everything in reach, setting the tone of a person's life and those of everyone around him. Few of us enjoy this sort of anger, but many of us do not know how to escape it.

Anger is uncomfortable for very good reasons. Whatever else may be said about it, it is unkempt and uncivilized. At full cry, it is also undignified and unreflective. Indeed, many northern European cultures have tried to consign it to oblivion. The British, for instance, recommend a stiff upper lip. However disturbed, a person is not supposed to show any feeling. To do so would be shameful and a sign of weakness. The Scandinavian brethren of the English are more likely to express their indignation in passionate outbursts, but strictly in private; they keep it within the family, so to speak. Since they perceive rage to be potentially dangerous, reputable people suppress it as long as possible and then release it only in the safest of environments.

We must look to southern and eastern Europeans for a more spontaneous attitude toward intense anger. Southern Italians, for example, are noted for the loudness of their arguments and the openness of their gesticulations. A true paisan will tell another precisely what he thinks, and do so with gusto. Yet he too may be uneasy, for he knows that anger can lead to vendettas in which people get dreadfully hurt. Russians, who also view themselves as a passionate people, have historically believed their despotic governments a necessary curb on their anarchic tendencies. They have perceived themselves in Dostoyevskian terms, namely, as burning with zeal but too unsophisticated to know how to handle it.

In the United States, we tend to be more ambivalent about our anger. As heirs to an English tradition, the emotion is not regarded as totally reputable; but as hosts to many other traditions, we try to be more tolerant. Perhaps as importantly, living in the land of the raw-boned frontiersman, we pride ourselves on a forthright directness. Real Americans are supposed to say what they think, at least men are, and to express themselves in ways that cannot be mistaken. If this means doing so angrily, then anger must be accepted.

WHAT IS ANGER?

There are many theories about the nature of anger. People have long questioned what it is, how it works, and what should be done with it. Many of their answers, however, have tended to be simplified and/or mistaken. For the most part the emotion has been viewed as nasty and violent, better extirpated than experienced. Consequently, as important and widespread as anger is, commentators have usually shied away from taking too close a look at it. Instead of appraising anger with a cool and steady eye, they have sought to contain rather than to understand it. As the psychologist George Bach has observed (Bach & Wyden, 1968), most people seem to have what amounts to a phobia concerning it. They act as if they were afraid of it. Despite misgivings, however, anger must be managed; and to be managed, it must be understood. We must pierce its contradictions and thrust aside the cant surrounding it. No matter how uncomfortable this endeavor, we must not settle for pious platitudes or scientific distortions.

Although many hypotheses have been offered to explain anger, none is universally accepted. Because the emotion is uncomfortable, it is difficult to scrutinize. People have been able to convince themselves that it is many incompatible things. Anger thus has functioned almost like a Rorschach test: People see in it what they hope to see. Though many true things have been said about anger, most explanations are incomplete. Indeed, some make it sound as if anger were a simple phenomenon, easily grasped and as easily manipulated. Express it or don't express it; be direct or be tactful—the solution is one or the other.

What then is this mysterious emotion that is so hard to pin down and so difficult to make work? One common answer is that it is a manifestation of our innate "aggression." In this view, anger is instinctive to our species: a baleful legacy of our animalistic past that is buried deep in our psyches and given to periodic violent flare-ups. We human beings are portrayed as vicious carnivores who revel in creating injury and disarray. Some say we are primitive hunters who take such pleasure in the chase that we can't help but extend it to everyday life. When not required to kill for food, we kill for sport. Our blood lust is so potent that, when hunting opportunities are insufficient, we precipitate wars in which our fellow human beings serve as the prey. According to this perspective, anger is but an emblem of aggression. It is both an inward and an outward sign of a need to inflict harm, the visible aspect of an internal engine that drives us toward crime and debasement.

Given such a vision, it seems obvious that the only way to control anger is to eliminate it. As an outmoded patrimony of our brutish past, it can safely be dispensed with in a postindustrial era where rationality, not passion, must reign. If anger belongs to the part of our brains we share with the crocodile, it should be overridden by our frontal lobes; in other words, anger must be quashed. This view is a venerable one, going back at least as far as the Christian fathers. For the doctors of the Church, anger was sinful, a sign of the devil's presence on earth. Perhaps its energy might be used to oppose evil, but the ideal was to contemplate the glory of God in peace and repose. Another classic expression of this attitude is found in the writings of Thomas Hobbes. This celebrated British philosopher described human beings as basically selfish warriors who, left to their own devices, would engage in a perpetual war of all against all; the result of which would be a life that was "nasty, brutish, and short" for all concerned. His solution to this dilemma was for a sovereign to impose his greater power and compel people to be nonviolent.

A century after Hobbes, across the channel in France, Jean-Jacques Rousseau turned these views upside down. He too noted the viciousness of human society but, instead of ascribing it to an instinctive human aggressiveness, blamed society itself for teaching people to be brutal. In a state of nature, Rousseau reasoned, we are basically gentle and kind. As fundamentally noble savages, our anger is activated by iniquitous social arrangements. The emotion itself is therefore not a problem; rather, the problem lies in the environmental constraints used to control it. Change these, make life more equitable, and no one will have cause to be angry.

In raising this possibility, Rousseau introduced what is today recognized as the nature/nurture controversy. Hobbes and the Christian fathers had both implicated human nature as the source of problem anger. According to them, we are born with it and have difficulty controlling it without the assistance of an outside agency such as the government or the church. Aggression is thus portrayed as an ineluctable fact. It can be confined, but cannot be made to disappear. Rousseau, however, blamed "nurture." To him, people are born pure. If they are subsequently corrupted, this is attributable to the way they are brought up or the way they are ruled. Change either of these, and we will all become mild and loving. Anger is thus not inevitable, but a reaction to an impure world.

In our own century, this debate has not flagged. Contemporary scientists continue to dispute whether people are inherently aggressive or merely the victims of an imperfect society. Both camps now use scientific evidence to bolster their cases, though neither has been able to claim a definitive victory. One of the most noteworthy parties to this controversy has been the towering figure of Sigmund Freud. Coming down squarely in the middle of the quarrel, at different stages of his career he presented evidence favorable to both sides. As the man who discovered the vicissitudes of the Oedipus complex and the discontents of civilization, he was aware of how social institutions, including the family and state, can cast a shadow on the tranquility of the individual. Likewise, as the popularizer of the *libido* and the *death instinct*, he detected an instinctive element in all human affairs. Freud noted that people seem to have a need to injure themselves and others, that they are constantly repeating timeworn mistakes. For him, both individuals and their role partners are a source of irrationality, and thus capable of great harm.

It is also to Freud that we owe the classic statement of what has come to be called the *hydraulic theory* of instinct. He envisioned libido, otherwise known as "sexual energy," as a fluid-like substance that gradually builds up inside a person until it can find a suitable release. In this view, anger also builds up inside people. As a standard part of our human equipment, it must be expressed in a controlled fashion, or it will accumulate to levels where it can explode. The prescription for excessive anger is therefore to open a safety valve and gradually lower the pressure. The idea is to be moderately angry so that one won't have to become dangerously so. This theory, seductive in its simplicity, provides the rationale for *catharsis*. It proposes that an open expression of anger is positive because it cleanses the soul. Indeed, this proposition has dominated recent discussions of anger management. Almost everyone seeking to address the subject seems to be aligned either for or against it.

It should also be noted that this dispute retains the moralistic edge it had in the days of Christ, and of Hobbes and Rousseau. Anger and its expression are still described as either good or bad. The very term "aggression" is symptomatic of this tendency. It implies that when people get angry, they intend to cause pain or injury. Clearly, if this is so, infuriated people are engaged in a dangerous activity that must be stopped, through social sanctions if necessary. Similarly, advocates who view anger as "natural" prefer that its release be encouraged. For them, an open appearance of anger solves more problems than it creates. It does not cause harm; rather, it "clears the air" and "gets things off a person's chest."

In this dispute I am not entirely impartial. In the coming chapters, I will advocate a "functional" theory of anger. This theory too will make judgments about the emotion but, instead of accounting it merely good or evil, will portray it as facilitating—or failing to facilitate—the achievement of important personal or social objectives. Rather than attempting to reach an overall conclusion about its moral status, we will enquire into its "effectiveness." Anger will be understood as a tool for living, albeit one capable of producing great harm. Further, it will be depicted as inherently social and incapable of being divided into exclusively individual or exclusively social components. Anger sometimes accomplishes positive things and sometimes negative ones, yet these all occur within an interpersonal context. There is no fight between nature and nurture per se, merely an unfolding of nature within an unavoidably social milieu.

HOW SHOULD ANGER BE MANAGED?

Before we move on to explore how anger works, we must pause to examine some of the recommendations typically proffered by those seeking to manage it. These come from many sources, but have in common the view that anger is a problem to be handled, not a tool to be used. Historically there have been two major trends in anger management; one advises people to express the feeling, the other not to express it. As Albert Ellis has put the matter, "Some advise you to assume a passive non-resistant attitude when others treat you unfairly, . . . [while] a multitude of [experts] advise you to openly and freely give vent to and to express fully your feelings of anger and rage." This states the issue quite succinctly and, one might think, should open the way to nondichotomous thinking.

But one would be wrong. Even Ellis goes on to endorse one side of the equation. He advises his readers to reinterpret the affronts they receive from their role partners to no longer seem offensive. He tells us that if a friend promises to share an apartment and then defaults, we must recognize that he is entitled to change his mind and that thinking otherwise is patently selfish. We must realize that there is no need for us to get angry because there is no reason to. This, it should be clear, establishes Ellis as recommending the suppression of anger. He is not even handed, despite initially staking out neutral ground. From this and from similar performances by other experts, it appears that it is almost impossible not to fall into one camp or the other. It seems we must either be in favor of catharsis or against it, that there is no third alternative.

Because these two factions are so dominant, let us examine them in slightly greater detail. We can begin with the pro-catharsis school, which operates on the premise that, if suppressed anger is dangerous, expressed anger must be better. They tell us that the objective should be to inform others exactly what feelings are present and to be direct and forthright with them. Saying the worst out loud at least allows it to be worked on.

To mix metaphors, as the advocates of catharsis sometimes do, repressed anger acts like a toxin. Retained in the body, it poisons the spirit and damages organ systems. Unanswered transgressions committed against a person by others leave residues in the brain that pile one upon another until they form a critical mass that can bring psychological and physiological functions to a crashing halt. Obsessive hatred becomes the theme of a person's life, preventing positive action.

Obviously, lancing the wound would be a better course, for it would allow the poisons to flow out. Though not pleasant, release would limit the tissue damage. No longer would a person's bitterness compound itself, for the fetid matter would have an opportunity to dissipate. Of course, such a release has to be achieved carefully. Anger must be directed at those persons who have committed an offense, not at innocent bystanders. Even malefactors who merit our fury deserve to have it meted out in civilized doses. Although we may fantasize their destruction, it is not this, but an open expression of our ire that will bring relief.

Advocates of catharsis assure us that anger, while it can be dangerous, need not be. A person does not have to discharge fury all at once or overwhelmingly. Liberating it in modest, but honest, portions can be equally effective. The idea is to show how one feels, not to demolish the other person. This means being assertive, not aggressive. One should say what one thinks energetically, not viciously. Indeed, many therapeutic programs are founded on this strategy. Group therapy, in particular, features a "let it all hang out" mentality. "Feel what you're feeling" and "Tell the other person what you really think" have become anthems for a liberation of the spirit. Expressing one's feelings, including anger, has thus become a goal in its own right, uncritically accepted as a good to be sought and disseminated. Clients are counselled to take lessons acquired within the safety of the therapeutic hour and apply them everywhere. They are promised that channels of communication will then open up to improve their prospects for satisfactory living.

Yet anyone who has had a tyrannical boss will have reason to doubt this injunction. As Carol Tavris and others have pointed out, a mere expression of anger does not necessarily make things better. It can even make them profoundly worse. Angry words do not automatically clear the air or ease the spirit. He who gets angry at his boss generally finds his boss getting even angrier at him; he becomes the recipient of retribution rather than understanding. Likewise, he who screams out a car window or pounds on a hapless punching bag may, after a period of exhaustion, find his internal stress returning.

This world is not always fair. Expressing anger at a person, even at one who deserves it, even when it is carefully phrased, does not guarantee success. When directed toward someone with greater power, anger can invite disaster. It takes an especially wise and confident boss to suffer derogation at the hands of a subordinate. More commonly, the ground rules will stipulate that authority be respected. A boss may allow mistakes to be exposed from time to time, but permitting angry denunciations of oneself is virtually unknown. Anger toward authority is interpreted as insolence. In hierarchies, its expression usually moves down, not up. A subordinate who gets overtly angry can be crushed by an intimidating display of counter-anger from a superior. Indeed, the ability to make anger stick is one of the most salient marks of authority.

Even between equals, a display of anger can cause more trouble than it dispels. A role partner who is feeling vulnerable may feel compelled to protect his or her dignity rather than recognize the legitimacy of another's grievance. Openly declaring one's anger can lead to a fight rather than to a negotiation. Thus, friends, relatives, and spouses must be careful about what they say or do. The fact that people are on the same level and even love one another will not ensure that they don't trespass on each other's rights or sensitivities. Because others, including equals, both deserve and demand respect, anger cannot be used at any old time in any old way. Tact and responsiveness are required.

When anger is directed at a subordinate, the risk of unfairness escalates. Overwhelming power tends to court abuse. Many authority figures have underestimated the weight of their wrath and ground defenseless underlings into the dust. Despite any desire to be just, their emotions carry more of an impact than they realize. In fact, tyrants are often convinced they are fair and helpful. Although sometimes subordinates must be coerced, the possibility of inadvertent damage dictates caution. Too often, power is blind to the needs of others.

In sum, expressing anger is a tricky business, the outcome of which may not be the improved interpersonal relationships predicted by the catharsis model. Anger should not be ventilated indiscriminately, lest it create pain either for the person who expresses it or for those at whom it is aimed. Nor will a more private expression of rage always overcome this difficulty. Merely making sure that no one else is around when giving voice to fury is no warranty that it will subside. Someone who screams into his pillow at night may feel just as bad in the morning. Nor will a wife who has become unhinged upon learning of her husband's betrayal obtain relief just because she goes on a screaming jag. If her husband's infidelity is not addressed, her rage will soon mount to its former intensity. Those who are addicted to exercise as a release find themselves in a similar predicament. As long as they are engaged in an act of emotional discharge, they may not have the energy to be angry; but once their exhaustion has dissipated, their anger will reassert itself. Relying on a physical workout for comfort can thus lead either to an exercise addiction or to a shattering disillusionment.

Is the answer then the opposite of catharsis, namely, repression? Should we keep a stiff upper lip or attempt to merge with the cosmos? Must we clamp a firm control over our feelings and refuse to reveal them or dissolve in a haze of feelinglessness that completely obliterates our rage? Common sense tells us that if an emotion causes trouble, will-power should be used to prevent its expression or, better yet, its experience. Instead of being tight-lipped and hostile, we should try to be warm and altruistic. Dale Carnegie assured us that if we are pleasant with others, they will be pleasant in return. Why shouldn't the same apply to anger? Repress it and/or excise it, and others won't have a reason to be angry. We will thus have initiated a positive cycle in which non-anger generates a further reduction in anger. What's wrong with that?

Albert Ellis and the cognitivist psychologists offer a special case of this philosophy. Ellis, as he himself avows, is a follower of the Stoic tradition. For him, it is usually not rational to become angry. As he explains, in this world there are many problems about which we can do little and therefore we should learn to bear them with dignity. To scream in rage at the inevitable is merely self-indulgent. One may tell the world it "should" be a certain way, but the "should" is one's own invention, not a fact of nature. The reality is that when we don't get our way, we have a right to feel disappointed, not enraged. We may be sad that our friend has gone back on his word, but we should not get angry. This realization will save us from a great deal of pain, for as long as we are aware that it is our decision, we can decide not to be upset. Ellis claims that he opposes the repression of anger, but his version of anger management essentially recommends talking oneself out of the feeling. It denies the validity of anger, rather than forcing it into quiescence.

Cognitive psychologists take a similar tack. In their view, people get angry because they talk themselves into it. We are supposed to have an inner voice that tells us when we have been denied something essential. Often, however, this voice is deceptive and stimulates rage when there is nothing to get angry about. If, therefore, we can change our "self-talk," we can avoid creating anger. If we can just tell ourself that nothing terrible has transpired, that what appears to be an insult really is not, we will subsequently calm down.

Behavioral psychologists are even more direct in their assault on anger. For them, excessive emotion is simply a form of illogical conduct that can and should be retrained, because it reflects inappropriate social conditioning. If a person is given to angry outbursts, reinforcement schedules can be devised that will punish unacceptable acts and reward suitably mild behavior. This may mean delivering an electric shock when anger is shown or a warm smile when calm is manifested. In the end, the person's anger will be diverted in directions that cause no harm.

A version of behaviorism that has been especially crafted for dealing with anger is *assertiveness training*. In a sense, this approach harkens back to catharsis; yet it is catharsis with a difference. Assertiveness theory promotes an expression of anger, but indicates that some expressions are better than others and that the unworthy must be ruthlessly expunged. Specifically, assertiveness trainers divide expressions of anger into three categories: the passive, the assertive, and the aggressive. People in the first category are said to be insufficiently expressive. Instead of speaking up, they allow the world to proceed as it will. Passive people may sometimes be manipulative or resistant, but these tactics too are described as unproductive, that is, as creating enemies through obstructionism. The third category, aggression, is regarded as a form of excessive anger. Instead of modulating their attitudes, aggressive people act hurtfully and immoderately, creating foes by bashing others over the head. Only in the middle category, assertiveness, is a golden mean theoretically achieved. People in this category are neither too much nor too little angry. Rather, they are forthrightly direct in a manner calculated to realize their ends. Assertiveness is therefore the correct form of anger. Clients are instructed to behave in this fashion, for it is believed that if they do so, anger will cease to be a problem for them.

What then should a person do? Should he express or not express his anger? Should he be direct and open, or reasonable and reserved? Apparently there is much to recommend each approach and much to recommend against each. How then are we to choose? Indeed, do we need to choose? Perhaps there exists some other, preferable, option?

Fortunately, although assertiveness training and catharsis sound like opposite approaches, both can contribute to anger management. Indeed, the dichotomy between expressing and repressing anger turns out to be false. Both are necessary aspects of a larger process. They can be joined together to form a more inclusive enterprise better suited to controlling anger than either is alone. By itself each may have its drawbacks, but in concert they are remarkably effective. As we shall see, the real question is not whether to express or not to express, but how to use anger. We must ask ourselves how the emotion makes things happen, not whether it should be given voice.

Anger management also turns out to be a multistage process. It appropriates bits and pieces from many sources and integrates them into a harmonious whole that is more effective than its parts. As our intuition suggests, governing anger is a complex affair that varies in its particulars. How the process works depends on who is getting angry, what he or she is angry about, and how the social environment is arranged. All these factors must be considered before devising a program to control anger. Moreover, any satisfactory methodology must encompass the needs of people with a diversity of problems. It must prevent omnipresent rage from bursting forth into violence, uncover deeply buried furies, and provide counsel when a forthright direct-ness does not bring expected results. In order to work, it must be flexible and capable of adjusting to the specific case.

Despite their justified fears, when anger is properly understood, people will find that it is not something to be loathed or suppressed. But neither is it something to be celebrated and promiscuously dis-played. In itself, it is neither evil nor sacrosanct. Our object should be to turn it to advantage. To put the matter succinctly, people who wish to stop being angry must learn to win the game they are playing or to change it. Moreover, anger is an essential part of our social life. It is not an aberration. Without it, we would be very different crea-tures than we are, and not nearly as powerful. Contrary to its detrac-tors, the emotion of anger is not an obsolete legacy of our barbaric past, but a crucial element in the perpetuation of our kind. Rather than denounce it or convert it into a magical talisman, we must un-derstand and implement it with intelligence and scruples.

2

A Theory of Anger

A FUNCTIONAL EMOTION

Anger is no mere ornament; it is decidedly not a useless appendage derived from our primitive past. We do not become angry only because our remote ancestors were once hunters or because we are descended from lower animals. Rather, the emotion is an essential part of our tool-kit for living that has critical tasks to perform in the here and now. In fact, without its services, we would be unable to function as social creatures. Moreover, any person who is unable to get angry—or unable to do so effectively—is at an appalling disadvantage relative to his peers. He or she loses the possibility of equal relationships and will fail to have essential needs met.

In the original Star Trek television series, Mr. Spock represented the ideal of perfect rationality. He was not swayed by his passions, while his rival, Dr. McCoy, was a florid romantic whose heart bled in all the wrong places. We were invited to believe that Spock's logic was dependable in a crisis, while McCoy's confused sentimentality, although endearing, was less reliable. Usually, in a conflict between the two, Spock got the upper hand. The crew might tease him about his impassivity, but in a crunch they accorded him great respect. Indeed, he seemed the epitome of our more efficient future.

In contrast to this view, our emotions, and anger in particular, are indispensable for very practical reasons. In their own way they too are efficient and reliable. To be specific, they help us get things done that no other part of our biological equipment can. Even the Star Trek creators knew this. The utility, even necessity, of anger is nicely illustrated in an episode in which Captain Kirk, the commander of the starship Enterprise, is split into two beings—one mild and reasonable, the other pugnacious and villainous. Though the first captain is loyal to his ship and crew, he is ineffectual. It is the second, the aggressive captain, who is audacious and compelling. At one point in the action, the bridge crew considers whether they should kill the violent captain, only to decide that doing so would cause the first to die as well. In the end, the two halves are reconciled. The moral of the story is obviously that although anger is difficult, it is what makes a person formidable; and that relinquishing it converts a person into a social weakling. The point is that anger has a vital job to perform; it achieves social goals that cannot be achieved otherwise.

All emotions, including anger, have what amount to goals that they press hard to achieve. Unlike rational thought, which can be turned on and off fairly easily, emotions tend to remain active until these critical objectives are reached. When this has been accomplished, the feelings evaporate and the person who experienced them no longer feels angry, afraid, or embarrassed. People aiming to fulfill an important objective benefit from having their feelings engaged; they provide the impetus for success.

The goal of fear is easy to see: clearly, it is safety. Fear warns us when we are in danger and mobilizes us to elude it. The fight-or-flight response, first enunciated by W. B. Cannon (1929), is really a mechanism for obtaining safety. It is an innate motivational package triggered by fear, without which we would be in far more jeopardy than we usually are. The person who has no fear can literally walk off a cliff. Like the individual unable to feel pain who inadvertently cuts off a finger, the fearless person cannot correctly evaluate a risk or make a suitable effort to overcome it. Fear is nature's alarm system. It is a shot of adrenaline, a first line of defense against mortality.

Of course, unbridled fear has negative consequences. Although natural, it does not provide all the answers we need in times of danger. If we rely solely upon its instinctive promptings, there are bound to be moments when we overreact or react incorrectly. Fear must be controlled in order to be effective. When fear spills over into panic, it almost guarantees disaster. It can then impel us to run from our enemies, only to be cut down from behind. Fear has to be coupled with courage and common sense. Though we need to feel afraid, we must be able to perform rationally even when we don't want to be rational. Thus effective fear is a complex phenomenon, partly innate and partly learned; neither aspect can be prudently neglected.

Other emotions are similarly constituted. They too have both an innate and a learned component, and they too promote objectives essential for survival. Sadness, for instance, specializes in relinquishing that which has been lost. When a person feels sad, his internal machinery warns him that some important attachment has been broken: perhaps that someone close to him has died. He is then able to undergo pangs of mourning that break his ties with the past and prepare him for the future. Without this feeling, he might remain enmeshed in relationships that are no longer viable. His sadness may feel terrible; but when a loss occurs, it is a vital step in the process of feeling better.

Shame is another indispensable, yet troublesome, emotion. It warns us when we are acting in ways that others will reject. The negative attention they direct our way tells us that we are providing an unacceptable model, and through our embarrassment we are motivated to hide so that they will not have to perceive our wayward performance. Shame thus moves us to conform. It is a tool for coordinating social activities and for establishing the norms that regulate society. Guilt has a similar function, though it is more complex in its implementation. It is not a unitary emotion. Rather, it is an internalization of anger that was once directed at us by others. Whether they told us they were angry or threatened a withdrawal of love, their displeasure at what we were doing frightened us into wanting to comply. Our internal anger then coerced us into acquiescing in their desires. The goal became their forgiveness, for we believed that if we did as they wanted, they would no longer be upset. Guilt thus enforces social conformity. It ensures that people follow rules initiated by others. Because we are born into a world overflowing with preexisting regulations, guilt is a mechanism for ensuring that these are perpetuated and that each individual does not have to reinvent society.

Anger, our main concern, is what might be called a teleological emotion, that is, it has *purposes* incorporated within it. Anger arises for several reasons, but the most important is to help people overcome their frustrations. To be frustrated implies that one is trying to achieve something but is not obtaining it. As Alfred Adler noted almost a century ago, anger exists because human beings have intentions that are sometimes thwarted. It then serves as a battering ram to obtain what they want. When it functions successfully, the person is then able to rest content, no longer impelled to push for success. When it does not, however, the individual's engine remains engaged and will continue the fight for the objective.

A half-century ago Dollard, Doob, Miller and Sears (1939) enunciated their famous frustration-aggression hypothesis. They theorized that a frustrated person automatically becomes aggressive and tries to inflict injury or pain on the frustrating object. After a good deal of research, it has become evident that not everyone reacts this way. Many people are able to contain themselves and do not attempt to hurt others. The real equation turns out to be between frustration and anger. Aggression is just one potential manifestation of anger, and a primitive one at that. An angry person, like a frightened person, has the option of controlling himself. He does not have to resort to stereotyped or ineffectual displays.

The fundamental purpose of anger, it seems, is to influence others, not to injure them. The idea is to get them to comply or to back off, not to put them in the hospital. When people get angry, they assume that a human agency has caused their distress and that if this other can be motivated to change, the source of their frustration will be removed. Killing or disfiguring the other may achieve this end, but is not itself the end. Indeed, if injuring the other does not remove the frustration, an angry person will remain angry. The provocation will persist, and a different approach will be necessary.

Raw aggression, it must be remarked, is usually a poor instrument for removing frustrations. It is so intimidating that it is as apt to trigger retaliation as to dislodge a barrier. Indeed, most people learn that aggression is not a productive expression of anger and hence try to avoid it. Unrestrained aggression is like a panic attack. It is anger gone wild and is ill-calculated to achieve its goal. Far from being the normal reaction to frustration, it is the response of someone too frustrated to think straight.

Because anger is such a stalwart emotion, it has another function besides alleviating frustration, namely, that of answering the anger of others. Because their anger is also powerful, often the only way to counter it is with more of the same. With an emotion designed to extract compliance, there may be no alternative available, except instigating an equally energetic counterattack. A target of anger says, in effect, "I'm not going to do it your way; you're going to do it my way." Though "my way" may entail no more than having the aggressor back off, the outcome will be different from what the aggressor envisioned. Counter-anger is therefore an instrument for establishing independence and for gaining respect. It declares, "I am a person to be reckoned with and will not be blown away just because you are angry with me." This is no mean statement. It changes anger from a one-sided game entailing compliance into an active two-sided argument.

The reader may have noted that, as described, both anger and counter-anger presuppose the source of a person's frustration to be another human being. Yet we get angry at nonhuman agencies too. It has become a cliche that one should give a malfunctioning electronic device a "good kick." Though we know that machines don't respond the way people do, we try to motivate them the way we might motivate a reluctant enemy. We seem to feel an almost inborn assumption that some person will prove responsible for our troubles; consequently when in doubt, we feel comfortable acting as if one were culpable. In any event, this sort of reaction gives us the persistence to grapple with nonhuman frustrations even though we cannot influence them psychologically. A different kind of "fighting" may be required, but it too can be effective.

However anger is employed, it should be implemented effectively. Because its goal is the removal of frustrations or the counteracting of external threats, one or the other must be achieved for the angry person to stop feeling angry. Just expressing anger or injuring another is insufficient. If the underlying purposes of the emotion are not attained, the result is further anger. Nor is the suppression of anger an answer. People who hold back their rage while their intentions remain blocked will continue to be distressed. Though the emotion may not remain at the front of their minds, they will have to expend considerable energy to keep their anger from breaking through.

Influencing others is an extraordinarily convoluted enterprise. Getting them to comply or to back off is not merely a matter of saying "Do this!" or "Don't do that!" Much depends upon what is wanted, which resources are available, and who the opponents are. Although we are all born capable of getting angry, it may take a lifetime to discover how to do so effectively. We must ascertain the right words, the correct tone of voice, the most efficacious point of entry, and so forth. As none of these is contained in a simple formula that is always applicable, there is a great deal to learn. Nor is this process just a matter of acquiring facts; it entails developing skills. To remove frustration, people must be able to implement their anger, not merely to understand it. They must be able to win or to change the game.

HOW ANGER WORKS

Let us pause for an example. The one that follows may be a bit regressive, even archaic, but it vividly illustrates the central mechanisms of anger. A more realistic story line, perhaps detailing an argument over the family budget or an incident involving sexual jealousy, would introduce distracting complexities. Needless to say, the example could as easily have concerned a woman angry at her husband for forgetting to mow the lawn or for bringing home the wrong groceries.

A person—let us call him John—comes home after a long day at the office. He is tired and out of sorts. For the past several hours all he has been thinking about is having a good dinner and planting himself in front of the television set. On most nights his wife, Mary, has his evening meal prepared when he arrives. She is a good cook, and he enjoys being pampered by her. Mary too seems to value this ritual. Tonight, however, things are different. When John walks through the front door, no enticing aroma wafts from the kitchen. Nor is Mary scurrying about finishing the last-minute details before dinner. Instead, she is ensconsed on the couch, watching television herself. After his initial astonishment, John's brow knits and his jaw clamps shut. Why isn't dinner ready?

John's reaction to being frustrated is a "feeling" we can all recognize. He is unhappy at not having his expectations met, and the tensing of his body is a sign of this. His unhappiness will take a specific form, namely, anger. If he can bring himself to notice it, he will find that he is squinting at the world with disapproval and that his body is beginning to prepare for battle. These assorted changes in his perceptions and muscle tone can alert him of his displeasure. As he mutters "damn" under his breath, he may be jolted into the realization that he is upset and that he misses his meal. His anger can thus notify him as to how much he has been looking forward to dinner. After this, he can begin asking himself what he intends to do about it. Most of these reactions will occur subconsciously, but he will sense that he is annoyed and that the missing meal has something to do with this.

Mary, lying on the couch, will have noticed John's arrival. From her vantage point she will see the flash of his eyes and the set of his jaw. She too will realize that John is unhappy. Since she knows that he was probably expecting dinner, she will have a pretty good idea of why he is disturbed. The signs of his displeasure, however subtle, will alert her that a storm is brewing and she will begin preparing to meet it.

Meanwhile, John is not only feeling angry; he is readying himself to act. Suddenly he wheels around, glowers at Mary in an accusatory manner, and demands, "Where's my dinner?" When she responds that she hasn't cooked any because she was busy, he may glare back and hiss, "What do you mean? It's dinner time and I'm hungry. How can you not have prepared a meal?" Because of his anger, John wants to make something happen. He will not merely shrug his shoulders and say "Oh well, I guess I'm angry." Far from it, he will swing into motion and direct his wrath at Mary. With all the emotional voltage at his command, he will try to move her in the direction of the kitchen.

For her part, Mary will not be unaffected by John's anger. To her, it is not some antiseptic display to which she can remain indifferent. When someone is, as they say, "in one's face," and it will feel to Mary as if John is in her's, one has to respond. An honest expression of anger directed one's way requires an answer. (Even when a person is in the presence of third parties who are angry at each other, he will often feel called upon to do something.) Nevertheless, there is no single predetermined response in this situation. Mary has options. One of these is to be overcome by guilt. Despite having had a hectic day, her conscience may demand that she quickly attend to her duties. She may be afraid of John and eager to do as he wishes lest he lose control and injure her. In other words, Mary may be motivated by John's anger to comply with his expectations. If she is, this can end the matter. When John settles down to enjoy his evening repast, his displeasure will evaporate and Mary's guilt may lift too. Both will have obtained some of what they were aiming for.

But Mary may not be so compliant. At the first blast of John's wrath, she may be moved to anger herself. "Why isn't dinner ready, you ask? Am I your servant? I've been busy too, and I'm in no mood for your nonsense. Make your own damn meal!" All of this may be said with considerable passion. Since Mary's anger has been aroused, she will try to motivate John to back off. She may even make counter-demands, and, in this era of equal rights, will probably stipulate that there are certain responsibilities John has been shirking, one of which is to prepare the evening meal with equal regularity. Now it is John's turn to respond. And he too has options. Having heard Mary's side of the issue, he may decide that he has actually been quite selfish and that having a hot meal is not such a vital concern. Or contrarily, he may get huffy and the two engage in a knock-down, drag-out donnybrook, the end of which may be mutual adjustments or further discord. There is no inevitable conclusion to this sort of conflict. Sometimes it ends with a couple resolving their differences; sometimes it terminates in murder.

Though the above scenario is simple in its outlines, and does not do justice to all of the complexities of human motivation, it presents the basic components of anger. Among other things, it demonstrates that it is not just a feeling, but part of a larger social tableau in which it may advance or impede the action. While feelings are involved, so are communications and motivations. Anger is not merely a private affair between a person and his psyche: it is a pivotal agency in the management of interpersonal relationships.

Like all emotions, anger has several aspects. As suggested above, it both communicates and motivates and in each of these modalities can be directed either toward the self or the other. In the case of fear, these aspects are very clear, so perhaps it may be useful to examine them first. When people are afraid, this feeling signals them that there is a danger present. In essence, it communicates with them and provides essential information about the status of their environment. In this it operates as a direct channel for evaluating their danger, one that by-passes slower acting cognitive channels. (See Zajonc, 1980.) In particular, it informs them that something is happening that is capable of damaging them.

When people are afraid, the terror in their eyes and the tremor in their voices also communicate to those with whom they are in contact. Just as members of a herd of wildebeest become alert when one of their number anxiously scrutinizes the savannah to detect an oncoming lion, so too do human beings when they are in the environs of another person who is afraid. This other's emotion is contagious and flits from one individual to another, albeit perhaps below the level of anyone's awareness. A person to whom fear is communicated suddenly feels uneasy and may begin scanning the horizon to see where the potential danger lies.

But fear does not merely communicate; it mobilizes people to avoid dangers. If being afraid only provided information, it would be a flimsy mechanism for coping with hazards. When we are in peril, it is imperative that we move into action with dispatch. The frightened wildebeest who perceives a lion had best start running immediately and energetically; otherwise, the probability of his becoming a meal increases geometrically. We human beings have a similar mechanism for preserving us from harm. As psychologists, beginning with Cannon (1929), have observed, we are born with a fight-or-flight response. When seriously alarmed, our bodies prepare us either to stand and challenge the danger or to flee it as expeditiously as we can. This disposition is not a matter of conscious choice: We do not calmly debate whether to move or not; rather, we move—and think about it later.

Our motivation to avoid danger is not, however, completely stereotyped. An impulse to act can be modified in the process of maturation. Thus, when a person finds himself in an impending automobile accident, his eyes open automatically in disbelief, but the countermeasures he implements have been shaped over time. Neither an impetus to step on the brake nor the skill to steer into a skid is part of his biological equipment, yet he may feel impelled to perform either as is appropriate. In short, fear motivates people to act in ways that they have learned will reduce their danger. Although we sometimes err about where our safety lies, we are propelled to move toward it anyway.

Similarly, others who are influenced by our fears are moved to act. Because they too have a fight-or-flight mechanism, they will wish to avoid danger as promptly as do we. Therefore, when our consternation has been communicated to them, it will not stop at sharing information; our evident alarm will prompt them to defend themselves. As with the wildebeest, when one animal takes off, other members of the herd leap to flight.

Anger is not unlike fear in its outlines. It too communicates with the self and other, and it too motivates both. The difference is that the information shared is not the same and that the impulse to act operates dissimilarly. Since the job of anger is not to protect us from danger, it obviously would not signal danger. Rather, it alerts us that we have been frustrated. It directs our attention to the fact that something has been denied us and helps us become aware of what this is. Likewise, when we are angry, our role partners quickly learn that we have been frustrated. The play of anger on our face will be very visible to them and will enjoin them to observe what has happened.

In its motivation dimension, anger mobilizes us to fight for what we want. It gives us the energy to pursue that which we have been denied and hopefully increases our prospects for obtaining it. An angry person is not merely content to pine away for what he wants; he feels compelled to act in ways that make things happen. One of the unique factors enabling anger to be effective is that it also motivates those at whom it is directed. Because they are not neutral in its presence, it can induce them to furnish missing goals. Whether through fear, guilt, sympathy, or a combination of these three, they can be inspired to comply, or perhaps to resist.

Communication

The communication function of anger has been recognized for a long time. Charles Darwin realized that anger is part of our biological equipment and hypothesized about its serving social purposes. Likewise, Freud acknowledged the physiological reality of the emotions, and he too speculated about their functions. One of his more fruitful concepts was *signal anxiety,* wherein he explicitly suggested that fear alerts people to danger. By analogy, a signal function can be attributed to other emotions, including anger. Nevertheless, Freudians have not been particularly diligent in following through on this lead.

From about the beginning of this century, there has also been a tradition in psychology which has virtually denied the signal function of the emotions. Under the banner of the James-Lange theory, even contemporary psychologists have attempted to demonstrate that people do not have specific internal feelings to which the common emotion-labels apply. They believe that there are general arousal states, which when experienced are interpreted according to their context as being one emotion or another. Thus, a person undergoing an adrenaline rush would consider himself angry if he also noticed he had been frustrated. This theory thus turns the communication function of the emotions on its head with the recognition of a frustration signaling that one is angry rather than vice versa.

William James, one of the originators of this perspective, also indicated that people learn about their emotions from internal stimuli. Though he denied that there is a specific feeling of anger, he believed that a person could notice his anger by becoming aware of when his muscles tighten or his eyes narrow. Kinesthetic feedback from these physiological changes would then be interpreted by his brain as anger. Thus, while anger might not be a primary sensation, like the color yellow, a combination of bodily sensations might fuse into what seems to be a primary sensation.

Recent research (e.g., Caroll Izard, 1977) has demonstrated that there are at least several primary emotions. Studies of human facial expressions have made it evident that unique patterns of muscular contraction are associated with specific emotions and that these patterns are universal. As anthropologists have documented, an angry face can be recognized anywhere around the world. In Izard's words, "The muscles of the brow move inward and downward, creating a frown and a foreboding appearance about the eyes, which seems to be fixed in a hard stare toward the object of anger. The nostrils dilate and the wings of the nose flare out. The lips are opened and drawn back in a rectangle-like shape, revealing clenched teeth. Often the face flushes red." Also, "In anger the blood 'boils,' the face becomes hot, the muscles tense. There is a feeling of power and an impulse to strike out, to attack the source of anger. The stronger the anger the stronger and more energetic the person feels and the greater the need for physical action. In rage the mobilization of anger is so great that one feels one will explode if one does not bite, hit, or kick something, or 'act out the anger' in some way."

Whether or not this multitude of physiological responses, extending over the face and the body, is associated with a specific inner feeling, it certainly does constitute a stable pattern of internal and external indicators that can function as a signal of anger. Even if there is no specific feeling, something is happening inside people that is capable of alerting them when they are angry. This something is obviously more than a generalized arousal state, though it may be less than a qualitatively specific feeling. In fact, how the feeling is constituted is irrelevant to its competence in signaling frustration. As Izard's description makes evident, most of the factors adding up to anger are very riveting and are difficult for a person who experiences them or witnesses them to miss. Moreover, when one has an impulse to strike out in a particular direction, this may be good evidence of where one believes the source of frustration to lie. In other words, not only can anger signal someone's frustration, it can also point toward that which has been denied.

Anger, however, unlike fear, is often better at communicating with others than with the self. People who are seriously frightened rarely doubt that they are afraid. Though they may deny their terror to others, not wanting to appear cowardly, inside they are usually so consumed with fear that they cannot fail to recognize its presence. Anger, on the other hand, very frequently goes unrecognized. This phenomenon is so common that it can be turned into a joke. Many a situation comedy has revolved around enraged people furiously denying their anger. Apparently, when people become enraged they can be so focused on a goal that they do not perceive their own feelings. Though they loudly disclaim their anger, they are not trying to hide a feeling they are ashamed of. They simply do not recognize its presence. They are aware only of the other party's presumed transgression, not their own reaction to it.

An angry person's role partners, however, will be in no doubt that they are seeing anger. Witnesses to a full-blown display of rage have difficulty ignoring it even when they close their eyes. To be sure, like fear, anger can be disguised, in which case its target may be oblivious to it, but when the normal indicators are present, they are easily discerned. Facial cues, tones of voice, bodily postures, and social contexts all go into creating a gestalt that demands attention. This seems to be so because the function of anger is different from that of fear. While the latter protects individuals from dangers impinging on them, anger attempts to remove obstacles imposed by others. Because it seeks to terminate frustrations by influencing others, it must be made palpable to them in order to work. A frightened person can achieve safety by running away, but an angry one cannot be satisfied unless he induces others to cooperate, which points up the importance of salient communications.

Motivation

A thwarted purpose, one that is capable of arousing rage, generally possesses substantial value to the person who holds it. An ephemeral goal rarely generates anything more than an ephemeral response. To become really angry entails wanting something very earnestly, or at least believing one wants it. But things worth having are worth fighting for. If something is really consequential, then one should be prepared to expend effort in its pursuit. If one isn't, the probability of obtaining it plummets and one will likely fall short.

Moreover, the frustrations that generate anger are often overcome only with difficulty. Barriers blocking our path do not vanish just because we are displeased. One of the more disquieting discoveries that most adults make is that the world does not revolve around us and that, in fact, most others are indifferent to our happiness. Because these others are concerned primarily with themselves, they are not prepared to be responsive just because we desire it. Often they must be persuaded to expend energy in our behalf. Indeed, they are frequently geared to work against us and must be persuaded to desist. Even nonhuman agencies can resist us. Sometimes it seems as if anything worth having requires a struggle. Indeed, it may be that this very effort is part of what makes things valuable. Among the most important tasks of anger is providing the power for a sustained drive toward worthy objectives and for smashing through obstacles that bar the way. It furnishes the persistence and the energy to make consequential things happen. Like all emotions its very nature is such that it is tenacious and dynamic. Its very reason for being is to enable us (and animals) to battle long and hard for meaningful targets.

When someone is gripped by a strong emotion, he can be sure that it will not evaporate in a trice, especially if its object has not yet been reached. For example, when a person has been seriously frightened, he will stay frightened until he is convinced that he is no longer threatened. He will not relax his vigilance just because someone tells him he is safe. Though he may try to push his fear out of his mind and operate as if it were not justified, the emotion will be ready to erupt at a moment's notice. Just as a soldier who has convinced himself that he is no longer concerned about falling bombs may leap for cover when he hears a car backfire, so may anyone be frightened when an old danger reemerges. No matter how cognitively persuaded he is to the contrary, the appearance of an old threat will reactivate the time-tested reaction.

Intense emotion is also well known to increase the vibrancy of memory. If an event takes place under conditions of emotional arousal, it is difficult to forget. Is there any married person who doesn't recall the most trivial details of his marriage ceremony? What he ate for dinner two weeks ago may have completely disappeared from his memory, but an occasion where he was simultaneously anxious, hopeful, and confused will last though the decades pass. Similarly, an event that has been seriously threatening will not lose this character quickly and, even after the passage of years, will be evaluated as dangerous.

In the case of anger, a person doesn't forget either. Imagine a world in which any time someone was seriously frustrated his mind wandered and he soon fixed upon another objective. What are the odds that this sort of distractibility would favor his obtaining important goals? Obviously they would be slim. The point is that anger keeps us focused. Particularly when a goal is significant to our survival (and/ or happiness), we do not lose sight of it. An angry person tends to be an unforgiving person. He remembers his disappointments and awaits the moment to strike back. He does not suffer defeat gently or absent-mindedly. If he did, he would not be able to reverse many unfavorable decisions. Some people even wait a lifetime to undo a galling frustration. They engage in vendettas and attempt to avenge themselves years after the fact. While it is true that anger can motivate us in petty ways, it is also a guardian of our most precious interests and enables us to fight for love and respect with real verve.

Besides being persistent, emotions are energetic. They not only fight long, they fight hard. The person who is emotionally indifferent to an objective puts up a token effort and then moves on to another goal. He does not dedicate himself to a cause with a "passion." This word, by the way, is revealing. To be passionately involved is to care and to try. To be without passion is to be neutral and unconcerned. We also talk about dedicating ourselves with a "fury." To do so is to fight ferociously for a cause. It is to put every fiber of one's being into an effort and thereby increase the chance of victory.

With fear, our energy goes into fight or flight. Frightened people (unless they have panicked) do not put up a tepid resistance or saunter peacefully into the sunset. Rather, the mother who is afraid because her child is trapped under an automobile acquires the strength of ten; the soldier who decides to run away from a battle keeps on running until he reaches the next county. Such energy can be misapplied, but when judiciously exploited it is an invaluable asset. Athletes, for instance, know that to achieve their best performance, they need an "edge." Having a suitable level of anxiety enables them to compete more effectively than if they were so relaxed, they simply failed to care.

With anger, our energy goes into both influencing others and trying harder. Because anger is designed to remove animate sources of frustration, an energetic display is more persuasive than a mild one. The person who inoffensively informs another that he is "a bit unhappy" is less likely to be noticed than the one who is "very upset." A powerful exhibition of anger can almost blow another person away, while a pallid demonstration inspires yawns. To be seriously angry (other things being equal) increases the chances that one will be taken seriously. It is a red flag that declares "look at me and pay attention."

An angry person is also more inclined to make an effort. Even with nonhuman frustrations, anger keeps a person in the game. The persistence of his anger is not only in memory, it is in action. Angry people try harder. Politicians know that when a population is aroused against an enemy, it is capable of performing heroic exertions. This is one of the prime reasons for exciting their wrath by caricaturing foes as villainous. In more ordinary circumstances, anger keeps people working tirelessly, for long hours. Because they are determined not to lose, they do what is necessary to succeed. This is why it is so frightening to have an aroused opponent; one realizes that he is unlikely to give up.

If we look toward the direction in which the motive power of anger operates, we see that, for the self, anger instigates an enduring and robust performance. It is the spark that ignites the continuing pursuit of one's interests. Consider what might happen to someone unable to tap the reservoirs of his rage. His would not be an enviable fate. Indeed, his very meekness would mark him as a target for all comers. Because he gives up after only a token resistance, he can be counted upon to lose. He is the ideal victim who can be either ignored or exploited, depending upon the interests of his adversary. Of course, energetic anger is not always successful. Should the worm turn and a meek person become more assertive, unless his anger is controlled, it can motivate unguided and automatic actions whose consequences seem feeble. Anger must incorporate a fair degree of planning or it can wreck havoc. Only controlled emotions are capable of motivating actions tailored to the particular objective.

When we look at the motive power of anger as directed toward others, we see first of all that it can put the fear of the Lord into them. It warns of the dire consequences of a failure to comply, and its energy is a warrant that it can back its promises. The person who wields it as his sword, far from being a dishrag, commands respect. Serious anger is both frightening and capable of producing guilt. It has shock value precisely because it can be dangerous. Indeed, if it is directed one's way, one may not think twice, but accede immediately. The emotion comes up so suddenly and forcefully that one is taken by surprise and attempts to appease its source by meeting the expectations raised, thus preventing further attack.

Furthermore, the target of someone's wrath may already be primed to deliver what is wanted. If, earlier in life, guilt was implanted in one's psyche regarding the issue at hand, an external display of anger can reactivate previously established commitments and an inner rage can become the ally of an aggressor's demands. As guilt is often the internalization of angry demands made by one's childhood role partners, if it is switched on, ancient mandates can add to a current opponent's power. They will set off reverberations of an anger one was unable to resist in the past and hence is ill-equipped to resist today. Whereas then one became guilty by being pressured into doing something, now guilt will cause one to act as if an old nemesis is still at one's throat.

Arousing guilt is therefore an extremely efficient way of exploiting anger. If, for instance, a woman has learned that it is her duty to prepare dinner for her family, when her husband becomes angry about an absent meal, she may not enquire into the equities of the current situation, but immediately accuse herself of being an unsatisfactory wife and mother. Her husband will then get his way, not because he is particularly persuasive or meritorious, but because her history has set her up for defeat. Though we as outsiders are appalled by the unfairness of his demand, his anger has a potency it would not otherwise enjoy, except for the fact that internalized injunctions imposed on her when she was young have persisted into the present.

Even if a person at whom anger is directed is not frightened by it or betrayed by her own guilt, the emotion can still be influential. It can motivate cooperation by making it clear that a current demand is meaningful. Because anger is riveting, it draws attention to that which is being requested. Their role partners quickly recognize that angry people mean business and that what they say they want they want. If these hearers are sympathetic, they may actually choose to be helpful. Because they care, they will be motivated to provide what they can. Having learned what is important, they will bend every effort to cooperate. A passionless appeal, on the other hand, is easily passed over.

Yet anger hangs on a knife-edge. It can as readily motivate massive resistance as it can submission. Instead of cooperation, it can call forth strong counter-anger. Because one of its functions is to confront the anger of others, this very reaction may be activated by what is ostensibly a demand for compliance. If it is, cooperation will be forestalled. Invoking anger in order to influence others is consequently a very delicate matter. Because the emotion is equally capable of inducing obedience, mutual modifications, or outright rebellion, it must be handled gingerly. Before expressing it, a person would be well advised to have some indication of how the other person is likely to react and to make the appropriate adjustments. Thus, a mildly angry request that is guaranteed to elicit the sympathies of one person may be interpreted as trampling on the sensibilities of another. It is an uncomfortable fact of life, but the balance between compliance and defiance lies in different places with different people.

Social Negotiations

The dance between anger and counter-anger forms a dialogue that is fundamental to many social transactions. It often explains how people interact with one another and why they structure their relationships as they do. The roles people play are usually the outcome of negotiations in which they have tried to reconcile their competing interests. When they make bargains that are mutually beneficial, each one wins; but it is equally possible for them to engage in destructive conflicts in which both lose. How anger is utilized in such negotiations is often the critical factor in determining whether they will be fair or injurious.

Dean Pruitt (1981) has provided an interesting paradigm for how negotiations can occur. In his "dual concern" model, negotiators are described as asserting (a) only their own interests, (b) exclusively the interests of their partners, (c) the interests of neither, or (d) the interests of both. It is only in this last permutation that they truly have an opportunity to solve problems and satisfy each other. This does not mean that each must be totally altruistic. On the contrary, it helps if both are moderately selfish. As they know their own interests best, it is useful if they can advocate for themselves. As long as they stand up for themselves, without invalidating each other, both will have a better idea of where they stand, which will facilitate mutual accommodations. The most productive posture, according to Pruitt, is "firm flexibility," that is, energetically asserting one's own goals while being pragmatic about the means through which they are achieved. It may then be possible to construct a deal in which both parties make adjustments that allow them to receive more than they would have had they not cooperated.

Controlled anger is an ideal instrument for firm flexibility. As long as it does not become an enraged demand for supremacy or a lust for injury, it is well suited to self-assertion and to genuine efforts at compromise. Because well-crafted anger both communicates and motivates, it can teach the parties what each must know about the other, as well as influence both to take account of the demands of the other. In a social negotiation, the anger of one alerts the other of what is desired, as well as calls forth an appropriate response. It also encourages each to be persistent in finding a solution and in developing viable options. Without a passionate attachment to their respective positions, the negotiators might be misled about what is really at stake and too casually deal with essentials. In particular, people who cannot angrily assert their interests are bound to lose. Rather than contributing to the final agreement, their interests will be ignored, for their passivity may be interpreted to mean that they don't care.

Anger also enables people to prioritize their concerns. When two individuals have competing interests, how else are they to know what is most important to whom? The degree to which each is frustrated will provide the key. If one feels especially thwarted, her anger allows her to know how unhappy she is; and when this feeling is communicated, the other may realize the extent of this unhappiness. The two can then jockey for position to see precisely how comfortable each is with a variety of potential alternatives. Although they may not verbally quantify their frustrations, their tone of voice, the number of times they come back to a particular subject, or the length of time needed to accept an unexpected proposal will all furnish more eloquent testimony to their real interests than will any rationalized schedule of priorities. As long as both parties can tolerate their own anger and that of the other, both can learn a great deal. In a sense, anger is nature's way of making mutual adjustments between people without their having to recognize everything they are doing or thinking. It provides them with a kind of "intuition" about what's important that is available nowhere else. Indeed, people often don't know what they want until they hear themselves angrily demanding it.

Contrary to what many critics suppose, anger is the governing principle behind a great deal of social structure. Besides creating chaos, it also helps pattern enduring relationships and ultimately contributes to social predictability and even fairness. Anger, for instance, helps decide the relative power of two individuals, which in turn helps them determine their respective status. We human beings are often like big-horned sheep butting our heads together to ascertain who is dominant. We use our anger like a battering ram to establish who is stronger and consequently who should have priority. Those who forge a reputation for strength thereby improve their chances in subsequent social negotiations and hence increase their access to many valuable resources, including power. While this may not be fair, it does help to create the hierarchies through which we coordinate complex social activities. In other words, without anger we couldn't have governments, large corporations or a highly differentiated economic order.

Morality also turns out to depend upon the good offices of anger. Indeed, it could not exist without it. It is moral outrage that underlies the ethical structures of society. For a precept to have moral standing, it must be backed by anger. Moral rules not so established have all the legitimacy of unenforced laws. Moreover, as guilt is too at the heart of morality and it would not exist except as a reaction to potent anger, it likewise confirms the importance of anger. As an internalized form of wrath, it keeps people virtuous, even when others are not present to uphold particular principles.

Although both morality and hierarchy can be unjust and indeed hurtful, it is difficult to imagine a society functioning without them. Although they have harmful side-effects, their omission would be even more devastating. In their absence, human interactions would be thoroughly disorganized and arbitrary. It therefore becomes imperative to regulate the amount of unfairness created by anger. Dominance must not become oppression, nor morality, moralism. When anger is controlled and seeks to promote mutual interests, collateral damage can be reduced, and even its victims will benefit from bargains that meet their needs.

A SOCIALIZED EMOTION

In order for anger to motivate or to communicate effectively, it must go through a period of development. Though everyone is born with an ability to get angry, how the emotion is expressed must undergo a transformation before it is useful for adults. The situation is not unlike that of language. Despite the fact that we all inherit a capacity to communicate verbally, this cannot come to fruition except through a process of social learning. As the linguist Noam Chomsky has taught us, people have an innate capacity to understand the deep structures of language, but this is activated only in interaction with other language speakers. Without such stimulation, children are capable of no more than gibberish.

Anger must be socialized. The mechanisms through which it is implemented have to be acquired by way of transactions with others who already know how to get angry. Otherwise, a person would possess only the primitive reactions of early childhood. When we are born, anger takes a few stereotyped forms. Babies cry, kick, scream, and bite. Even the youngest child hates to be frustrated, but the techniques available to him are limited. Fortunately, parents sense the unhappiness of their infants and are motivated to remove it. Thus, the angry cry of a hungry child brings the comfort of the maternal breast. The neonate may not know why crying works, but it does.

Some of those who talk about innate human aggressiveness imply that one of the purposes of anger is to cause injury. But it is evident that this is not the primary goal of infants. Frustrated babies do things that are hurtful, without understanding that they hurt. Thus, when a neonate bites his mother's nipple, it is because her milk isn't flowing freely, not to punish, much less to injure her. As children get older, anger does impel them to inflict pain, though still not necessarily injury. A toddler who gets angry at a playmate may push or slap, but not with the object of causing major damage. The purpose is to acquire a toy or perhaps to attract attention. Between the time of the terrible twos and school age, a child may begin to take pleasure in creating pain. When frustrated, a child can seek revenge and even giggle when a friend winces. Such a child when seriously angry may feel cheated unless the other hurts as much as the child does.

Nevertheless, primitive anger is overwhelmingly directed at terminating frustrations. If it reflexively inflicts pain, that is because pain is an excellent vehicle for motivating others. It certainly gains their notice. Injury, when it occurs, is only a by-product. Indeed, its occurrence can be both frightening and surprising to a very young child. Moreover, since young children are not particularly effective at causing physical damage, even when they have murder in their hearts, they don't actually hurt anyone. Their pleasure in inflicting pain goes little beyond the joy of startling someone with a bite or punch.

For adults, however, the repercussions of reflexive anger are very different. Adults are capable of causing substantial, even lethal, damage. When they engage in the equivalents of childhood slaps and bites, the results may not be as desired. Instead of motivating compliance, their primitive anger is more likely to generate resistance and mayhem. We adults know the destructive power of our blind rages and, for the most part, try to keep them in check. We also take pains to teach our children not to engage in them. Though we may tolerate a baby who bites an older sibling, the school-aged child who tries a similar maneuver will be upbraided.

Moreover, adults who engage in unsocialized anger find that their tantrums are not honored. Kicking and screaming brings assistance to a young child, but derision to a grown-up. The kinds of display necessary for influencing other adults are very different from the ones with which we were born. Hence they must be learned. A child must be indoctrinated into the customs of the tribe to discover what works and what doesn't. "Big boys don't cry." "Big girls act like ladies." These are instructions on how to get mad. They are guideposts that convey another's likely reactions. The child who pays attention will gradually redirect her natural impulses to make them conform with the emotional lexicon of the society. Just as children are taught words that others understand, so too they obtain an education in the anger displays others comprehend.

This is not to say that children are formally instructed on how to get angry. Rather, their lessons gradually unfold during the course of their growing up. It is in the relationships to which they are a party that they discover what others find acceptable. Thus, all children make demands of their role partners and these others make counter-demands of them. As the years pass, the nature of this dialogue is altered. What works at one stage does not work at another. The oedipal child, for instance, may discover that breath-holding gets a rise out of his parents, while an adolescent garners amused laughs with the same maneuver. Similarly, teenagers who belligerently demand a late curfew because all of their friends are allowed to stay out late will at least obtain a hearing, while the adult who tries a comparable gambit with a spouse will elicit an incredulous smile or an unamused scowl.

Among the most important competences that must be acquired through socialization is an ability to control one's emotional impulses. The springs of primitive anger do not disappear just because a person adds years. Nonetheless, as our frustrations build, we must be capable of engaging in rational planning. We cannot afford to let intemperate anger get in our way by impelling us to thoughtless action. This means remaining cool enough to recognize our situation and to act accordingly. One of the primary areas in which this sort of restraint develops is the games children play with one another. Sports and board games provide a reliable store of interpersonal frustration, which, if not dealt with competently, transforms a child into a "loser." Typically, we describe persons who become paralyzed by anger in competitive settings as "psyched out." Their brains become so clouded with fury that they cannot coordinate the efforts needed to prevail. It is not without reason that high school coaches are fond of portraying the process of coping with powerful emotions as character building.

If, despite having primitive impulses, children cannot learn both to communicate clearly about what they have been denied and to motivate others in ways that elicit a positive response, they will fail. The parents of young children know that their offspring have a limited ability to do either. They therefore expend a great deal of effort in translating the frustrations of their offspring and may even try to provide them with what is wanted, despite their inability to ask for it. With adults and growing children, the situation is different. It is expected that their messages be clear and civilized. If not, they will be dismissed as pests. The result is that most people eventually become proficient at communicating and motivating with anger regardless of their primitive impulses. Unfortunately, some psyched-out individuals tend to remain poor planners and continue to be inept in dealing with others. Since they did not learn to cope with coercive anger when young, they are not likely to be heard or respected as they mature.

Let us review the issue of timing a little further. A frustrated child acting on impulse may tug at a mother's sleeve when feeling thwarted. Though annoyed, she may comply because she makes allowances for the child's immaturity. Adults, however, are not granted such liberties. They are expected to have sufficient foresight and self-control not to act on the spur of the moment. When adults see that those to whom they wish to direct anger are otherwise engaged, they must be sufficiently composed to recognize that a delay may serve their interests—that, for instance, another person may be more inclined to comply when not diverted by other purposes. Likewise, an adolescent, while playing basketball, must not let the specter of loss generate an ill-considered tantrum. The best ally here is quiet determination. Though anger urges the athlete toward immediate physical retaliation, its gratification must be delayed in favor of playing hard and smart. Yet such control and foresight are not easily acquired; it takes many years of experience, including years of failure, before these can be applied well.

Once anger is controllable, it can be pragmatic. If primitive reactions are not automatically activated, people obtain the luxury of observing what works and what doesn't. Sometimes they can use others (e.g., parents, siblings, and friends) as models of effective anger, but sometimes they must experiment with new techniques on their own. What they learn will in large part be a reflection of their social setting. Who their parents are, their social class, the kinds of school they attend, whom they marry, and the sort of job they select can all have a profound impact on the way they manage anger. Of course, the temperaments with which they are born also play a part, for instance, in determining whether they prefer to be active or passive. Still, the very vocabulary with which people express their anger is socially transmitted. Hence it is that children from upper-class backgrounds may be punctilious about sharing their ire, while someone with working-class roots can project the coarseness of the streets. Similarly, people raised by abusive and undisciplined parents may find it difficult to believe anger can ever be controlled, whereas those brought up with compassion and kindness will find it incomprehensible that anger can ever be used to inflict pain.

By now it should be evident that the socialization of anger is a strenuous enterprise consisting of many lessons. But despite this complexity, the emotion must be socialized in one way or another. Some people are fortunate in how they are raised, and for them anger becomes an asset in overcoming their adult frustrations. Others, less blessed, find it a liability. One of the challenges of anger management, therefore, is to overcome the drawbacks of poor initial socialization and to see to it that people are put on a relatively equal footing.

Rage

Anger comes in all shades of intensity, from the very mild to the cataclysmically severe. When it is extremely intense, it may be said to be transformed into "rage." Although rage is but a variety of anger, there is almost a firebreak separating it from other manifestations of the emotion. Once the boundary between them has been traversed, a qualitative difference arises. Enraged people are typically wild with anger. It is as if a form of madness has transported them and made them forget why they are angry. All thoughts of ending their frustrations are banished, and their goal becomes destruction and damnation. Rage aims at revenge and injury, not fulfillment. It is crazy and without a plan. People in its throes see red and want only to strike out. The impulse to act is overwhelming.

Where then does rage come from, and why is it so destructive? The answer apparently lies in primitive anger. It seems that when people become intensely angry, they short-circuit the effects of their socialization and revert to the primordial springs of their emotions. That rage is dumb and planless is no more than an artifact of their innate impulse to act. Infants' fury is also dumb and planless, and they too strike out unthinkingly. The difference is that an adult's unthinking anger is far more dangerous. A reflexive bite from a child can cause pain; the blow from an adult's strong right arm can put someone in traction.

Rage is almost always self-defeating. As a result of its stupidity, it rarely terminates the frustrations that called it forth. Because it is self-involved, it doesn't care whether it influences others or whom it hurts. While the rest of us are appalled at its fury, it doesn't notice that it is disproportionate. Although its goal may not be to inflict injury, in its blind rush for instant gratification it does not stop to repair the damage in its wake. Nor can rage be reformed. Once the genie has been set loose, it cannot be taught manners; it can only be put back into the bottle. Only when anger is under some kind of restraint can it be employed effectively. Thus, the first objective of anger management must be to cool enraged people down so that the lessons of their socialization can be respected. Only then can they thoughtfully decide how they want to express themselves or to motivate others.

Among the manifestations of rage that should set off warning bells are revenge and spite. People who are so angry that they seek only to get even set themselves up for defeat. Revenge loses sight of its reasons for being and strives to injure the object of its wrath. It becomes more important to hurt another person than to achieve an underlying goal. Thus what was originally a mechanism for influencing others takes on a life of its own. Like all intense emotions, revenge is persistent and energetic, and capable of inflicting pain indefinitely. This, however, will provide cold comfort for the enraged person. In seeking to injure, his anger no longer influences, and so there is no satisfying it. No matter how much the other person is made to suffer, the enraged person will be moved to inflict more pain. A strategy of revenge does not allow for a stopping place; for, in its lust for punishment, it doesn't permit the other to deliver what was originally wanted. It therefore provides no way to terminate the frustrations that summoned it into existence.

Spitefulness, especially against the self, is similarly mortifying. To get even with another, enraged people can destroy what they love, including themselves. As long as they deny the other person victory, they will consider themselves triumphant. The old saw about "cutting off one's nose to spite one's face" is completely forgotten, and they revel in the other person's frustration. Though the scales are weighted heavily against them, they use the only weapon they feel is available, even if it is certain to blow up in their hands. Such stupidity can only be the consequence of a brain clouded by passion. It is a manifestation of rage impelling someone to ignore real interests in favor of immediate action. As such, its logical conclusion is misery for the person who invokes it as well as for the person at whom it is directed. Spite, like revenge, is anger run amok, and can be deactivated only by lowering the emotional temperature and seeking what is really wanted.

3

Integrated Anger Management

MANAGING PROBLEM ANGER

If anger is a social tool that can be both used and misused, how should it be handled when it causes difficulties? What should be done when people lose control and fail to meet their own needs, while simultaneously behaving in ways that inflict injury on others? What of people who do not lose control, but become so angry that they only leave themselves further frustrated? What also of those who are so intimidated by their rage that they cannot admit that they are unhappy? How are these to deal with an emotion that they cannot help having and that won't go away, but has the potential for generating much trouble? Can they find routes to keep it within bounds and perhaps even to make it productive? If they cannot do so on their own, can others, including professional helpers, support them in this endeavor?

More particularly, can a functional theory of anger, that is, one that concentrates on the goals of the emotion, provide clues for successful anger management? Can it point the way toward intervention strategies beyond those currently in favor? If anger has a purpose and that purpose is to overcome frustrations and/or to resist the angry impositions of others, will techniques that aim to conquer frustration or to oppose external anger reduce the intensity of problem anger? Can such strategies remove the cause of the emotion and convert it from an enemy to a friend?

When we keep an eye on the mission of anger, it becomes evident that it is not merely a feeling that is either present or absent. Instead of appearing as an irreducibly dangerous internal sensation, which for some unfathomable reason occasionally erupts in perverse displays, it will be perceived as part of a larger process through which people negotiate their social worlds. Rather than an isolated event that can be expunged, it then becomes something that must be used to achieve individual and social objectives. Contrary to how the issue is usually posed, anger management involves more than a decision about whether a particular feeling should or should not be expressed. Far more important than its mere expression is the question of how it is employed. If invoked in a manner such that significant frustrations are terminated, the intensity of the feeling will wane. But if frustrations remain, no effort at diluting the feeling can succeed. Although covered over or temporarily diverted, eventually it will return, if only in a disguised form.

Anger must be utilized in such a way that it both communicates and motivates effectively. It has to make things happen so that it precipitates positive, not negative, outcomes. In this regard, primitive anger is the enemy. Because it is unsocialized, it is both dangerous and simple-minded. It is not so much that its raw energy is a problem, but that in its atavism it institutes problematic courses of action.

As has been emphasized, the competent use of anger is a complex affair. Keeping one's eye on the ball and influencing others to collaborate in eliminating frustrations is not the automatic product of having decided to do so. The process of recognizing why one is angry and then doing something about it involves several stages. Although these do not always occur in sequence, they do possess a logic that gives them coherence. They form an integrated whole in that all have the same ultimate objective and each facilitates the next. Together they move progressively toward the end of obtaining what a person has been denied.

The several steps that together constitute the core of integrated anger management (I.A.M.) have often been employed separately by programs designed to control anger. Indeed, they are part of our commonsense notions about how to handle anger. I.A.M. simply places them in context. Too often approaches to addressing problem anger have an ad hoc quality. One takes a little bit of this and a tad of that, and behold: anger management! Unfortunately, without an overview of what is happening, even potentially useful procedures become myopic. Instead of reducing frustrations and thereby reducing anger, they become ends in themselves and are pursued so single-mindedly they become counterproductive.

None of the steps comprising I.A.M. possesses magical properties. Each by itself is useful, but ensemble they become truly potent. When given structure by the overall objectives of reducing frustration and countering external anger, they are compelling. What then are the steps that form integrated anger management? There are five stages, four of which are almost always present. They are (1) assuring safety, (2) developing incremental tolerance, (3) evaluating underlying goals and methods, (4) relinquishing impossible goals, and (5) using the emotion to achieve its ends.

For the moment, these steps may sound cryptic, but they are actually quite commonplace. We all engage in them at some point in our lives and often help others to navigate them as well. Briefly, assuring safety refers to the need to make certain that problem anger does not go out of control, and specifically that it does not become so intense that it runs amok and causes injury. The second step, developing incremental tolerance, is but a fancy way of saying that a person must gradually get used to experiencing intensely angry feelings without their switching automatically into rage. The third step, an evaluation of the goals and mechanisms of anger, becomes possible only when someone is able to experience the emotion and examine it carefully. The gravamen of this stage is that, before proceeding into action, an angry person must determine which objectives have been stymied. It is also essential to know whether these goals or the means used to achieve them are feasible. Should it be determined that they are not, it will be necessary to move to step four. Obviously relinquishing a goal need occur only if it is found hopeless. But when it is, it is imperative that a person reorganize priorities and head in a more promising direction. Finally, once a suitable goal has been selected, a person must utilize anger to obtain what is wanted. Judiciously deployed, anger can actually help to procure what is sought.

We must now set about the task of unpacking what is built into these five steps. Although they were easy enough to label, in practice they are difficult to execute. The problem is that each can be achieved in many different ways and that in concert they require coordination. Moreover, implementing them is more arduous than is deciding to do so. It requires skillful application and astute decision making. For the balance of this chapter we will explain in greater detail how each can be instituted and how it is related to the others. In subsequent

chapters, we will explicate the specifics of crisis management, catharsis, self-assessment, and social influence. As we move toward these
particulars, it will become apparent just how complex they are and
why easy answers are not viable.

ASSURING SAFETY

Once anger has gone out of control, attempts to use it effectively
become irrelevant. When someone is on a rampage, questions about
what will terminate his underlying frustrations are beside the point.
The very energy contained in rage gives it the potential for creating
tremendous damage. Should it be unleashed, the consequent destruction rightly becomes the focus of attention. Because this can include murder, and worse, it constitutes a problem of greater magni-
tude than mere frustration. Clearly, when there is blood on the floor,
this deserves a higher priority than the circumstances that produced
it. In particular, concerns about tolerating, evaluating, or utilizing anger should pale, and those affected by the emotion must devote their
efforts to damage control.

Before attempting to use anger to increase one's happiness, it is
essential to impose a minimum of control. Ways must be found to
ensure that the emotion will not go wild. Its primitive manifestations
must be kept in check, and those persons experiencing it or being
exposed to it must sense that they are safe. Though not all intemperate anger poses a threat, when it is overheated the possibility of injury is ever-present. In consequence, the first step of I.A.M. must be
to ascertain whether danger is imminent and then to intervene to
prevent it. Even if danger is not impending, it is necessary to remain
vigilant, for irrational anger can be unpredictable and, once loosed,
difficult to contain.

While the best way of assuring safety is to interdict danger before
it arises, an anger management program must also be prepared to
confine it after it appears. Such a program must encompass techniques for controlling angry people both before and after they turn
violent. The principal object is to prevent injury without inflicting
further damage. To this end, sufficient force must be deployed to
counter the energy of the anger, while not employing so much of it
that the force itself becomes a danger. If the cure is worse than the
disease, there is no point in taking the medicine.

Perhaps the best means of restraining problem anger is to help
people establish self-control. If they can learn how to refrain from

erupting violently, safety will have its best guarantee. Since people live with themselves, they are admirably situated to determine when they are about to lose control and can catch themselves before going too far. Moreover, they can impose limits that are commensurate with the danger. Because they will be able to recognize the degree of peril impending, they can be firm without being coercive.

It should also be noted that the danger to be controlled may be internal. It is relatively easy to perceive when a tantrum threatens harm to others; it is less simple to determine when someone is engaging in self-torture. Yet many people become so angry that they institute an orgy of self-recriminations and self-denial. They are so furious at their own transgressions that they lose all sense of proportion and engage in a frenzy of self-abuse. Should this be the case, it is especially important to establish self-control. Because only those who experience an internal rage know the depths of its savagery, they themselves must subdue it. They must recognize and restrain the fury that is making them so cruel to themselves.

Whatever techniques are used to assure safety, they must protect both angry people and those around them, including those who attempt to help. Professional helpers, relatives, or friends who try to impose control must be as aware of the threat to themselves. It is no good to prevent injury to an angry person only to sacrifice oneself. In the long run no one benefits when a helper becomes a martyr. Even if a given act of self-sacrifice pays off, no helper can sustain continuous punishment.

Nor should we forget that assuring safety is part of a larger process. Efforts at controlling anger are not an end in themselves. If the emotion is only perceived as a behavior to be eliminated, a person may forget what inaugurated it. If so, the frustration at its heart will be neglected. One of the primary reasons for pursuing safety is to establish the conditions in which the succeeding steps of I.A.M. can proceed. Without it, neither incremental tolerance nor an accurate assessment of one's goals can occur. Still, while assuring safety may be the sine qua non of dealing with the dangers inherent in anger, if today's problem is merely effaced, one's mode of attaining security may constitute a dead-end. It may bring momentary peace, but at the cost of long-term happiness.

There are many ways to ensure safety besides prohibiting whatever seems dangerous. We will find that removing the sources of the angry feeling, namely, frustrations or another person's anger, is usually efficacious. Generally, when not immediately confronted with the cause of the emotion, an angry person becomes momentarily less angry. In the next chapter we will discuss specific means of achieving this end, but for the present we will generalize and talk only about how "safe places" can be established.

Several kinds of safe place can reliably be used to defend against problem anger. The first of these is the *safe location*. A literal place, where provocation is not present, can douse a spark before it becomes incendiary. When such a place exists, it can be treated as a fortress into which one can retreat in times of need. Next, there are *safe persons*. These too create envelopes of security. Someone who is not provocative and/or is able to control various sources of external frustration can have a calming effect. Indeed, we human beings are capable of behaving in ways that are biologically soothing, for example, by talking quietly and calmly to one another. Third are *safe activities* that can keep a person busy. These serve as diversions that prevent someone from obsessing about causes of frustration. Fourth come *safe objects* that capture a person's attention. Something as simple as a security blanket, or as sophisticated as a work of art, might qualify in this category. Next are *mental processes* such as daydreams, which, if soothing, are equally adept at removing a person's awareness from what is upsetting. Last come *competences* that enable people to cope effectively with threats and hence certify that they are able to protect themselves. Though these cannot be manufactured in response to a momentary danger, if developed ahead of time, they can be used to meet many predictable dangers. If I know that I have the verbal facility to deflect the insults issued by my enemies, I am less likely to be agitated when I encounter them on the street.

Assuring safety thus takes many forms. It can involve physical controls, calming techniques, literal safe places, and cue training to deflect internal and external threats. Although none of these is infallible or appropriate to all circumstances, if invoked with an eye to their ultimate objective, they can be very effective. They can enable people to begin the process of finding out why they are angry, without having to worry that they or anyone else will be harmed.

INCREMENTAL TOLERANCE

As important as is a guarantee of current safety, it may not be sufficient to initiate an accurate assessment of why a person is angry. Because it only guards against problems in the here and now, it may allow some dangers to endure. While it prevents current explosions, it can not in itself make intense anger feel less dangerous. Thus people who are in the thrall of rage may still want to avoid the feeling because they fear its consequences. They will worry that when they become angry they may go wild unless contingent protective factors intervene. Though they may have reason to believe that they or others can forestall injury, they will not be one hundred percent certain. There will remain the thought that, should they lose control, horrors will ensue. Better then to suppress the emotion and take no chances.

But if, in order to assure safety completely, people won't allow themselves to feel angry, how can they evaluate the emotion or its message? If at the first whiff of distress they shut down, they will clearly have a difficult time ascertaining why they are upset. Objective safety is not the only factor that counts here; people's internal perceptions also have consequences. Only when they feel confident enough to feel their feelings will they be able to examine them and determine what they are about.

Another way of stating this is to say that people must be able to tolerate their anger. They must be able to allow themselves to experience the feeling without reacting as if its mere appearance portends a loss of control. They must recognize that even intense anger can be experienced without being acted upon. Intense anger is, to be sure, very uncomfortable and seems to have a mind of its own; its ability to motivate the self is so strong that it can appear impossible to master. Yet vigorous anger can be controlled; one can feel like acting, without actually doing so. A person can tolerate substantial discomfort while consciously deciding not to suppress its cause.

This ability to tolerate passionate anger without spontaneously succumbing to it is not easy to develop. Young children have great difficulty acquiring it. When they are very angry, they are impelled to do something, and often do. Even adults are challenged to maintain their equanimity when under the sway of a powerful emotion. If a feeling is sufficiently vibrant, it clouds the senses, and any of us can act against our better judgment. Mastering an angry impulse may consume every ounce of strength a person possesses.

Often when having difficulty acquiring a skill, we are urged to press forward. People say that if we fall down while learning to ice skate, we should pick ourselves up and try again. We may fall once more, but eventually we will succeed. The same advice is frequently proffered to people trying to develop impulse control. They may be told to continue expressing their anger until they conquer it. The problem with this approach is that if people allow themselves to experience anger they have not yet conquered, it can conquer them. An inability to tolerate the emotion may establish precisely those conditions that make it impossible to control. Because in this case what they feared might happen does happen, it can further erode their ability to cope. Intense anger, when swallowed whole, is so robust that it can take over and leave no room for learning. Its victims are then motivated only to continue avoiding it. The moral they deduce from their turmoil is that a strong emotion is not be trifled with, that in fact it cannot be controlled.

In any event, the question of whether to plunge into intense anger is generally academic. People not already out of control usually won't do it: the feeling is simply too frightening. Bad experiences have taught them that intense emotions, especially anger, must be handled with care. Consequently they tread lightly. Fortunately this tendency can be turned to advantage. People can learn to tolerate their anger precisely by manipulating it warily. In fact, a greater problem may exist when it is not handled at all than is posed when anger is handled deliberately.

The development of incremental tolerance is predicated on the proposition that any emotion can become less threatening if it is experienced slowly and carefully. Thus, people can first allow themselves to feel a form of anger they are comfortable with, then gradually expand to its more ominous incarnations. They may, for example, find that they are able to get angry when alone, but not when others are around. These others' presence may be so intimidating as to make feeling rage unendurable. To get used to this sort of anger, they may find it advisable to get angry when only one other person is nearby, perhaps a stranger at a considerable distance. Once they are at ease with this situation, it may be possible for them to work up to being angry while in the environs of a close friend, and so forth.

Those familiar with contemporary psychology will quickly recognize this process as comparable to desensitization. Joseph Wolpe (1973), the originator of this treatment, did most of his work with fear and anxiety, but the principles he developed apply equally well to anger. By gradually allowing oneself to experience more intense versions of this emotion, a person can, in time, tolerate considerable quantities of it. As long as it is part of a progressive process that is not pushed faster than he can sustain, incremental learning will occur. The person essentially practices with instances of anger he can marginally accept until they lose their terror. This, in turn, allows him to endure slightly more threatening instances, until ultimately comfort is achieved with them too.

As with the prototypes pioneered by Wolpe, acquiring a tolerance of anger can occur both *in vivo* or *systematically*. What these approaches entail and how they can be achieved will be discussed further in chapter 5. For the moment, however, we may note that both involve much of what is usually labeled catharsis. In Freud's hydraulic model an excess of feeling is controlled by gradually releasing it. The goal is to reduce the pressure by venting it to the outside world. Yet this same process can be interpreted very differently. If it is construed as a form of desensitization in which a person incrementally experiences more intense emotions via a process of talking about them within a safe environment, then catharsis can be understood as promoting the gradual tolerance of anger. Instead of being perceived as the solution to problem hostility, it will then be recognized as but a step toward its management. On such a view, ventilation is not an end itself; it is only a means toward more efficacious control. By preparing the way for an accurate assessment of particular cases, it promotes the eventual dissipation of anger.

EVALUATING ANGER

Once tolerance to problem anger has been achieved and people are able to "feel their feelings" without their automatically escalating, it becomes possible to inspect these feelings to see what they mean. Anger always engenders a message and a mechanism. As an emotion, it is impelled to communicate and to motivate. Therefore, people need to examine where the emotion is trying to go and how it proposes to get there. Its goal, and the means for achieving this, must both be understood if success is to be attained.

Evaluating anger means taking a sharp-eyed look at the objectives of a particular instance. It especially entails becoming aware of the internal messages of the feeling. What goals have been frustrated, and what end points will satisfy those experiencing it? The answers to these questions must be specific, for it is concrete events, and not abstract ambitions, that relieve the inner press of our goal-oriented natures. Evaluating anger also encompasses a reassessment of the mechanisms employed to realize goals. How do people get angry? In what ways, for instance, do they express themselves? What kinds of technique will they institute in order to enlist the compliance of others? Specifically, how is the energy and persistence implicit in the emotion enlisted to make positive things happen? Because anger can be and often is used in a stupid, counterproductive manner, it is essential to consider whether a particular means makes sense. Only then will people be poised to alter ill-advised strategies.

But often the springs of people's anger are hidden from view. They may not hear the message of their rage no matter how loudly it reverberates. Although they may be violently angry, they won't have the faintest idea of why. Yes, they know something is wrong; they just don't know what. Neither the goals at which they aim nor their modes of action are apparent to them. This is especially true of "problem" anger. Because it is overly intense, and frequently misdirected, it routinely makes egregious mistakes. All too often it is primitive and visceral, rather than considered and deliberate. While it makes a lot of noise, it does not move things where they need to go.

Unexamined, primitive anger, while compelling, is unenlightened, and therefore frequently an obstacle to success. As we have already seen, unrestrained anger is usually stupid. It is unsocialized and ill-equipped to influence the complex adult world in which it must operate. Rage, therefore, is usually a prescription for trouble. The mere fact that it is a genuine does not save it from being ineffective. Suppression, however, is rarely the answer. It too is stupid, albeit in a different manner. While rage clouds the brain, suppression freezes it in a stultified and limited universe. In this latter case, because a person is terrified of his feelings, he simply forbids himself to recognize what might otherwise be readily apparent. But self-imposed ignorance is no better calculated to confront hard truths than is a violent tantrum. Both interfere with a person's ability to evaluate his situation. The upshot is that the message and means of his anger become increasingly confused.

Even if neither rage, nor suppression are present, a pessimistic person may still be unable to recognize what he wants. A lack of success in dealing with anger usually breeds further failure. People accustomed to impotence simply stop trying. Because they spend much of their time hiding from their emotions, they have little experience evaluating them. Consequently their ignorance becomes a liability. They simply don't know what needs to be achieved. When they do decide to extricate themselves from this dilemma, they may be surprised to discover what is there to be seen. Because we human beings are adept at fooling ourselves about reality, our actual aspirations can be more of a mystery to us than to our intimates. We may literally convince ourselves that we want things that we hate and that we don't care about things we crave. If we are convinced that an intense desire causes us more pain than it is worth, we can persuade ourselves and others that it is not present or that something else more salient is.

We human beings have many secret desires, some emanating from the obscure dynamics of our distant childhoods, some arising from the complexities of our here-and-now relationships. Desires are generated by all sorts of circumstances, some of which we perceive and some of which we do not. As paradoxical as it may seem, life entails not always being aware of how we are living it. Many times we act on impulses that have not been examined. A desire comes, frequently in the shape of an emotional reaction, and we move without reflection. Moreover, because others are not neutral about what we do, they may feel entitled to tell us how to act. Although we may resist their urgings, sometimes we do comply, all the while not allowing ourselves to realize what is happening. The connection between our desires and their demands is lost on us, and we imagine that underlying our motives are a rationality and independence that do not exist. Though few of us would willingly acknowledge these facts, they are very much the rule.

Instead of examining what they are doing, or why, people typically adopt social explanations for their actions and desires. They, and we, tell ourselves and others what these others want to hear. Socially acceptable formulas proclaim that we are attempting to do something because we are trying to "help" or because we are defending a vital "principle." That our real objective is to gain someone's respect by beating a third person into submission is unlikely to be acknowledged. Nor is a desire to be the family favorite apt to be openly asserted. We know full well that a candid admission of either would not promote our cause. Indeed, too much candor with ourselves is also dangerous because we might slip and say things out loud.

Shakespeare advised "to thine own self be true," but his counsel is more honored in the breach. In fact, it seems that few people acquire the habit of honest introspection. For most of us, it is an unfamiliar and even risky exercise. The thought of looking closely at our desires or our real modes of interaction arouses images of wanting monstrously dangerous things or of pursuing them in ferociously destructive ways. The reality is that most of us feel it is best not to know why we are angry or how we are trying to secure our aims, for fear that the answers will be unacceptable.

The irony is that, for the overwhelming majority of us, an examination of the goals and mechanisms of our anger will reveal no scandals. When these are honestly evaluated, it turns out that what we want is fairly modest and that our strategies are reasonably civilized. Few people really want to commit murder so that they can rule the world. Despite having fantasies of this sort, in our more lucid moments we generally think better of them. Yes, we want to win, but not everything, and not at all costs.

How then do people recognize their actual goals or reconsider the mechanisms used to achieve them? How do they arrive at an understanding that it is uncontrolled, primitive anger, not what they truly desire, that is dangerous? Some people may think that having desires, or trying to realize them, is itself the problem, but were this true, it would be virtually impossible for anyone ever to achieve satisfaction. If, in consequence of their trepidations, they decided to feel nothing, their life might be as placid as that of the proverbial clam, but it would also be as empty.

One of the most important mechanisms for surmounting this "nirvana myth" is the standard therapeutic advice to "feel one's feelings." Nothing is better suited to persuading people that what they want is valid than actually experiencing their desire. Nevertheless, in order to evaluate the message of their anger and to see what it really implies, people must have the courage to feel and to observe. They must be able to stop and ask, "What am I feeling, and why am I feeling it?" "What am I striving for, and what is thwarting my efforts?" Then they must stay to hear the answers.

Obviously more than one question is involved here, none of which can be asked only once with definitive results. Rather, finding out about underlying goals and means is a process that entails keeping on the alert. It is surprising how much people can ascertain once they are receptive to learning. Insights pop up unexpectedly. They may come as awe inspiring revelations or subtle changes in orientation. A person might, for example, suddenly realize, while preparing to go to a party, that her husband is emotionally distant in the same way her father was, that his focus is more on what he is wearing than it is on her. Or it may gradually become apparent that she hopes to extract a kind of love from him that he is incapable of giving. After years of fighting, she may slowly comprehend that this tactic is backfiring and that he is, if anything, being induced to be less loving than he might be if he were allowed to approach her on his own terms.

Whatever the realization, and however it arrives, when it does, the next question will be how to apply it.

It may be, however, that introspection is unfruitful. No matter how much effort we employ or how honest we are, nothing may come of it. In this case, other people may be needed as a kind of mirror. Their perceptions about what is happening can prove pivotal. This is where friends, relatives, and professional helpers come in. Assuming that they have our interests at heart and are reasonably insightful, they may see and share things that we, in the grip of a strong emotion, do not. They may point things out, which once identified, we will later be able to distinguish for ourselves.

But why should others possess an ability to perceive what we ourselves cannot? If our anger belongs to us, how can they gain a better fix on it than we do? There are several reasons. First, others may be more disinterested. If they are not bound up in our emotion—or their own—their vision may be less obfuscated by passion.

Second, because emotions communicate, they too can hear the message of our anger. Indeed, the import of a particular piece of anger is often more clearly conveyed to the person at whom it is aimed than the one who experiences it. Third, others may also be the recipients of our efforts at influence. As such, they have special access to how these efforts operate. (This is related to the therapeutic modality called *transference*.) Fourth, helpers can engage in roletaking. They can empathetically place themselves in the shoes of an angry person and use introspection to distinguish what the other cannot.

RELINQUISHING IMPOSSIBLE GOALS OR MEANS

The fourth stage of I.A.M. involves relinquishing unattainable objectives and strategies and is a direct consequence of the preceding evaluation phase. Frustrations cannot be terminated nor anger quieted, if the goals a person is pursuing are not achievable. If in fighting for a particular purpose, it slips forever over the horizon, the fight can be drawn out indefinitely. Indeed, it may escalate dangerously. Therefore, one may have to change one's goals rather than keep up the struggle. But such reversals entail letting go of previous directions, which can be a problem in itself.

Of the five stages of anger management, the relinquishing phase is most likely to be optional. It need occur only when an examination of one's goals proves them unworthy. Only when it is discovered that they are impossible or incommensurate with the effort necessary to obtain them is it incumbent upon a person to let go and move on. Similarly, only if a strategy proves hopelessly ineffectual is it necessary to renounce it in favor of other alternatives. Typically, however, people's attachments to their goals are stronger than to their means and thus are more difficult to relinquish.

One of the more terrible discoveries people can make when scrutinizing their goals is that they preclude success. Recognizing that one can't win is a horrible twist of fate. After all, persons who have been fighting strenuously for particular goals generally believe them to be important. Their impossibility will not be a matter of indifference. They can't just shrug their shoulders and move on, yet it may be imperative that they do precisely this. If, for instance, they are seeking love from someone who is incapable of giving it, they will continue to lose unless they change their purpose. No matter how meaningful a goal, if it can't be obtained, continuing to pursue it implies perpetual failure. Lost causes, like dead horses, do not suddenly spring to life. Although it may be difficult to tell when a defeat is unavoidable, one must be prepared for the possibility and acknowledge it when it becomes evident.

The relinquishing phase of I.A.M. exists for the same reason that anger itself exists. We human beings are teleological creatures. We have purposes that we work mightily to effectuate. If we did not, we would not need anger to help attain them. Likewise, if we did not have attachments to goals, we would not have to let go of them when they fail. Were the things at which we aim as interchangeable as grains of sand on a beach, when a hope evaporated, it would be simple to pick up another grain. But important goals are not like this, so when we make a commitment, to find that we must surrender it is agonizing.

Sometimes we even commit to the strategies used to obtain specific goals. It is not unknown for a means to become an end. When this happens, instead of being flexible, we persist in contending in the same old patterns despite their having proved ineffectual. We make repetitive demands; we throw tantrums; we twist arms. And then we get angrier because our techniques don't work.

So how do we let go of an impossible objective or an ill-conceived means? How can these sturdy attachments be ruptured? The answer lies in mourning. Grief is nature's way of breaking ties with things that have been lost. When someone dies, we grieve; that is, we become sad and withdrawn and do not feel better until we have said our good-byes. This process may take time, but without it we remain mired in the past.

Losing an important goal is not unlike a death. Think of how it might feel to discover that one can never obtain the love of one's parents. We all know how important such love is and how fiercely we would be prepared to struggle for it. But imagine the impact of realizing that one's parents are incapable of such love. For years one may have believed that if one tried a little harder or was a little more dutiful, a parent would relent. Surely, someday there would be a tearful reconciliation in which everyone admitted that a terrible mistake had been made. But what happens when it becomes clear there will never be such a reconciliation because the parent is an emotional cripple, too engaged in self-defense ever to reach out and offer love? The bottom will drop out of a person's world. The agony of realizing that the desired love will never be available can be unendurable, as if someone special had truly died. Certainly, the person's hopes will have. Nor should it be surprising that he feels as if he too has died.

Grieving over the passing of a vital goal is one of the more painful experiences any human being can endure. It is never welcome and usually resisted. People would rather go on fighting hopelessly than suffer the anguish of an acknowledged loss. They perceive the pain they are experiencing not as a barrier to be breached, but as a conclusion to be avoided. Because they are not prepared to separate from the loss, they shun the reevaluation phase of I.A.M. or act as if they had never made the dreaded discovery. At such moments, they may need help facing reality. It is here that family, friends, and helping professionals can provide a critical service. At the very least, others can be supportive and help those who suffer such a fate to hold on to life, even though they feel like releasing it. In particular, helpers can give permission to grieve by instilling the hope of ultimately prevailing. Though people may not initially see a connection between sadness and anger, a more dispassionate outsider can keep these emotions in perspective and thereby facilitate the normal workings of mourning.

But because grief is almost as painful to those who observe it as to those who experience it, the former may have a tendency to reinforce the desire to avoid grief. If overcoming anger depends on another's being able to accept and even encourage the feeling, this need can be a terrible liability. Helpers have to understand the nature of sadness and allow it to proceed, or they may inadvertently strengthen the trap holding their "client."

USING ANGER

It does no good for people to recognize which of their goals have been frustrated or even which are feasible if they do nothing with this knowledge. Achieving goals, not just perceiving them, is what reduces anger. People have to go out into the world and make things happen. During the evaluation phase of I.A.M., they should have reconsidered the means they have been using to procure objectives. Because they are coping with unresolved anger, it is a sure bet that whatever mechanisms they have been employing will, to some extent, be found wanting. From this, they should acquire valuable lessons. Though they may not yet know how to obtain what they want, they will better understand how not to achieve these things. This is no trivial accomplishment, for often we zero in on our best strategies by first eliminating the worst. It is also important to realize that, because anger has hitherto not worked, does not mean anger per se will not work. Despite false starts, anger is still a necessary emotion. It should not be viewed as a foe. Rather, one must avoid its previous incarnations.

The purpose of anger is to obtain goals. The trick is to execute it appropriately. To repeat what has been said earlier, with anger the question is not whether to express it, but how to utilize it. Anger is a resource, not merely a compelling passion. But using it effectively is a delicate matter. It is easy to execute wrongly and difficult to employ suitably. Although anger can motivate both the self and the other, it does not always push in the right direction or with the correct amount of force. Instead of making things work, it can boomerang, leaving a bigger mess than existed before.

Many contemporary anger management programs fail to appreciate that anger must be socialized before it can operate satisfactorily. People do not merely retain or expel the emotion; they must learn to do so in specific ways within specific contexts. What happens when they do will depend both on how their anger is expressed and on how it is received. What works in interactions between angry people and those at whom their anger is directed is not always easy to determine. So many variables are involved that results can be hard to predict. What is certain is that anger is not a phenomenon that has only an on-and-off switch. It is not just a doing or a not-doing, but a how-to-do.

Sometimes anger is portrayed as a three-way switch that has aggressive, assertive, and passive positions. One is then told that only the assertive position should be turned on. Aggression is described as causing injury and passivity as permitting it, while assertiveness is said to be direct, temperate, and successful. Unfortunately, this portrait describes only an aspect of reality, which it simplifies enormously. Assertiveness does not always work, for as we've seen, directly and forcefully calling one's employer wrong can get one fired. Nor is passivity always wrong. Sometimes it is the only way to evade the wrath of a tyrant. Even aggressiveness can be appropriate, as, for example, when used to stop a bully. The fact is that each position is sometimes appropriate and sometimes inappropriate, depending upon a complex set of social factors that can not be known in advance. A person may need to figure out which is best when the time arrives.

Nor is individual strength the only arbiter of successful anger. Force of personality may be an important variable in determining whether someone will succeed, but it can not sweep everything before it. Many people remain victims of a fable carried forward from childhood that urges them to believe some people are inherently so vigorous that their anger can overpower all conceivable opposition. They may feel weak and incapable of overpowering many others, for they are acutely aware of the countless times others have not trembled before them, but they think they should be invincible. This myth may be shopworn, but it is a potent illusion. It suggests than any door can be broken down if a person is strong enough or, as significant, if a person tries hard enough. This, of course, is arrant nonsense. We all know that there are some doors too sturdy to be shattered. Yet the myth persists, and many angry people believe that if only they become a little angrier, their opponent will suddenly capitulate.

As we shall later see, the decibel level of anger does not correlate very well with its effectiveness. "Louder and more passionate" does not always equate to "more persuasive." Actually, it is quiet, intelligent anger that is more likely to be efficacious. Planful anger, not an intemperate outburst, is better calculated to exploit the motivation of another and so tends to work better. Blind rage is generally only a prelude to equally violent counter-anger.

Many factors need to be considered when preparing to be angry. People must assess the relative strength of their role partners, have an awareness of what motivates them, evaluate the current tactical situation, and survey potential allies. It makes an enormous difference whether they are dealing with a superior, an equal, or subordinate, what the other persons' goals and norms are, how many other battles they are engaged in simultaneously, and whether there will be a backup if they begin to lose. Each of these circumstances requires a different quantity of energy, which must be applied in a different place. Hence, no single plan can fit all contingencies.

The title of this book, *I.A.M.*, was meant to underline the functional nature of anger and to indicate that how people implement the emotion is complex and consequential. Anger management programs frequently imply that the proper use of anger is virtually automatic, that as long as a person is entitled to be angry, its judicious expression must work. This, however, is far from the truth, in large part because human relationships are so diverse. People need to learn a great deal before skillfully exploiting the emotion. They must not only know what they want and be able to control their impulses, they must also be capable of judging the impact of their efforts. In subsequent chapters, we will consider some of these intricacies. We will then ask the questions of when, how, and with whom.

4

Assuring Safety

FIRST THINGS FIRST

Safety is essential. It cannot be emphasized too strongly that without safety, anger cannot be controlled. Evaluating anger or putting it to use are empty gestures without the presence of security. When on the rampage, anger is so dangerous that mechanisms for terminating frustration become pointless. The first priority for dealing with problem anger must therefore be avoiding injury. There must be no blood on the floor and no irreversible physical damage. It is even a good idea to shun emotional damage, for it too can be difficult to repair.

Yet people often have trouble guarding against their own anger. It is so frightening, so potentially explosive, that they prefer to pretend it does not exist. Using an Ostrich defense, they convince themselves there is nothing to worry about, even when there is. Their hope is that it will somehow go away and everything will be all right. They may also use a Chicken Little defense that detects catastrophes lurking everywhere. At the merest whiff of an argument, they will feel endangered and scurry away before the sky can fall. Such persons typically demand that their role partners refrain from yelling at them, even when they are in fact whispering. To them, anger is loud and menacing whenever and wherever it appears.

Because anger really can be dangerous, it is crucial to ascertain when a threat is imminent. Otherwise, efforts at defending against it will be futile and disorganized. The best way to protect against problem anger is to perceive it coming and to accurately assess its dimensions. Because efforts to guard against it must be directed toward appropriate hazards with a suitable degree of force, it is vital to recognize what these are and how powerful they are. Yet potential countermeasures also hold the prospect of danger. Unless they are intelligently managed, they can create greater problems than they deter.

Protecting against the ravages of anger can occur both before and after it has gone out of control. It is possible to prevent it from escaping its boundaries, or, once it is loose, to contain it and limit the damage. Prevention is, of course, the superior alternative; but when one is unsuccessful in this, techniques must be available for returning anger to the reservation. These methods, however, should themselves be controllable. They must be calculated to assure safety, not to blast unwanted anger out of existence.

The best way to contain anger is obviously through self-control. Whether before or after the fact, people who can guard against their own violent impulses are most likely to keep themselves and others secure. Because the people experiencing anger are best able to see it coming and can be counted upon to be present when it explodes, they are best fitted to limit it. As useful and necessary as external constraints may be, they are often several steps behind events. Moreover, they may not be available when needed. Helpers are not always nearby or inclined to be helpful. Therefore, the safest form of control is personal; if people can be taught to exercise such control, they will be the gainers. Among the mechanisms that can be used to achieve self-control are physical restraints, calming techniques, and cue training. The most important form of control, however, is frustration management.

AVOIDING FRUSTRATION

Because it is usually frustration that initiates anger, it makes sense that avoiding frustration can forestall anger. To use a cliched analogy, if frustration is the red flag that enrages the bull, why not take away the flag? The stratagem is simple: remove the cause and inhibit the effect. But how is this to be accomplished? There would seem to be two general strategies possible: one is to remove the source of frustration, the other to prevent it from being perceived. Since it is usually much more difficult to eliminate a frustration than to disguise it, the latter tactic is more important in containing violent anger. Because it is often essential to do something quickly, one manipulates the more easily alterable perception rather than the obdurate reality.

Though this may be only a temporary remedy, when safety is at stake, the value of a momentary reprieve must not be underestimated. Changing the actualities of a frustrating situation and attaining more durable benefits will have to await the completion of a more lengthy anger management process.

Still, we are left with the problem of preventing a person from perceiving that which is frustrating him. How can it be arranged so that he does not recognize that his goals are being stymied? Once again there would seem to be a number of possibilities. 1. A person can literally move away from the source of his frustration. 2. The object or event exciting his wrath can be removed from his vicinity. 3. He can be prevented from seeing what is happening, for instance, by diverting his attention toward something else. 4. Someone, or something, can intercede between him and whatever it is that is setting him off.

1. Suppose a woman is having a fight with her husband. She wants him to take out the garbage, but he refuses. Instead of staying toe-to-toe and nose-to-nose, she can leave the room. She might go for a walk. Once she has removed herself from the source of her annoyance, she should be able to calm down. Without him around to remind her of how exasperating he is, her irritation will subside. And once calmed down, the chances of an explosion are reduced. Indeed, even if there is a loss of control, its natural target will not be accessible.

2. But if it is a woman's husband who is causing her grief, she does not have to be the one who leaves the room: he can. The source of her frustration can literally be relocated. One can, as it were, physically remove the flag from the bull. This will not make the problem disappear, but for the moment it will seem to. Such is the tactic of the enraged parent who shouts at her child: Get out of my sight!

3. An object of frustration does not have to be physically manipulated for it to become less visible. Looking in a different direction can have the same effect. Distractions, diversions, and even jokes can take a person's mind off of that which he cannot tolerate. It is difficult to attack that upon which one is no longer focused.

4. Even if a person can see what is irritating her, it may not be possible to get at it. When someone physically intercedes between two disputants, the angry person can usually recognize that there exists a greater operational distance between her and her target. This physiological distance will then create a psychological barrier that allows room to cool down. Though someone's trigger may have been

pulled, if the firing pin has been removed, she may think twice before pulling the trigger again.

All of the above techniques can momentarily obviate frustrations. While not eliminating or making them invisible, such measures can obscure frustrations, thereby buying time. Though all diversions may do is calm people down, they will allow them to take other measures before heating up again. Furthermore, a series of postponements can prevent an explosion from ever occurring, for they may never get back to the original source of irritation. In the meantime, they can get so involved with other projects that their goals change. Better still, if they can learn to introduce diversions whenever an outburst impends, they can throttle further outbursts. Frustration avoidance may not be an optimal solution, but it can extend over a wealth of hazards. Though it does not answer all dangers, it can guard against a multitude of them.

It should also be noted that sometimes safety is achieved not by diverting frustrations, but by marching straight into their teeth. The object may not be to interdict an explosion, but to allow it to occur under favorable circumstances. Not all bombs are protected against by defusing them; some are rendered harmless by detonating them in a bomb-proof container. When an explosive has gone off in such an enclosure, its energy is muffled and others can breath more easily. With anger, we confront a warhead with a potential to explode repeatedly. Nevertheless, if a person can discharge his rage in safe directions, he may become exhausted and hence more easily managed. One way to implement this stratagem is to have a person aim his anger at a target that will not be overwhelmed by it. For example, if a man is enraged by his wife, his getting angry at her may result in her being grievously upset. If, however, he takes this same anger and directs it at his psychotherapist, she may be barely perturbed. The satisfaction he obtains from verbally berating this third party may not be the equivalent of verbally abusing his wife, but it can temporarily reduce his rancor. It may then be possible to address what is really upsetting him and to make some changes.

The reason it is sometimes necessary to allow explosions to occur is the so-called Zigarnec effect. This phenomenon, discovered by gestalt psychologists early in this century, involves what they called "closure." It seems that we human beings usually feel impelled to complete things once we have started them. Thus, we attempt to fill in the empty space in an unfinished circle and strive to complete a paragraph once we have begun reading it. This same tendency afflicts us when we become angry. When something has ignited our fury, we do not want to rest until we have expressed our feeling in some fashion. Thus, we may feel driven to yell at someone who has frustrated us before we are ready to settle down and change directions. In other words, it may be impossible to prevent someone from saying what is on his mind once he gets going. The only option may be to allow him to act out his indignation, excepting that we will arrange for this to occur in a safe environment. Then after psychological completion has been achieved, other methods of frustration avoidance can be implemented.

EXERCISING PHYSICAL CONTROL

As has been noted, anger is frequently confused with aggression. While the two are not identical, it is easy to see why they have been confounded. Out-of-control anger does often result in aggression, and enraged people do make efforts to injure others. They are motivated to do more than merely tell their role partners about their anger; they feel impelled to do things like beating, shooting, and stabbing them. Violently angry people also engage in mutilations, torture, and vendettas. Such persons may actually take delight in causing anguish to others.

Given these possibilities, aggressively angry people cannot be allowed to wreck their will unchecked. They must be controlled, whether or not this is in their interest. If, in preventing someone from implementing unfair anger, his frustrations are deepened, this is something he will have to bear. While his interests remain important, they cannot be allowed to obliterate the well-being of others. While we, who must interact with him, may care about his unhappiness, we do not care so much that we are ready to acquiesce in injustices to innocent parties. Even here it is best if the angry person controls himself, but if necessary we must oppose him from the outside. Whatever force is required must be considered. Though this can entail acts we would in other circumstances abhor, we may have no choice. The alternative, namely casual violence, would be tantamount to anarchy.

How then is physical control to be imposed? First, it must be recognized that this is not the automatic responsibility of passing strangers. It is not incumbent upon us to intervene personally, whenever we see someone exploding in violent rage. Despite the dangers he represents, an aggressor may be bigger or stronger than we are, and we may not be able to prevent his depredations. Remember that rage enhances a person's strength; therefore personally opposing him just because we perceive him to be unfair can be foolhardy. It tempts fate and begs to become a target oneself.

What then to do? The answer should be self-evident. We often need to call for help. When our own strength is insufficient, or when criminal violence is being committed, we must have access to others who can assist in asserting control. Fortunately, this is not a new problem, and society has developed institutions to serve in remedying it. Thus, we have police forces, armies, prisons, social work agencies, religious institutions, and the like, the purpose of which is to impose constraints on malefactors and deviants. This world is no utopia, so it is essential that we possess stable social arrangements for maintaining fairness. In particular, specific individuals have been delegated to implement social control and consequently are authorized to become expert in the requisite skills. They are available to be called upon when needed and should be. Our safety, and that of our loved ones, may depend on it.

This is not to suggest that we need a police state in order to defend against violent anger. Far from it, a dependable constabulary and readily available protective services decrease the prospect that they will have to be used. There is less indiscriminate use of force in the modern world than there was in ancient times precisely because force is more reliably available. Since potential aggressors can predict that their violence will be resisted, they are less apt to engage in it. Despite appearances derived from the media, the physical restriction of aggression via prisons, fines, and mental hospitals is a crucial, and more or less effective, check upon unrestrained anger. Moreover, in spite of recent evidences of police abuse, well-organized police departments greatly decrease the incidence of random destructiveness by social authorities themselves. Back in the Middle Ages, if a nobleman felt his honor was being besmirched by a serf, he could with impunity cut him down. As recently as the ante-bellum South, a slaveholder could whip a recalcitrant field hand to death. Contemporary social institutions strive to prevent such atrocities and consequently have rules aimed at deterring arbitrary action. Those charged with maintaining control are instructed that they are not supposed to lose control themselves, and usually don't, in spite of the obvious exceptions.

One of the formulas used to define this limitation is the "least restrictive force" rule. Those who intervene to prevent violent explosions are enjoined to interfere with a malefactor's freedom as little as possible and to use only the degree of coercion needed to avert injury. The injury referred to is that of the potential victim, the restraining official, and the perpetrator. In the real world, of course, it is difficult to juggle these respective rights. Often it is also difficult to ascertain how much force is adequate. Because those charged with maintaining order are merely human beings, their judgment is not always perfect, and when their emotions are engaged, they too can become unfair.

Nonetheless, this is the best option we currently have. Both vigilance and reform may be necessary to make social control work, but we cannot on this account renounce it when dealing with anger. The simple fact is that when problem anger threatens, it is valid to call upon the police or child protective services. Likewise, if court orders are necessary, or a hospitalization indicated, these should be accessed. Too delicate a sensibility or an overdeveloped sense of equity intent upon avoiding all mistakes open the door to unspeakable brutality and/or to vigilante justice. Nor should individual heroics be loudly applauded. No one ought feel compelled to prove competence by confronting an enraged person alone. Though our sources of help are admittedly imperfect, they are far superior to playing the lone gunslinger.

This same counsel applies to the professional helper. Too often those with therapeutic responsibilities feel inadequate if they cannot by themselves restrain potentially violent clients. They do not ask for help lest it appear that their clinical skills are deficient. Yet professionals who attempt to tough it out put themselves under unnecessary pressure. They should know that the frightened clinician is the one least likely to be helpful and that placing oneself in avoidable danger is a sign not of competence, but of insecurity. It is experienced and secure counselors who keep their office doors open when interviewing a client on the edge of rage.

Among the mechanisms professionals have developed for physically controlling dangerously angry clients are "takedowns," "wraps," and "touch-control." They have also evolved mechanisms for fending off blows and for breaking a client's grip on their hair. The object of all of these maneuvers is to interfere with a client's ability to inflict harm. Putting violent people down on the floor or wrapping one's arms around them prevents them from lashing out. Likewise, the martial arts can be used to turn an attacker's energy against himself. Since rage is dumb, its incoherent violence is particularly suscepti- ble to countermeasures that redirect its force.

Touch control is a particularly elegant way of implementing non- restrictive force. Frequently, all that is required of helpers is that they place a reassuring hand on the shoulder of a person who is about to lose composure. Gentle contact from someone who clearly means no ill and who appears competent to intercede physically signals the presence of dependable physical control. It can therefore stimulate a person's internal controls. The touch of a powerful other says in ef- fect: Stay calm lest more forceful restraints be imposed. Nevertheless such reminders are only effective with those who are prepared to accept them. Touch can actually be provocative when applied to someone who does not wish to be touched.

CALMING TECHNIQUES

Most of the time, even in the case of potential violence, it is not necessary to get physical. Enraged people usually can be helped without the use of force. Although intense anger feels automatic, it can generally be brought under control by lowering its temperature. A whole panoply of procedures are specifically designed for this pur- pose. These "calming" techniques can be implemented by an angry person himself or by those with whom he is in contact. They include reassuring talk and reassuring actions and can encompass the use of safe places, safe persons, and safe activities. They also entail the ap- plication of distractions and alternative motives, all of which can be deployed separately or in concert.

Safe Places

The object of a safe place is to remove people from frustrating en- vironments that might set them off. They can be expected to calm down once they are no longer provoked. A safe place is one where provocations are not visible. Thus an individual or circumstance that signals frustration is physically removed from the whereabouts of the angry person, or the angry person is transferred to a neutral location. As previously indicated, the simplest way to accomplish this is to encourage the angry person or an adversary to leave the room. This is standard operating procedure in institutions charged with control- ling violent inmates. Whenever a fight impends, staff members attempt to separate the protagonists. Moreover, individuals who do not get along are assigned to different parts of a building or placed on different schedules. The assumption is that if their paths don't cross, untoward incidents will not occur.

A corollary of this procedure is that an interposition of space can be reassuring. The more distance between people and whatever upsets them, the more confident they will be that they won't be provoked. This, in essence, is the theory behind vacations. These are justified on the basis of stress reduction, but what this can come down to is removing people from those day-to-day frustrations over which they have little control. Even psychotherapy is dependent upon establishing safe places. Thus, a therapist's office is usually arranged to be nonthreatening. Persons a client finds nettlesome are ordinarily not admitted, and the room is designed to be quiet, safe, and warm. An observer would find it furnished with comfortable chairs, nonjarring decorations, and a diminished level of lighting. All of these provide sanctuary by purposefully excluding stimuli reminiscent of frustrating elements in the outside world.

Safe Persons

Of course, no safe place is sufficient unto itself. If it is occupied by unsafe persons, the effect is lost. The single most frustrating, and therefore dangerous, element for a human being is other people. If these are present, and discernibly threatening, defensive anger is virtually inevitable. To calm people, it may consequently be necessary to surround them with nonthreatening, nonfrustrating others, who must not be provocative or even appear to be.

In contrast, soothing others can symbolize safety. For this to occur, such peoples' voices should be reassuring and their demeanor nonthreatening. Few sharp edges should be exposed, which means that voices should not be grating or language harsh. Similarly, body language must exude an air of relaxation and avoid any indication of mobilizing to attack. The message safe people want to deliver is that they are neither angry nor frightened and therefore have no reason to be frustrating. Of course, the best way for helpers to seem safe is to be safe. Those attempting to calm an intensely angry person must carefully evaluate their own motivation. If they are angry or disingenuous, this will usually be discovered. Successful calming depends upon trust, which is rarely extended without merit. People, including angry people, are sensitive to the machinations of dangerous others. Their vigilance is not disarmed unless they can be satisfied that they really are safe.

Safe persons must usually demonstrate that they are on the side of the enraged person. They must not be moved to counter-anger or have hidden agendas. When an angry person's wrath tries to blow them down, they must stand their ground and behave in a nonconfrontational and nondemanding manner. Likewise, they must be sincere and nonmanipulative, not given to airs or to talking down to those they are ostensibly helping. Because not everyone is capable of such self-restraint, not everyone is equipped to be soothing. Those who themselves operate on hair triggers or who are grappling with intense personal frustrations should recognize their limitations and not overextend themselves.

Sometimes being a safe person entails more than avoiding further mayhem. Sometimes it translates into offering positive assistance, that is, into helping angry people overcome the frustrations inflaming them. This is the strategy of the parent who calms an enraged baby by producing the lollipop for which the infant has been clamoring. When dealing with people of limited ability, such as the mentally retarded, this approach can be invaluable. Often one cannot seem safe to such persons unless one helps them obtain what they cannot obtain on their own. One would otherwise be perceived as part of the problem. In other words, safe people are often those who protect people from themselves. The gratifications they supply may not be long lasting, but they do provide a warrant that the helper means no harm. Because they remove occasions for anger, they give the world, and their provider, an aura of benevolence.

Safe Activities

Since frustrations arise from not attaining desperate desires, seeking other objects can help reduce them. When people change the activities in which they are engaged, their priorities change. What had been the cynosure of their efforts loses its salience and hence its ability to be provocative. Thus, if violent anger can be deflected into different channels, angry people can be calmed down. The energy they have been expending to break through one door will be dissipated by directing it against another, possibly less breakable, door. Intensely angry people can be encouraged to go for a walk, to take a swim, or to go jogging. Any kind of sport that requires an effort can be substituted for an unfruitful struggle to overcome an intractable frustration. As their energies have already been mobilized, they can be exhausted by trying to do something different and presumably safer. Instead of punching an opponent in the gut, a person can be encouraged to slug a heavy bag. While this will not solve his problem, the person may become temporarily less dangerous, for the moment hobbled by the tranquility of the weary.

Intensely angry people can even be encouraged to break things. Primitive rage often feels driven to smash small objects. Happily, this impulse can be appeased by breaking things that are unimportant and cheap. Popping a paper bag or throwing a light bulb against a wall can cause a gratifying noise without creating much collateral damage. A similar effect can be had by yelling or cursing as loudly as one desires. Doing so in a place where one will not be heard—for instance, in a moving car with the windows rolled up and the radio blaring—can ensure that no damage is done. Screaming can make a person feel as if he is doing something and will be appropriately tiring, without alienating potential adversaries.

Changing the activities in which people are engaged also redirects their attention. Persuading them to look elsewhere encourages them to look away from the source of frustration. While out walking or swimming, they are no longer face-to-face with their opponents; and the effort they expend will lead to thoughts other than a thirst for revenge. If no other safe activity is effective in instituting this sort of calm, it may be possible to impose a "time out." Instead of asking people to engage in an alternative activity, we can urge them to do nothing, at least for a time. People may even be placed in a quiet room, thereby allowing them an opportunity to "think" about their situation.

Distractions

It is also possible to change people's state of mind more directly. Instead of altering the surroundings or their activities, we can aim at modifying patterns of thought. In particular, if their attention can be diverted, they should become less angry. If their thoughts are turned to less-provocative objects, they will be less frustrated. This is the purpose of telling angry people jokes. It may seem absurd trying to be funny with those who are about to explode, yet if they can be made to laugh, they will no longer be intent upon causing injury. Think of how parents make faces at children who are about to throw a tantrum. Their hope is plainly that if the child can be induced to giggle, he will forget what happened. Though a child may be more easily diverted than an adult, even an adult can be pacified by a good comic movie.

Attention can also be redirected by other means, such as telling a story, asking questions that require an answer, or starting to watch television or listen to music. What will work depends upon the nature of the angry person, the helper, their joint situation, and the cause of the person's anger. There is no one best way to be distracting. The respective interests and strengths of the parties, as well as the availability of engaging alternatives, will be the determining factor.

A very generalized technique for distracting people is to slow them down. If, instead of swinging into action, they can be induced to delay their response, it may be inhibited entirely. The traditional advice to "count to ten" depends upon this mechanism. Counting gets people thinking about something else, at least for a few moments. Likewise, asking them to take deep breaths diverts them from their initial purpose. Though the time involved is not great, it may be sufficient to derail them and enable them to regain control. Time-outs also work by diverting attention and creating a setting that encourages people to reflect on their defects. Even getting angry at one's helper can divert anger from its original object. Many a knife fight has been interrupted by companions who have interposed their bodies so that they interfere with an aggressor's line of sight and make themselves the target. As long as such Samaritans can keep from being sliced up, they can help a person forget the true source of his anger.

Alternative Motives

A particularly effective way of distracting people is to appeal to motives beyond those underlying their present anger. Everyone has goals in addition to those whose frustration has excited current rage. If these other goals can be made more salient, they can generate efforts that will replace those directed toward achieving the initial goal. If this new aspiration can be made to seem more important than the old, obtaining it will take priority. For example, it may be pointed out that a person's impending actions are in conflict with greater values than the ones she is currently seeking and that, in striving for the latter, she interferes with the former. Thus, if someone can be persuaded that a current behavior is not "kind," or that a loved one needs help more than an enemy needs to be harmed, these newly aroused goals may take precedence.

Often this strategy includes what has been called "self-talk." People on the verge of losing control can be asked to give themselves what amounts to a pep talk. For instance, if about to commit violence, they can stop and implore themselves "not to do anything stupid." Should physically or emotionally violating other persons contravene their strongly held convictions, they may be able to convince themselves to desist. Or if they can persuade themselves that the long-term consequences of initiating a battle go against their interests, they can decide it is more prudent to still their hand. When people are not inclined to engage in this sort of internal conversation, it can come from someone else. Friends can remind friends of values both hold dear. "You're a good guy; you don't really want to do this. We can work it out." It is sometimes even possible for a physically small individual to calm an intimidating peer by appealing to the latter's self-interest. For example, a helper who is being threatened with assault would find it less useful to say, "I forbid you to hit me," than to say, "I don't think you genuinely want to hurt me." The first response is confrontive and virtually dares the other to act, while the second calls upon underlying goals. Making people feel good about themselves, perhaps by mobilizing their central commitments, is usually more efficacious in gaining cooperation than is trying to extort it.

CUE TRAINING

A technique specifically aimed at helping people induce self-control is "cue-training," which is based upon the assumption that few people willingly lose control. When they go wild, it is not because they enjoy the display or relish causing injury. Rather, their anger simply gets out of hand, and they find themselves unable to restrain it. Because they are intent upon achieving a specific objective and yet are being consistently frustrated, their anger accelerates until it becomes primitive and blind. Such people may be eager to discover more effective ways of obtaining control. If they can be persuaded that they have a better chance to win when they take charge of their efforts, they will usually want to assume command. Once they realize that someone who is not enraged can think more clearly and hence can act more effectively, it will make sense to them to avoid the worst aspects of their rage.

Perhaps the best way to manage rage is to catch it before it goes on automatic. One must, as it were, "catch it on the rise," while it is still controllable. The secret here is to recognize the point beyond which constraints become ineffective and to make changes before then. To remain safe, anger must be kept on the tame side. Nevertheless, how does one recognize the place beyond which extensive damage is virtually inevitable? How are people to perceive when their anger is becoming too intense for their own good? This may not be as easy as it sounds, because excessive passion induces myopia in those under its sway. When people are in a state of fury, they are often the least able to discern that they are going overboard. Their rising state of agitation interferes with their judgment and precludes a determination of the point of no return.

Because anger is dangerous, it is frightening; and because it is frightening, people refrain from observing it too closely. They are far more likely to repress it than to recognize it for what it is. Indeed, they may be inclined to deny it just when they should be trying to ascertain whether it is becoming too vigorous. Instead of noticing the danger signs, they march blithely over the precipice. The trick, therefore, is to see the signs of impending trouble before it arises. If people can be alert to the changes in themselves that occur when their anger is escalating, they may be able to recognize their situation and act in a timely manner. If they know that particular feelings or movements generally occur before they become enraged, these signals can be monitored and heeded.

There are many potential cues to approaching rage. The signs vary from person to person, but everyone has some. It thus becomes incumbent upon us to know ourselves, especially those of us who are subject to problem anger. We may, for instance, notice that we clench our teeth at moments of frustration. Or perhaps we tighten our fists, or our stomach cramps, or our face turns red. For some people, the activities in which they engage are a dead giveaway. They may pace the floor or begin talking more rapidly than is usual. Also, because anger motivates us to fight, it can prepare our bodies for action in visible ways, such as in a jiggling foot, tightened eyes, or a piece of cloth twisting in our fingers. In any event, these occurrences can be observed by individuals and by those in contact with them and therefore can serve as indicators of danger. Unfortunately, they often go unnoticed. People can be so riveted by the central drama of their anger that they overlook these ancillary phenomena. It may take an explicit effort to perceive them.

Often this awareness must begin with a helper, rather than with the angry person. The dispassionate helper can more readily observe small details and will then be in a position to share these observations. This is the essence of *cue training.* In it, people are taught to recognize signs of impending rage not previously noticed by them. They may thus discover that when they begin to rubbing their fingers together an angry incident is about to transpire. Now that they can see it coming, they can interdict it, perhaps by removing themselves from the scene. Cue recognition sets the stage for various mechanisms that then assure safety. It can provide the signal for calming techniques, safe places, safe persons, or safe activities, which complete the task of preventing foreseeable rage.

When anger can be consciously controlled, it becomes much safer and does not have to be shunned or disguised. The potential for using it well increases dramatically, and it ceases to be a problem. What is not helpful is trying to control rage by ignoring or burying it. If someone's frustration is not assuaged, sooner or later it will reassert itself, often in harmful ways. Alcohol, in particular, is a terrible vehicle for dissolving anger. It merely introduces other problems. A rotted-out liver and despoiled relationships do not make for happiness. Even a simpering smile can be dangerous. Its message that there is no problem, when there really is one, only postpones the day of reckoning. Though it may prevent a violent outburst, in sending signals of submission, it invites exploitation. Telling other people that one is not angry when one is may lead the others to believe that they are at liberty to do what they will. In such a case, restraint via emotional denial results in further distress.

Trying to control anger by denying it strips a person of essential tools for self-protection. Much better to defend against anger by attempting to control it forthrightly. Physical restraints, calming techniques, and cue training can all contribute to maintaining safety as long as the enemy is correctly identified. Failing to acknowledge the existence or potential menace of anger only strengthens one's sense of grievance. Though people may tell themselves nothing is wrong, they know that there is, and so they feel more deprived than ever.

Yet even the best mechanisms for assuring safety have their limits. Aside from not addressing the underlying origins of a person's anger, they take energy and vigilance to implement. Constantly being on guard against rage is an exhausting business. Besides, if one slips, the consequences can be regrettable. Assuring security may be essential as a stopgap defense against volatile anger, but it is no panacea. What is also needed is a way of making intense anger less automatic, which is the function of incremental tolerance, our next topic.

5

Developing Incremental Tolerance

FEAR OF ANGER

When anger is demonized, it becomes unavailable for use. People run from it, thereby transforming it into the very specter they fear. To avoid the creation of such a problem, it is essential that they not be afraid of the emotion, but rather understand and become comfortable with it. This is the point of what is here being called "incremental tolerance." Its object is the gradual evolution of a greater ease with anger so that it can be harnessed and exploited.

Fear of anger is widespread. Most people prefer to choke it down rather than confront it. They perceive not its functions, but its dangers, and magnify these to such an extent that they are considered the whole of the phenomenon. To them, anger is a red-eyed monster capable of untold horrors, an evil to be assiduously shunned. When it is abroad in the land, they secrete themselves in the nearest cellar. Their hope is that, if enough people can be cajoled into doing likewise, the emotion will be banished from human affairs, and reason, justice, and compassion will prevail. Given such a perspective, the sensible reaction to anger is obviously suppression. If it can be throttled in its crib, there will be room for more appropriate emotions.

This strategy, however, does not accept anger as a fact of life, regarding it instead as an aberration to be rejected. Such a attitude, besides failing to recognize the value of anger, is oppressive. Not only are individuals denied help in coping with an inherently difficult emotion, they are encouraged to engage in self-punishment. For the crime of entertaining a natural response, they are urged to bind themselves in a girdle of guilt. But if they do, their anger will be turned inward and they will fall victim to their own frustrations. Some anger-phobic philosophers go even further and, in the name of virtue, advise people to seek feelinglessness. They advise them to give up their aspirations and renounce all attempts at satisfaction. The reality of this tactic, however, is an unending inner conflict, with a person's underlying desires forever pitted against his determination to do the right thing.

In fact, anger must neither be reviled nor be persecuted. Rather, its purposes and mechanisms must be appreciated and facilitated. For individuals to achieve this, however, they must be comfortable with the feeling. They must be far less sensitive to it than are the phobics. Instead of fleeing at anger's first appearance or lingering behind to club it to death, they must be capable of abiding with it on familiar terms. More particularly, they must be able to experience it without turning it off or springing automatically into stereotyped action. Ultimately it is crucial that they calmly examine the emotion and discreetly decide what to do.

It must not be imagined that the goal is to become indifferent to one's anger. The emotion's ability to communicate and motivate must remain intact for it to do any good. Fortunately, anger is highly stimulating. It rarely fades into obscurity just because it has been asked to do so. Nonetheless, it is dangerous and must be prevented from becoming primitive. Though it insistently presses for resolution, it does not have to be acted upon unreflectively. It can, in fact, be sustained without being impulsively heeded. Neither suppression nor automatic expression are the sole alternatives. It is possible to feel the feeling, then to behave judiciously.

To achieve an effective execution of anger, people may also need to become less sensitive to other emotions that may prevent them from coping with it. If fear, guilt, or shame obscure their understanding and/or acceptance of their anger, these emotions may need to be addressed and extirpated. We will shortly be discussing mechanisms for desensitizing intense emotions; and although these techniques will be applied primarily to anger, they can be understood as equally applicable to other feelings. Thus, if fear makes it impossible for people to confront their anger, they may need to become less fearful before they can properly evaluate the anger. Just as uncontrolled fury is stupid and dangerous, so too is unbridled terror. In preventing people from seeing what is truly dangerous, it can induce them to protect themselves from what is safe or to welcome what is damaging. Desensitization is aimed at reducing such errors.

DESENSITIZATION

The term *desensitization* is an evocative one. Most of us have an intuitive feel for what it means to be too sensitive. We know that sometimes we react sharply to stimuli that should not be very arousing and wish that we could take them in stride without making them such a "big deal." Sometimes when an unkind word is directed our way, we flare up as if we had been assaulted. Later, we ask ourselves why we were cut so deeply and are sorry we didn't have a "thicker skin." If only we could learn to be less tender.

Yet the concept of desensitization is itself relatively new. It was introduced into the helping professions by Joseph Wolpe in the 1950s as part of a behaviorist campaign against traditional psychotherapy. Wolpe himself was especially concerned with fear. He considered it an inappropriate, even destructive emotion, which he sought to extinguish. His goal was to replace it with something less damaging, specifically by inhibiting its expression and substituting an antithetical response. This he believed could be achieved through the so-called relaxation response. Wolpe argued that people would gradually learn to feel less anxious if they could be taught to relax when a particular instance of fear appeared. He called this process *reciprocal inhibition,* and it seemed to work. From our point of view, what is important is that a gradual exposure to an intense emotion does appear to have the effect of making people less responsive to it. Whether this entails its replacement by a competing response or some other mechanism is of less importance than that it does occur and can be harnessed to help a person develop tolerance of problem anger.

Still, it is useful to consider an alternative hypothesis. It may be that desensitization occurs not because of reciprocal inhibition, but as an aspect of *emotional learning.* As we have discovered, emotions communicate vital information and motivate germane actions. Signal anxiety, for example, warns of danger and motivates a fight-or-flight response. But when a danger passes, so too should its signal and/or our tendency to act on it. We don't want these to change too quickly, lest we fail to run from a genuine threat, but neither do we want them to remain in effect when the world has become safer. In the long run I.A.M. aims to achieve this objective by altering the way we evaluate the anger message and how we implement anger. But on the way to this end point, desensitization can begin the process by muffling the message of the emotion and partially detaching it from what may no longer be an appropriate rejoinder.

The essence of desensitization entails gaining a gradual familiarity with an intense emotion so that its intensity can become less compelling. Repeated exposure to an emotion, within an environment where it is no longer so intense that it impels immediate action, allows people to habituate to it. Its message then begins to sound less strident, and the need to launch into a stereotyped action is less urgent. People conclude that, although the emotion is still screaming for relief and continuing to press for familiar solutions, these calls need not be heeded. In a sense, the power of the emotion is reduced, and people are given time to reflect on its nature and perhaps to choose a more suitable response. Exposure to it in an attenuated form apparently removes some of the energy pushing for action and buys us time. In effect, the stimulus that initiates the emotion is temporarily separated from an individual's prior reactions to it, and he is thereby enabled to regain control. Instead of being in the grip of what was virtually a reflex reaction, he begins to regain mastery.

In the case of anger, desensitization occurs when people gradually discover that an apparently intolerable frustration is actually tolerable. There is still something important about what they want, but the deprivation is not so egregious that instantaneous action is mandatory. Eventually it sinks into their psyche that the discomfort of this particular frustration can be endured without a tragedy intervening. Besides, it may yet be possible to plot a more effective course toward achieving a goal once they have calmed down. Just as with fear, a secure environment, in which immediate action is not essential and where there is sufficient time to habituate to the message, is crucial.

The same sort of protective strategies used to assure safety in the face of rage also turns out to be useful in promoting an incremental tolerance to anger. If these can be actuated when the emotion threatens to go out of control, people can learn that their anger is less compelling than they once thought. When they allow themselves to experience it, but with safeguards readily available, two positive results can accrue. First, they can discover that they have reliable defenses against violent outcomes. They should experience a growing awareness that they can protect themselves and will be assured that they are in less jeopardy than they previously imagined. Second, the greater the exposure they have to a particular frustration, the more they will realize that its demands are not so overpowering that they are unable to resist them. Although they may not recognize the nature of their underlying objectives and may not have learned how best to utilize their anger to obtain them, increased familiarity will lessen the emotion's ability to generate precipitous action. Having heard its siren call without being moved to act, they will find its song less seductive.

Of course, all this entails the passage of time, often considerable time. The recognition that a frustration is tolerable does not come easily. As anger is a persistent and energetic emotion, it does not readily desist in its attempts to move people. In consequence, there is a constant pressure toward repression. For a long time it will feel to them that the only practical way they can handle their anger is to avoid it. It will take many exposures to a given instance of the emotion and many repetitions of successfully controlling it before they react differently. Only when they have had time to allow the lesson that their anger can be controlled to settle to their emotional core will it feel less threatening.

Systematic Desensitization

Now let us briefly review Wolpe's paradigm. According to him, helpers and their clients should together explore the clients' intense emotional reactions and arrange them in a hierarchy of increasing potency. With each labeled, they can then be dealt with in turn. The clients will be instructed to expose themselves to a first fairly modest example of a situation that arouses their emotion, while carefully avoiding more powerful stimuli. Because their initial reaction will be relatively tepid, clients should be able to experience it without fleeing in panic. If not, a new, less-potent first step can be formulated. When clients are able to endure this, they will gradually recognize that their feeling is both controllable and safe. The impulse to act will dissipate, and the emotion will become more tolerable. In the case of anxiety, people can begin by confronting a moderately fearful situation and gradually move toward more terrifying ones. If they are dealing with agoraphobia, they may want to start by looking out a window, then slowly progress to visiting sports stadiums, and so on. Whatever the mechanism through which this procedure works, in time they will grow less sensitive and more able to live with their feelings. If this process is construed as a form of emotional learning, its slowness may be understood as necessary for allowing a subjective reinterpretation of what has previously been an all-consuming experience.

The safety devices required to implement such a progression work only when they are addressed toward moderate emotions. Thus, many of the calming devices described in chapter 4 would be overwhelmed were they asked to deal directly with terror. Only after a particular device such as the reassuring presence of a soothing other has successfully neutralized a small fear will a person gain the confidence to apply it to more extreme fears. Because problem emotions are devastating when confronted en masse, they must be surmounted in manageable doses. Too much fear or too much anger, and they become the proverbial snowball caroming down a mountain, not slowing until ending in an avalanche of destruction.

Incremental tolerance must be initiated by partializing intense emotions such as problem anger. These feelings must be cut into small portions, as it were, none of which is overwhelming in itself, and then each can be worked through in turn until it is mastered. In the end it will be possible to reassemble the pieces and tolerate them as a whole. For example, instead of being angry at the whole world because it metes out love stingily, a person can be angry at a particular individual for a specific act of denial. The whole world is a terrifying enemy, but one mean-spirited human being can be contemplated without panic. Only then should another, more intimidating individual be confronted, and then another, and another. If this sequence is handled carefully, in the end it should be possible to tolerate the niggardliness of the entire universe.

Another way to describe this procedure is to suggest that people remain within a "comfort zone" when trying to master an intense emotion. An analogy may be made with learning how to ski. Novice skiers are often advised to work almost at the edge of their competence, but not quite at it. If they press too hard, perhaps by heading straight down the slope, the odds are that they will become alarmed and wipe out. If, on the other hand, they are too timid and do not attempt new, but uncomfortable, skills, they will never improve. What is needed is to work within a range where they feel nervous, but not excessively so. It is here that emotional learning occurs and where incremental tolerance is advanced.

One of Wolpe's more valuable distinctions is that between systematic and in vivo desensitization. *Systematic desensitization* involves the kind of hierarchy building discussed at the beginning of this section. It utilizes explicit lists of fears and frustrations and makes conscious efforts at confronting them in succession. It is not, however, the only means of instituting incremental tolerance. *In vivo desensitization* can also be effective. It is desensitization that occurs in real life and is consequently less structured. This modality leaves the safety of the clinical office and braves the vicissitudes of the street. Obviously, out in the real world well-ordered hierarchies are less achievable. Still, anger (and fear) can be mastered in a relatively unguided, back-and-forth fashion; it may be messy and unconscious but may nevertheless succeed. What happens is that sometimes people move forward, then retreat, then move forward again. Ultimately, as long as their anger is experienced slowly and safely, they can progress without being overwhelmed. As we shall shortly see, much of psychotherapy is organized in this manner. It facilitates progress without being systematic or even being labeled as incremental tolerance. Ordinary living can also provide an arena for desensitization. Professional helpers are not always required in order to actuate what is after all a natural process.

CATHARSIS

Many therapists recommend that their clients "feel" their problem feelings. They claim that if people first experience and then express an emotion such as anger, they will feel better, that the very act of public confession will make the feeling dissipate. This "catharsis" approach has a wide following, but it is not clear why it should work. Its champions make strong claims about its beneficial effects but offer relatively little evidence about how it accomplishes this. Without being precise about what they mean, they seem to conclude that catharsis has a "purging" effect. Much like the bloodletting once prescribed for releasing bodily poisons, an effusion of emotion apparently cleanses the soul.

We have already noted that Sigmund Freud was one of the most important advocates of catharsis. His first efforts at psychoanalysis aimed at uncovering childhood traumas and encouraging their emotional expression. Once this had occurred, he presumed that his clients would be freed from their neurotic chains. Unlike many of his detractors, Freud was at pains to propose a scientific rationale for his speculations. In the case of catharsis, libidinal energy was hypothesized to be dammed up by internal blockages. Emotional expression would then provide a release. The mechanism would work by shunting excess energy out of the psyche.

Later critics have derogated this viewpoint, describing it as a "hydraulic theory," and have seized upon its improbabilities to discredit Freud. They claim that his theory depends on an analogy of questionable merit. Does mental energy (i.e., libido) really operate like a tap emptying into a vessel of limited capacity? Although this makes a pretty picture, to what extent does it correspond with brain physiology? If there is no identifiable biological fluid, an hydraulic analogy, rather than providing an explanation, offers only an emotionally satisfying depiction of what is accepted on other grounds. It is reassuring, not informative.

But many people still find the hydraulic imagery compelling. They are certain that emotions do build up pressures that, if not released, will lead to explosions. Better then to reduce the pressure and clear the air. If angry people say how they feel, this should theoretically have two effects. First, after their anger is expressed, they will be less inclined to act impulsively. Their internal stress will be reduced, and they will not need to erupt in violence. Second, with their grievances made public, there will be a better chance at an equitable solution. The object of their displeasure will know what they want and may be able to provide it, at least in part.

But does this process work? Does overt anger always clear the air or reduce internal pressures? Research indicates that it doesn't; and common sense confirms this. We all know that angrily telling people we are upset with them does not inevitably lead to an amicable solution. They may just return our anger with counter-anger. Rather than working together toward a joint resolution, we may continue to dispute. And because we fail to agree, our anger may generate another explosion. Think of what happened when the husband in chapter 2 testily demanded that his wife prepare dinner. In some scenarios, they reconciled; in others they didn't. Think also of what occurs when a supervisor is angrily derided for "dumb" mistakes. It is the rare boss who contritely begs forgiveness.

Nor does an expression of anger always reduce internal pressures. Much depends upon what happens after its release. If frustration is overcome, people may, in fact, feel better. If it isn't, they can get angrier. Anyone who has shouted at another person only to have that rage answered by derision knows that this generates further anger. Someone red in the face with rage is not placated by the mere fact of having a flushed visage. Nor is giving voice to anger gratifying if all that happens is that vocal chords get exercised. Think of how it feels to yell at someone who stands there completely unmoved.

All this seems so obvious that one wonders how a catharsis theory of anger could ever have seemed attractive. One possibility is that clinicians have not really been thinking about anger. When Freud advocated catharsis, the primary emotion he seems to have had in mind was sadness. His patients, in recalling their traumatic pasts, reawakened many distressing thoughts. They agonized about what had happened to them, and in their agony they often did feel better. But what they were usually feeling was despondent. Sorrow, it develops, is a much better paradigm for catharsis than is anger. The fact is that people who are depressed do need to express their pain. When someone is enduring a grievous loss, it is beneficial to cry. The tears flow, they sob uncontrollably, and after awhile feel better. Thus, the consequences of a good cry are very close to those depicted in the hydraulic model. Wracking tears do release tension and help a person to adjust.

Anger, however, is not the same. It has a different function and operates through different channels. The two emotions may share an impulse towards expression, but what happens when they are expressed is quite dissimilar. Ventilation is rarely the complete remedy for anger. Unlike sadness it is typically destructive and without a cleansing quality. Still, an expression of anger is natural and widespread. When upset, people do feel pressed to say so, and therapists do encourage this expression. Even though the rationale for catharsis may not be compelling, professional helpers act as if it were. Furthermore, they tell us that their clients do improve when stimulated to vent their rage, that anger does have a curative effect.

So what is going on around here? It unlikely that legions of competent professionals could be so wrong. Something beneficial must be taking place, even if it is not as described. When we take a closer look at the catharsis, it becomes evident what this process is. In the hands of professional helpers, catharsis promotes incremental tolerance, not just an emotional release. The mechanisms through which it works encourage emotional learning and therefore desensitization.

When we nudge aside the veil of sanctity guarding the therapeutic consulting room, we notice several things. First, clinicians encourage an expression of anger. They say to their clients, "Tell me how you are feeling. Don't be afraid of it; say it out loud." And when an emotional disclosure occurs, they continue, "Stay with it; feel your feeling," apparently in the hope of intensifying and extending this experience. Second, the more emotive are their clients, the more clinicians reward them with praise. Whether client-centered, gestalt, or Freudian, virtually all assiduously avoid being punitive.

What then is happening? It will be recalled that incremental tolerance works by encouraging the safe experience of an intense emotion over an extended period of time. This helps decouple feelings from actions by providing a secure space where the rupture can occur. Isn't it true, however, that therapists arrange these very conditions in the name of catharsis? Don't they too provide emotional security and time? Specifically, when they reward a disclosure of anger, don't they avoid reacting the way a normal role partner might? Although awash in client anger, they fail to respond as if the emotion had been directed against them. Instead they strive to be neutral. If this means eschewing irascible, and/or punitive, responses, they do so. Thus, we see that, although anger might be dangerous when expressed in its natural setting, in the therapeutic situation things are purposefully arranged so as to be nonthreatening. Emotional learning is consequently facilitated, and clients are provided an opportunity to adjust to the intensity of their sentiments. Since they do not have to fend off counterattacks, they have the luxury of examining and reorganizing their reactions. Because they are not overloaded by the turbulence of normal interpersonal conflicts, they can reflect on what is happening and learn from it. In short, more is transpiring than a mere discharge of emotion.

Time is especially important in this scenario. Therapists allow their clients to voice their anger repeatedly. They do not expect one all-consuming discharge, after which there will be a complete remission. On the contrary, it is understood that clients need to speak about their frustrations many times before feeling less pressured. This emotional expression also provides a bridge to the other stages of integrated anger management. Although no panacea, it prepares the ground for a dispassionate reexamination of the underlying goals of anger and for their effective execution. Catharsis, it develops, is not wrong; like anger management in general, it is just different than advertised. If one understands it as promoting incremental tolerance, its potency is actually enhanced.

DESENSITIZATION STRATEGIES

Emotional tolerance can be achieved in a variety of ways, all of which depend on the safe experience of a threatening emotion over time. The most important of these utilize talk, fantasy, and structured conflict to remove the sting of anger. Each can be implemented by an angry person alone or with the assistance of a helper, but if the support of a second party is enlisted, it must be someone who is safe and capable of promoting the proper conditions.

With their emphasis on catharsis, therapeutic interventions reveal how incremental tolerance can be attained. In particular, they demonstrate the utility of talk in consummating desensitization. Freudian therapy began as the "talking cure," and virtually all therapies still depend upon discourse. In the normal therapeutic situation, client and clinician sit face-to-face, speaking to one another. Even group and family therapy are essentially forums for talk. While these may attribute their success to different curative agencies, they fully expect verbal exchanges to inaugurate movement in clients.

How can talk foster incremental tolerance? By itself, of course, it cannot. Empty words, drained of all feeling, make little difference. It is only when talk elicits emotion that desensitization occurs. When people verbalize their anger, it will generally make them uncomfortable. Their words will remind them of an emotion, and they will feel the feeling. Freudians early on discovered that people don't feel better unless they have what is called a "corrective emotional experience." Abstract talk alone is useless. Luckily, they also found that focusing upon an emotionally charged incident and asking tactful, but pointed, questions can bring its experience into a person's awareness. Subsequently gestalt and client-centered therapists found they too could enhance the reexperiencing of problem emotions. In gestalt therapy, for instance, clients are asked to role play incidents derived from their remote past and are encouraged to talk about them as if they were occurring in the present. This can make their recapitulation very dramatic, and what begins merely as a recitation of an anger-charged incident can end with a client trembling in rage. Client-centered therapists achieve a similar effect by reflecting clients' emotional reactions back upon themselves. As the clients talk, the nature of their current experience is revealed at the moment they experience it. This too can make it palpable.

As valuable as is talk's ability to arouse emotions, of equal import is its ability to do so without being threatening. Talk, not screaming and yelling, not sarcasm and ridicule, is able to gently prod people to encounter feelings they would otherwise find too frightening. "Conversation" is rational, civilized, and above all under control. Its latent message is that the subject, whatever it may be, is tolerable, that it can be discussed. Words are really tools we human beings employ to control our environment. They are used to "mentally" pick things up and turn them around until we get a feel for them. They thus enable us to approach frightening issues slowly and cautiously, which of course is the essence of incremental tolerance.

Talk also offers the possibility of social support. It not only builds a wall of rationality around intense emotions, it helps establish relationships with prospective helpers and tests whether these are safe. As the telephone company's commercials have been telling us, words can "reach out and touch someone." If gentle and reliable, they are reassuring. They almost constitute a lullaby that can enable us to maintain control over our anger while we are trying to assimilate its meaning. We know that our friends' words, even questions, can be calming when they indicate that they are not terrified of us. Serene talk is a warrant that they are not about to respond with rage. More than their specific conceptualizations, the timbre of their voice, indeed its very tone, will indicate that they can be trusted. So too will their selection of words and the posture they assume while talking to us.

In ordinary life people often feel compelled to discuss their anger with a friend. They seek out someone they trust, probably someone who also trusts them, and proceed to pour out their complaints. "Did you know that John did so and so?" "Can you believe that?" "It makes me so furious." "Wouldn't it make you?" This sometimes gets tiresome for listeners, but for the speakers it is marvelously liberating. The sympathy of their friends assures them that it is okay to be angry, and they no longer feel like going out and hitting someone.

But language is not the only mechanism able to foster desensitization. Images too are useful. It is possible for people to have fantasies about their anger and thereby make it safer. Most of us, from time to time, entertain vivid mental pictures of what we would like to do to those who have frustrated us. We may visualize inflicting a panoply of tortures that will extract a complete, and well-deserved, vengeance. In our mind's eye we skewer them with knives, spray them with bullets, and burn them to cinders. Best of all, they don't fight back and our victory is total. We can then sit back and mull over our glorious success. Though such daydreams don't change the world, they do make it momentarily more tolerable. Even mild-mannered people savor visions of a more just world.

We are often told that evil thoughts are as bad as evil deeds. Parents, in particular, are uncomfortable when their children have murderous fantasies regarding them. Nevertheless, images that don't culminate in action can provide a cathartic safety valve. In fantasizing about what we would like to do to our enemies and mentally experiencing the associated rage, our nasty feelings lose much of their severity. Just as words can be used to manipulate feelings and help work them through, so too can mental visions. Images are relatively trustworthy and are plastic enough to be molded to suit most needs.

Indeed, many therapists use a technique called "guided imagery." They encourage their clients to engage in lurid fantasies of death and destruction, advising them to muse about their anger in safe but graphic ways, so that they won't feel too distressed when life arouses similar emotions at a later date. "Think about it, but don't do it!" Guided imagery can actually be used to construct desensitization sequences. Hierarchies of anger can be rehearsed in one's head, until even violent rage becomes tolerable. These mental emotions may not be as potent as the real thing, but they can serve as a prelude to them. In a sense, they partialize anger by cutting it into imaginary pieces that can be as small as a person's fancy allows them to be. Fantasies can also be turned off in the blink of an eye and, as it were, made invisibly small.

Safety and time can similarly be provided by structured conflicts. It will be recalled that sports and other forms of competition constitute a mechanism through which anger is socialized. These create situations in which people get angry (because they want to win), but place a premium on retaining control. Neither an angry tantrum nor a psyched-out paralysis is conducive to victory. In the mock battles of the playing field, anger needs to motivate an energetic performance, not an enraged one. When in the midst of a game, players must be determined to feel their feelings, but all the while exercise authority over them.

This pattern is tailormade for implementing incremental tolerance. Indeed, the games of childhood contribute to the socialization of anger precisely by teaching us how to experience anger without going wild. Using these same devices in adulthood to inculcate lessons not earlier acquired can be poetic justice. If golf, tennis, or chess are used as venues for practicing safe anger, people who are excessively angry because their earlier life has been unfair can procure an emotional competence they did not previously possess. They can also have fun while doing so. What better way to demonstrate that anger does not have to be undisciplined or ultrapainful.

A less amusing, albeit no less stimulating, method for structuring anger is found in group therapy. Members of such groups are often instigated to engage in sham fights. Usually these involve role plays about real or pretend events, but they can get quite heated. Their saving grace is that they are refereed battles. Because a professional is available to ensure that the hostilities do not escalate, they can be used to test the tolerability of anger. Comparable constraints are provided in marital and family therapy. These too can permit couples and their offspring to practice and to master anger in safety.

Surprisingly, even some professional and religious activities provide an opportunity for controlling, and developing a tolerance to, anger. Politics, religion, and the law all contain what amount to rituals for expressing the emotion. Thus, the choreographed adversarial system of the courtroom, the conventionalized accusations of some religious ceremonies, and the mandated graciousness of parliamentary procedure all allow people to articulate what in other circumstances would be an inappropriate disdain for others and to do so in their presence.

Safe Helpers

To return to question of trust: as we know, anger can be dangerous, as will certainly be apparent to people trying to cope with problem anger. They will rightly be alert to any prospect of danger and may be prepared to foreclose all attempts at incremental tolerance lest they backfire. It is therefore vital that whatever method is used to promote desensitization, whether it be talk, fantasy, or competition, that it be safe—safe in itself, and safe in containing anger. Slip-ups can ill be afforded, for not only do they encourage an unregulated expression of preexisting rage, they can create additional breaches of security. They may, for example, instigate new frustrations that open fresh opportunities for indignation.

Among other things, angry people have reason to worry about the responses of others, including prospective helpers. They will rightly be concerned that helpers have hidden agendas or will prove ultrasensitive to their rage. Perhaps these people will be frustrated by them and choose to inflict harm upon them. The mere fact of offering help does not ensure that helpers will be either fair or helpful. People who appear to be safe often are not. This is something to be demonstrated, not assumed. Who knows what another's response will be when confronted with the actualities of intense anger? Angry people must consequently test the waters.

Psychotherapists are taught to beware of *countertransference*. They are expected to possess a degree of integrity and of self-knowledge despite the normal impulse to project their own feelings on others. It is believed that if they are committed to fairness and honesty, they will recognize their own hidden agendas and resist the temptation to visit their frustrations on those they are helping. Above all, they are expected to be non-judgmental. They must not harbor biases that incline them to reject a person's emotional reactions before understanding them. Having a therapeutic attitude entails withholding judgment pending the evidence. Angry people must not be condemned until one knows what they are trying to achieve.

Nonprofessional helpers tend to be a bit rash. They are often intent upon upholding their own status or so desirous of offering immediate help that they intercede with ill-considered enthusiasm. Instead of attending closely to what is happening with anger, they rush in to do what they consider right. Even if their interest is only in seeing that the other feels better, they may act precipitously. Thus they can say, in one fashion or another: "Don't be angry!" just when they should be asking: "Why are you angry?"

Helpers who don't overreact, who allow and even encourage anger through focused talk, fantasy, or competition, have another advantage. They not only permit incremental tolerance, they demonstrate how it can be achieved. Their ongoing calmness when confronted with belligerence serves as a proof that the emotion can be managed. In essence, they become models of how to tolerate anger. Their not reacting automatically proves it possible. A client may even ask how they do this, and they should be prepared to answer. They should especially be prepared to make it clear that self-control is within the compass of any human being who pursues it with determination and discretion.

Safe, reliable helpers may also function as coaches. Having developed skill in controlling their anger, they will understand some of its vicissitudes and be competent to pass this information along. When they perceive that a person is struggling with the emotion, they are able to verbalize what is happening. For instance, clinicians who notice that their clients are reluctant to speak about anger for fear that this will precipitate an explosion can counsel patience. They can explain that, although this feeling is quite common there are ways of forestalling explosions. They can also relate the importance of taking risks and explain that while anger is dangerous, it can be contained, that the emotion can be accepted, if not embraced.

In addition, coaches can further tolerance by regulating the pace at which people expose themselves to their anger. Timing is essential to determining when, and whether, people have the resources to endure their own intense indignation. If they rush ahead while feeling vulnerable, what in other circumstances would be an easy stretch may in this case portend disaster. Yet people accustomed to repressing their anger are poor judges of how close they are to losing control. A dispassionate helper may need to provide guidance about what they are ready for. Thus, people who are terrified of their feelings can be urged to press forward with more alacrity, while counterphobics ready to jump instantaneously into any scrape can be advised to restrain this audacity. Incremental tolerance takes time, but the right amount of time. A person may need to be slowed down or speeded up as the case may be. One who outpaces his preestablished controls may cause fears to reemerge and learning to stop. Tolerance cannot be accelerated beyond its limits. It occurs when it occurs, not when it is convenient or when it is demanded.

All of these complications make it unlikely that the desensitization of anger will be as systematic as described by Wolpe. The situations in which it is inaugurated and mastered almost never constitute a logical progression. They tend to arise as a person feels ready, which depends on a multitude of uncontrollable variables. Consequently, something akin to Freudian free-association transpires. Particular cases of anger come to mind and are expressed when something in the world or in the person's head triggers their emergence. What comes to mind may more closely match what is needed and can be mastered than would a predetermined sequence of emotions. One of the great advantages of the strategies elaborated upon above is that they are responsive to who a person is and what is to be achieved. In the hands of a helper with emotional courage and perspicacity, such strategies can facilitate adjustments based upon a person's actual reactions.

When nonprofessionals attempt to expedite desensitization, an even less systematic result can emerge. Helpers who have not had prior experience in facilitating the process may have difficulty in recognizing what is going on or in exercising skill in moving it along. Many mistakes may result, but fortunately they are rarely fatal. People can learn from their errors. This same logic applies when angry people are determined to provide their own salvation. Because they may be disinclined to expose themselves to the terrors of their intense anger, they may find ways to rationalize particular difficulties. Sheer grit may keep them going, and they may succeed; but then again they may discover it is necessary to seek a helper, if only informally. Though they may wish to retain control of their progress, others may be able to offer them the safe environment and relatively unbiased perspective they are unable to provide for themselves.

6

Evaluating Anger

A MYSTERIOUS EMOTION

For many people, for some of them most of the time, anger is a mystery. It comes unbidden and unwanted and moves them in directions not of their choosing. To them it appears to be irrational and uncontrollable, at best a legacy of their remote animalistic past. Rather than understand it, they would excise it and pursue more gentle pastimes. In particular, they fail to recognize that their anger may possess indispensable clues about what they want or are trying to do. For them, it seems to have no rhyme or reason, just a raging intensity. In consequence, they leave it unexamined, not pausing to observe it or to make inquiries. They hurry past, content to depart from its vicinity, happy if they can get away unharmed. It does not occur to them that they are ignoring information vital to their self-interest.

What is worse, many people actively cover up their anger. They enhance its mystery not merely by neglecting it but also by papering it over. They don't know, and they don't care to know. Every available psychological defense is thrown into the fray to ensure that it remains impenetrable. Repression, suppression, displacement, disguise, and denial are all invoked in an effort to pretend that it doesn't exist. The idea seems to be that if anger isn't visible, it can't cause trouble. Yet we all know that an ostrich strategy holds perils. In the case of anger, it is difficult for people to hit a target they can't see. As long as the goal of their anger remains concealed, the emotion will be difficult to control and is likely to take them places where they don't want to go.

Paradoxically those most in need of understanding their anger are often the least inclined to do so. People who are angry all of the time and those who never seem to get angry at anything may believe that the emotion is not a problem for them. Either they imagine that constant anger is a normal and effective way of living that is not in need of an explanation, or they personally are not troubled by it. They thus engage in a form of denial that hides the causes and consequences of their unhappiness from themselves and from everyone else. Examples of this tendency are to be found in people who are always in a bad mood but attribute this to the general state of the universe or in those couples who seem always to be fighting over trivia (perhaps about whether she has been serving him too many cheese sandwiches for dinner) but who refuse to acknowledge that they are fighting or that the real issue is whether or not they love each other.

Given this tendency, what sort of anger is most likely to be repressed, and why? Sadly, the answer is that it is usually the most critical instances. Because intense anger is apt to be perceived as dangerous, it is most liable to be denied. Yet this sort of anger is generally fighting for very meaningful goals. It is when people's truly important needs are being actively thwarted that their level of frustration is most exacerbated. It is when love, respect, or safety are effectively denied them that they are most strongly motivated to overcome the barriers to their goals. But energetic anger is also apt to be encountering determined resistance. One of the reasons it needs to work so hard is because it finds itself with so much to surmount. Also, when people are fighting hard, they can generate counter-anger, which will require still more energy to defeat. Thus, repression, suppression, displacement, and denial occur both because much is at stake and because the battle to obtain it is potentially so destructive. Either way, these people will be too apprehensive to see what is there to be seen.

A special case of repressed anger involves what Freud called the repetition compulsion. Often, someone who has been abused as a child tends to get into similarly abusive situations as an adult. Whether in the role of the aggressor or the aggressed-upon, such people may not want to understand that they are reenacting a past trauma. In essence, they are trying to gain control of anger that once terrified them; but, because it remains terrifying, they do not want to see it too clearly. Ironically, it is the joint task of attempting to overcome a terror while not perceiving it that can make their mission impossible.

They will then feel more frustrated and trapped than ever. Some people, sensing the imminence of this dilemma, try never to approach unfinished business emanating from childhood. In the process they damn themselves to eternal frustrations, which may be revealed not as unexplained anger, but as an ongoing, never-ending depression. Their real feelings are so horrific and so deeply buried that they find themselves in a hopeless situation, which they sense only unconsciously. One way people can tell whether they are in danger of this predicament is if they find themselves continually repeating the same sad scenarios. Being caught in an endless loop is good evidence that there is something they want badly enough to continue pursuing but which is nevertheless being thwarted.

Still, maintaining a veil of secrecy can be challenging; there is so much to be disguised. For starters, it will be important for people avoiding the true nature of their anger to repress their underlying goals. There must be no consciousness of what is being frustrated. Any awareness will be a painful reminder that vital needs are not being met. Thus, many people who have grown up in loveless homes convince themselves that they don't need love. Ask them what they think about intimacy, and they will tell you that it is a cynical ploy foisted upon a gullible public by the media. Despite the fact that they are in agony because they were cut off from all genuine human warmth, they compartmentalize their pain and squeeze it into as small a space as possible. When they take stock of their most cherished objectives, love is not numbered among them. Its recognition would rub a raw spot and might precipitate a conflict.

Also requiring concealment are frustrating agents. Not only must unmet goals be disguised, so must those situations in which they were thwarted. People have to deny any suggestion that there is a reason for their anger. Of course they don't need love, but neither was it ever refused them. Perhaps childhood was bleak, but their parents were basically very affectionate. Father wasn't selfish, and Mother turned her head away only because she was extremely busy. Thus, acts of frustration are reinterpreted to make them seem neutral or even positive.

Another factor requiring distortion is the way they reacted to these frustrations. Besides denying that there was a cause for their anger, they must pretend that they never responded belligerently. Since intense anger is dangerous, refusing to admit that it occurred can make it seem more controllable. If people can convince themselves and others that anger is not part of their vocabulary, it will seem less likely that they will want to resort to it. Thus, someone whose father was impossible to please will claim never to have been perturbed by this fact—never to have shouted for attention, nor sulked when it was withheld—for he is not that sort of person.

Similarly, a person's present reactions must be suppressed too. Because anger tends to be persistent, past frustrations have present consequences. Covert grievances can erupt at the most inopportune moment and puncture the placid facade someone is trying to maintain. If his anger is to be denied, it must be denied in its current manifestations too; otherwise, it will soon be evident that one is not immune to its siren call. Thus, those who were refused love in childhood will keep searching for it in adulthood. A man whose mother may no longer be available to provide love may use his wife as a substitute provider. When he perceives her to be frustrating, as he no doubt will, he will be placed in a quandary. Since he must no more yell at his wife than he would at his mother, how is he to respond? He may thus decide to sabotage her vacation plans rather than call her a bitch. His hope will be that this disguise will maintain the fiction that he has no problems.

Defenses

People who are going to understand what they have hidden need to know how they have hidden it. If they are to evaluate their goals, how they have been frustrated, or how they have tried to overcome these frustrations, it helps if they can recognize the strategies they have used to disguise them. Among the mechanisms employed to conceal the reality of anger are projection and displacement. In the case of projection, anger is disowned and its source reassigned. Rather than admit a hidden feeling or try to deal with it, people may fail to recognize it as their own and believe that other people, often those at whom they are angry, are upset with them. They sense hostility in the atmosphere but imagine that it has been instigated by these others. To them it will appear to be the second parties' problem, and hence theirs to resolve. Projection sounds as if it should be easy to unmask, but because intense emotions are disorienting, both the person making the accusation and the one at whom it is directed can be deceived.

Displacement is a bit more complex. It diverts anger by directing it toward targets other than the original one. Displacement does not deny anger or pretend that it is emanating from the wrong person;

rather, it disguises its objectives and methods. Thus, there can be displacement in people's goals from primary to secondary ones. They will admit that they are frustrated, even angry, but convince themselves and others that they desire something other than what they really crave. This surrogate goal then draws attention away from what they are too uncomfortable to seek directly. A familiar example of this mechanism is the person who desperately wants to be loved but spends his life grovelling for money. Although able to recognize that the failure of a business venture is unsettling to him, he may not be aware that the energy behind his distress comes from thwarted love. Were he to acknowledge this, his rage might rise to insupportable levels.

There can also be displacement in the means through which people seek their goals. Those pursuing love may do so in the wrong places with the wrong methods. They might, for instance, ask the wrong people for love. Because they expect rejection from those they really care about, they substitute others and try to extract it from them. But even if these comply, they will feel frustrated. Similarly, people may choose the right person but make the wrong demands. Instead of asking for love, they might substitute a request for attention, even for negative attention. Thus, they can create a fuss that requires notice, but that can't elicit the concern or tenderness really desired.

Sometimes people hide their anger from themselves, not so much because they are afraid of it or of the frustration causing it but because they feel guilty about being angry. The danger they wish to avoid is not an explosion, but the feeling itself. When in the past they used anger to get what they wanted, their role partners launched into a counteroffensive and attacked them for being angry. They were told that it was wrong to want what they wanted and even more wrong to use anger to obtain it. The focus was therefore shifted away from the frustration to the anger. Its suppression became the object and all other concerns were disregarded.

When anger is treated as a sin, angry people are placed in a bind. If they get angry, they become an object of wrath; if they don't, they won't get what they want. This conflict is usually resolved in favor of repressing the emotion. Because a condemnation of anger is almost invariably initiated by a parent against a child, there exists a disparity in power guaranteed to frighten most children into submission. It is simply too dangerous for them to persist. The best way to conceal such anger, however, is from the inside. Because such anger is always pressing for expression, children must be able to catch themselves before it causes trouble.

Feeling angry, especially feeling justified in anger, is dangerous in the face of external repression because people's real feelings may unintentionally leak through. Their body language, perhaps a tightness around the mouth, may reveal an inner resentment. What children have not been told to wipe a smirk off their face after being rebuked for a misdeed? No doubt they found it difficult to appear contrite when they felt wronged. It is difficult to pretend not to be angry when one is. Efforts to substitute an inauthentic emotion are usually betrayed by an artificiality that others find grating.

This is where guilt comes in. It squelches anger at its source and forces people not to feel it. By taking the anger of an oppressor and internalizing it, people learn to condemn themselves. Whenever their resentment rises, it is subjected to a tirade of self-abuse. Anger that would otherwise be directed outward is turned around and now orders itself to shut up. Such anger demands of itself that it disappear. Its possessors sputter with an impotent, self-suppressing rage until they get the better of it and expel it from awareness. Thereafter, what remains is the vigilance of guilt, ever prepared to pounce lest any signs of an outward-directed anger reappear. This guilt will feel uncomfortable, but will be preferred to the alternative. Indeed, guilty people may feel a sense of righteousness in suppressing their anger. After all, isn't it bad people who allow themselves to get angry?

Yet when anger becomes a sin, everything is lost. If all its manifestations are off limits, there is no hope of ever overcoming externally imposed frustrations. What people want will be totally obscured, and their best means of achieving satisfaction categorically disowned. Such people are victims of self-inflicted mutilation. They become cripples whose chance at happiness is canceled by the defenses they erect against their efforts to succeed.

This may be a good point to discuss a related phenomenon. So far we have elaborated upon a variety of mechanisms used to repress, suppress, and disguise problem anger. Our theme has been that the reality of anger is often obfuscated in order to protect against an assortment of dangers, either real or imagined. Anger, or its goals and consequences, are rendered invisible by being projected, displaced, or internally quashed. This then creates greater problems by reducing people's abilities to address their frustrations. In short, devices intended to protect against anger result in its being perpetuated in a disguised, but persistent form. Given all this difficulty, it may be surprising to learn that some people actually revel in their anger. They proclaim it to be a problem, but make few efforts to contain it. Such persons are provocateurs for whom anger is variety of theater. As much as they may holler for help, they really have a great time performing the role of the agitator.

Anger is very diverting. When at full cry, it grabs us by the throat and won't let go. What better means then for deflecting attention? So far we have discussed mechanisms for avoiding dangerous anger, but anger itself can be used to obscure more frightening emotions. This secondary anger, which seems for all the world to be a problem in itself, is really a cover-up for what a person fears is a greater problem. It is therefore an aggressive defense against other fears. Let us say that a person is afraid of being loved. To her, love may appear to be a form of interpersonal merger in which her very soul is in danger of being dissolved. This may sound overly dramatic, but many people raised by overprotective parents do feel this way. In any event, when such a person encounters someone who wants to be close, the other's warm smile will seem as threatening as a murderous attack. It is then that she may manufacture an incident over which to be angry. Perhaps she will criticize the other's clothing or his manner of speaking. Either way, the object will be to pick a fight and create distance. To others, this fight may seem menacing, but for her it will be very reassuring.

Sometimes provocateurs engage in pre-emptive anger. Because they fear the anger of others, they rush to beat them to the punch. In their uncertainty as to whether they can resist the demands of others, they try to keep them off balance. Their hope is that if these others can be put on the defensive, their demands may never be made. Conversely, confident people tend to be calm enough to state their case openly with moderation and conviction.

Because provocateurs are thought to have difficulty with their anger rather than with their self-confidence, it is often proposed that they learn to be less aggressive. But this is usually beside the point. Because their anger is not caused by frustrations, methods for reducing these have little effect on them. Their real problem is not an uncontrolled hostility but perhaps a dread of closeness, and if so, it is these feelings that must be addressed. Their fear of intimacy may need to be reduced by making it seem less dangerous. If this can be achieved, love will be less foreboding to them, and it will not prove necessary for them to protect against it by instituting social distance. The diversion achieved through anger will then be superfluous, and the emotion will melt away.

IDENTIFYING AND EVALUATING GOALS AND MEANS

When frustration is the cause of people's anger, a different strategy is indicated. Here it is essential to understand the reasons behind their frustrations as a prelude to removing them. The message and motivation of their anger must be deciphered so that these can be heeded and/or changed. But it is difficult to recognize the aims and mechanisms of anger when what it communicates is being obscured. A message distorted by repression, suppression, denial, disguise, displacement, or guilt may be rendered practically invisible. Penetrating to the truth will take dedication, skill, and energy.

Compounding this difficulty is the fact that most defenses are instituted long before people decide to confront them. Typically, although the repression of intense anger begins in childhood, attempts to disarm it aren't initiated until adulthood. The power of primitive anger is so overwhelming that few people feel capable of defying it until they are competent adults. Of course, much problem anger is initiated later in life, but the energy driving its most virulent forms usually has roots in the distant past. It is then that our most vital needs are first, and most formidably, frustrated. Not surprisingly, these grievances fester, remaining active into one's maturity.

Yet what happened a long time ago is often dim in the memory. It is difficult to recall exactly how a frustration was initiated when this occurred decades earlier. Even for people who heroically strip away their defenses, it can be difficult to get clear about what transpired. Fortunately, it is possible to tap into one's emotional memory. What is learned within an emotional context tends to be retained as an emotional reaction, which will help to recapture the events surrounding it if it can be re-activated. If, for instance, people can reanimate the joy they experienced during their wedding ceremony, they should be able to reconstruct the details of who was there and what they did, often with photographic clarity. The trick is to feel the feeling and to experience it as if it were happening now for the first time.

When people genuinely allow themselves to recapture the depths of their anger, they can transport themselves back to long-forgotten episodes or reanimate irritations that occurred only yesterday. Instances of frustration imagined too remote or too challenging to be recollected can be experienced as if in the here and now. For example, a man reexperiencing infantile rage will almost be able to touch his mother as she turns away from him to return to her cooking. If his wife is presently treating him the same way, he may recognize his mother's rejection superimposed on her. He will see, and feel, how his current anger recapitulates the past, but also how it is different. Moreover, he will begin to understand what he is actually demanding of his wife; what, for example, is the result of her actions and what is not.

An ability to tap into one's emotional memory lies within the province of everyone. Others may dimly fathom what we are experiencing by observing our behavior, but they do not have access to the details. Emotional memory is privileged. It is fully usable only when its possessor chooses to use, or to share, it. Relatives, friends, or professionals can assist in this enterprise, but they cannot take over. We ourselves must have the courage to enter upon it or it won't happen. If we really want to understand, and overcome, our anger, it is up to us to do so. It is our responsibility, not that of anyone else, no matter how competent or altruistic.

One of the primary reasons for developing an incremental tolerance to anger is to make the emotion available for emotional memory. Anger that cannot be experienced cannot be examined or fully understood. In I.A.M., desensitization precedes the evaluation phase specifically because it institutes a prerequisite for a successful review of the emotion. Because evaluating a feeling presupposes being able to perceive it clearly, an ability to tolerate it is an essential forerunner.

Indeed the way an evaluation of anger proceeds entails mechanisms very like those used to achieve a tolerance of it. One talks about the emotion, one thinks about it, one even dreams about it, because doing so will facilitate an awareness of what is being felt. This time, however, the goal is not habituation, but a clarity of observation. A person evaluating his anger is like a cow chewing on her cud. Whether by himself or in conversation with friends or relatives, he perpetually reviews what he is feeling until its features become strikingly evident.

Once anger returns to consciousness, people can ask themselves which goals have been thwarted. What do they desperately want that was not allowed? If they will listen to their anger, it will communicate with them. It will send them signals that they can decipher, if they so choose. Listening for these messages may not be an exact

science, but neither is it an arcane skill. Our normal human equipment furnishes us with the capacity for doing it. Thus, when people
are angry, they will almost feel that a barrier confronts them. If they
allow themselves to strain toward it, they can gain a sense of what is
on the other side. They will almost see what they hope is there, what
they believe will give them emotional release. Of course, when people are intensely angry, they often have no inkling of what this may
be. The interference generated by their defensive tactics can completely prevent them from experiencing their anger. Yet were they
more alive to their feelings, the outlines of these feelings would be
apparent.

When anger is fully aroused, it carries its context about with it.
People, things, and situations surround it and give it structure. Anger, even rage, does not float in space. It is directed toward specific
objectives. It wants to reach out and to push someone aside or to gain
his assent. When people's emotional memory allows them to recognize the faces of their interlocutors, they will be reminded of what
they are expecting of them. By reexperiencing the sounds and smells
of a room where one once met defeat, one can recall what has been
lost. To return to our example of a person denied love in childhood,
if his emotional memory returns him to the scene of his earlier misery, he will see his mother, behold the expression on her face, and
sense the tension within his own body. He will also recognize himself striving for her approval and know to the depths of his soul that
he wanted her unconditional love. He may even imagine being embraced by her tenderly and protectively. It is at this moment that he
will grasp his underlying goal.

Evaluating Goals

After the goals of a person's anger have been identified, it is essential that they be evaluated. Identification will tell him what; evaluation assesses feasibility. He must know whether his goals can be attained and, if attained, whether they will be satisfying. Just because
a person yearns for his mother's love, doesn't guarantee that he will
be able to get it, or that having gained it, he will feel better. If his
mother was incapable of loving him, he may be destined to fail. Even
if she does relent, today's love may not be able to erase yesterday's
sorrow.

We human beings are always constructing purposes. As teleological creatures, we do not merely blunder about like earthworms in a

compost heap; rather we select directions and move toward them. The particular directions we choose are based upon what we think the world is or should be; but when we are wrong and the world does not conform with our expectations, these pathways may lead nowhere. Consequently, an accurate determination of feasibility is mandatory. But this takes judgment. Both experience and good sense are necessary to establish whether a particular goal is worthy. When we are young or are confused by emotional turmoil, our logic can be defective. We can misperceive our social environment and miscalculate its dimensions. The remedy is years of living and an increasing emotional maturity. It is necessary to be exposed to the world and to develop a measure of disinterest before we can gain competence in assessing the validity of specific goals.

A person trying to overcome problem anger needs to be aware of reality. Rather than rely on fantasy, he must witness what really works and what doesn't. This means being ruthlessly honest and recognizing his failures as well as successes. He must also broaden the scope of his experience and the span of his options. The more he understands the world, the better he can recognize its possibilities. For instance, it is difficult to assess whether one's father is capable of giving unconditional support if one labors under the assumption that all fathers automatically support their children. A clearsighted ramble through life makes it evident that fathers are human beings whose ability to bolster their young is conditioned by many factors, including whether they were given support when they were small.

An ability to evaluate the goals of one's anger is also enhanced by avoiding excessive passion. During periods when a person is consumed by rage or transported by sorrow, his critical faculties are blunted. Because intense emotions are stupid, their judgment is not to be relied upon. Consequently, during the evaluation phase of I.A.M., a person must establish a certain degree of emotional removal. If he can act almost like a witness to his situation, he may more accurately perceive it.

Experience and emotional removal combine to give perspective. They enable frustrated goals to be appraised in light of the needs they serve. Ultimately the objectives we all seek are designed to meet our basic needs. If they do so with reasonable efficiency, we will be satisfied; if not, then not. It is therefore vital to ascertain whether thwarted goals are capable of meeting our needs. If they can not, then obtaining them will make no difference.

Among the most basic and universal human needs are those involving safety, love, and respect. If these are not fulfilled, they will press incessantly for satisfaction. A person in danger keeps seeking safety until he has it; an unloved person searches restlessly for love until he is loved; a disrespected person strives mightily to become important, until he is. To be sure, people deny having these needs, but a close inspection invariably reveals that they too are moved by them. Somewhere lurking behind their proclaimed motives, these wheels are turning. Consequently, when evaluating goals, it is a good idea to ask how they impact safety, love, or respect. A person may be too embarrassed to admit feeling insecure, unloved, or unimportant, but the possibility cannot be discounted. Most of us learn that admitting our vulnerabilities, especially with regard to our basic needs, exposes us to greater frustrations. Other people can and do take advantage of our weaknesses. In order to advance their own agendas, they will hit us where it hurts. Basic needs are therefore generally pursued under cover of darkness. Once this is understood, it becomes more possible to assess aims accurately. We, or those working with us, can gently lift aside the cotton batting protecting our sensibilities and zero in on what really matters.

Assessing Means

So far, we have stressed the goals underlying anger, but it is also necessary to identify and evaluate the means through which they are achieved. Emotions have a message that, if listened to, can be heard; but they also have a motive power that, if examined, can reveal the effectiveness of our efforts. How is a person's anger being expressed? What plans of action guide her behavior? Is she under the sway of a primitive impulse, or are more sophisticated strategies at work? In particular, who is she trying to influence and how persuasive are her exertions? Indeed, what are the consequences of her anger for herself and others? Are its goals being achieved or is it arousing negative side effects? Does it, for instance, incite counter-anger?

Perhaps the best place to begin assessing how anger is being implemented is to ask who a person is trying to influence. In talking about anger and thinking about it, we must recognize that it works, above all, by motivating others to comply with our wishes or to get out of our way. If it can frighten them into agreement or excite their guilt, it may change their behavior in ways that help us to achieve our goals. The relevant questions therefore are: who and how?

Who is the barrier to our hopes? And whose cooperation is necessary for attaining success? If this person (or persons) can be identified, we may figure out how to influence him. Usually anger is directional. Certainly effective anger is. People generally do not just blow their tops; they blow them at someone. When a person is so angry that he spits rage in every direction, this is a sure sign that he has already lost control. Primitive anger is directed at the universe; socialized anger has specific interlocutors. Unfocused anger can also signal that a person's defenses have gone up—that he is, in essence, displacing his anger in all directions, except the correct one. Thus, another function of incremental tolerance is to calm us down so that we can discern whom we want to influence. Instead of setting off indiscriminate fireworks, we must have sufficient control to select a particular, and relevant, target. Rather than beat up the furniture, we must determine whether it is a spouse, a parent, or some third party we need to change. Moreover, the people we select should be able to give us what we want. If they are peripheral to our frustrations, getting angry at them may prove useless.

The determination of an appropriate direction for interpersonal influence has both an is and an ought component. The *is* question identifies who has until now been our target, whether or not this is an appropriate one; the *ought* question evaluates the efficacy of our choice. For the moment, let us focus on the *is* question? Identifying the mechanisms of anger requires a recognition of actual targets. People hoping to be effective must perceive their starting point. They have to be honest with themselves even when this entails a recognition that they have been causing injury to innocent bystanders.

If not immediately apparent, the actual objects of wrath can be identified by observing when and where people get angry. Once more the context of anger provides clues about how it is operating. Generally, there will be particular individuals, or classes of individuals, who are present when an emotion is ignited. Angry people can then ascertain how these others are connected with their anger. Did they provoke it? Can they assuage it? Are they stand-ins for others who did or can? The answers may prove fascinating.

The *ought* component of the object of our anger has even more latitude. The potential targets of anger are unlimited. They are, however, intimately connected with how our anger is being used and hence may not be resolvable before we plan a strategy for getting angry. The clarification of these may therefore have to await the final stage of I.A.M., namely, that of using anger.

Identifying the current *hows* of anger can also be challenging. There is no single stereotyped expression of the emotion that occurs every time a person is frustrated. Nor do all its expressions produce equal results. While it is true that primitive anger is restricted in its manifestations, for adults it is not the standard manifestation. Socialized anger, with its far wider repertoire, is much more common, which also means that more things can go wrong. It becomes possible to employ the wrong words, an inappropriate tone of voice, or an ineffectual form of persuasion. Identifying and evaluating these cover a good deal of territory.

People trying to recognize how they get angry must determine whether they are using verbal, physical, or emotional means to effect change. Are their demands being communicated in language, or are they literally twisting arms? Is their emotional energy the persuasive element, or are they threatening to inflict physical penalties? To complicate matters further, just as people can disguise the fact that they are angry, so can they conceal the mechanisms through which their anger operates. In order to foreclose resistance, they may utilize indirection in their approach. Thus, they may be angry, but not look angry. They may, for example, promise to break someone's arm but deliver this threat with an ingratiating smile. While direct anger tends to be very visible, when it is packaged as something else, people, including the angry person, can become confused.

Indirection is possible both as to the person being influenced and the demand being made. A threat, for instance, can ostensibly be directed toward one person, but intended for another. Similarly, people can ask for one thing, while implying they want something very different. Another form of indirection involves the energy level being employed. Presumably the greater the intensity, the more frustrated the person; but this can be deceptive. The loudness with which a demand is expressed can be adjusted according to its expected effect. This means that ostensibly low intensities can sometimes achieve the best results. Perhaps the most celebrated form of indirection is passive aggression. Here no obvious demand is made. Instead of outrightly challenging another, people drag their feet. Verbally they promise compliance, all the while trying to sabotage the other's demands. Nothing may seem to be happening, certainly nothing the resisting party can be blamed for, but this is the point. "Yes, the garbage has not been taken out yet, but keep your shirt on, it will be shortly." Only it won't.

Once anger is identified as to its direction and manner of implementation, these can be evaluated according to their probable effectiveness. In general, determining the specific form anger should take hinges upon what is wanted and how others are likely to respond. As we shall see, effective anger is dependent upon many factors. People must understand the barriers in their path and comprehend how to breach them. Sources of resistance must be correctly estimated and instruments for persuasion wisely chosen. Is the right person being addressed? Is the correct message being delivered? Is belligerence in order, or perhaps more sugar? The answers to these questions are enormously complex and can take a lifetime to ascertain.

GETTING HELP

Even when people can tolerate their anger, it may be difficult for them to assess it. Anger is a distressing, frustrating emotion that tends to get in its own way. It may thus be necessary to call on friends, family, or professionals for help in making anger both safer and more visible. Such persons can act as a coachs, cheerleaders, protectors, role models, or mirrors. They can provide information, motivation, advice, or security; and because they are less involved, they can be the eyes and the voice of reason.

But first helpers must understand someone's anger. If they misperceive it, their judgment too can be distorted. To prevent this fate, they must open a window into the other's soul. One way of achieving this is through role-taking. When we interact with other persons, we typically play complementary parts; husbands interact with wives, teachers with students, and so forth. Indeed, without cooperation between the pair, their respective roles would be impossible. A "husband" without a "wife" makes as much sense as a fish without water. Yet coordination can be awkward. For people to work together, they must understand each other. This is where role-taking comes in. It is a mechanism for projecting oneself into others' shoes in order to determine what they are doing or feeling. We human beings can, as it were, mentally take one another's part in order to see what it feels like. Invaluable to this process is our capacity for empathy. It enables us to feel with another person. Thus, when helpers seek to facilitate an evaluation of problem anger, they must try to project themselves into their "clients'" feelings. By trying to feel as they do, helpers may be able to catch a glimpse of the goals and mechanisms lying behind the facade. Yet, because the anger is not theirs, the intensity of what they experience should be lower and less distracting. Helpers' observations can be more accurate and, when communicated, exceedingly informative.

Still, role-taking is not magic. Recognizing another's situation does not automatically reveal what is happening. It may be necessary to make an educated guess. In other words, helpers may have to generate hypotheses and then test them. They may have to use their self-knowledge and their knowledge of the world to fathom why others are angry and what they intend to achieve.

In formulating such hypotheses, it is salutary to keep several things in mind. First, when people are angry, there are always reasons. The purposes may be obscure and easily dismissed, but there will be a point to be unearthed.

Second, clients are almost always angry at some person. Even when no target is apparent, there will usually turn out to be a disguised one. This target may seem irrational to an outsider, but anger does not have to be sensible. It can be mistaken in its goals or its mechanisms. It can even be initiated by events that seem trivial. What an angry person interprets as unforgivable insult may to someone else seem no more than a mere slip of the tongue. The point is that a helper must look for some person and some reason, even when there is ostensibly none.

Third, helpers must be alert to suppressed goals and means. Because intense anger invites disguise, they must be prepared to penetrate one. Though clients' explanations seem plausible, they should not be accepted uncritically. Sometimes people rationalize. Sometimes they put forward socially acceptable justifications designed to placate themselves and others. This dictates that helpers must not be naive. They must have had experience with repression, displacement, and projection. It will be especially useful for helpers to understand their own defensive maneuvers, in order to recognize them in another.

Fourth, helpers must examine the context of clients' anger. Just as angry people may be able to diagnose their own purposes and methods by observing when they get angry, so too may outside observers. The mysteries surrounding anger often evaporate when it is studied in action. Unfortunately, the context of personal anger may not always be available or accurately reported. Accounts of sensitive events are notoriously subject to revision. Nevertheless, a Freudian discovery can come to the rescue. The phenomenon Freud called transference can transport anger generated in inaccessible circumstances into a here-and-now relationship. In transference, people enact roles with their helpers that were previously enacted with someone else. The other's motives and behaviors are projected onto the helpers, who are treated as if they were the other person. A female therapist, for instance, might be reacted to as if she were a client's mother. If the person's mother was unloving, the therapist can be blamed for being unloving, no matter what her real attitude. Though uncomfortable, this tendency can be exploited for therapeutic purposes. Because clients' current anger recapitulates what they once felt toward other people, it can be used to determine what the earlier anger was about. An important caveat, however, is that helpers must not be fooled by countertransference. If their own unresolved emotions are projected onto those they are helping, their perceptions can be distorted. It takes enormous self-control and self-knowledge to avoid this pitfall.

Fifth, whatever the hypotheses regarding clients' anger, they must be tested. As there are many potential sources of error, even good-faith judgments have to be tempered with skepticism. No specific speculation, no matter how plausible, should be granted the status of fact without being given an opportunity to prove itself false. If a mythology about a person's anger is created, even inadvertently, it can retard the resolution of difficulties. Undoubtedly, the best way to test a theory about anger is to see if it can terminate clients' frustrations. If readings about underlying goals or their disguised expressions are correct, it should be possible to construct a strategy for helping clients get what they want. If this is not possible and their frustrations continue, either the theory was mistaken or the goals were not feasible after all. Either way, the enterprise will have to be rethought.

Finally, helpers must not allow themselves to be blown away by the power of a client's anger; or else their role-taking, empathy, hypothesis generation, and testing will all go by the boards. A helper who leaves the scene or attempts to retaliate in self-defense loses the ability to understand or be helpful. Rather, helpers must let the client's anger wash over them, while they strive for ever better comprehension.

7

Accepting Losses

THE PAIN OF LOSS

The pain of enduring an irreversible failure is much more profound than is commonly supposed. If either the goals or means of anger make success impossible, the strain involved can be traumatic. The word *frustration* has a mild, almost technical sound, but its reality can be a torment. When evaluation of anger reveals that its subjects cannot win, that they can never obtain what they feel they must have, they will inevitably be shaken. Their desire to prevail will be no less, but the optimism that has sustained their exertions may evaporate. Suddenly they will be faced with a reality they have not been prepared to accept, indeed, one whose acceptance has probably been considered untenable. But accept it they must, for the alternative of continuing to fight and continuing to lose are worse. Still, they will be confronted with an unpalatable choice, for even if they do acknowledge the truth, they may descend into a period of protracted misery. Relinquishing long-held commitments is very painful and not easy to abide.

Step four of integrated anger management, in contrast to the preceding phases, is optional; its implementation depends on the results of what has gone before. But when it is indicated, it is essential. Attempting to move on and and act as if nothing happened, as if there was no loss when one has indeed occurred, can climax in further frustration. No matter how strong a person's desire to attain the impossible, if it truly is impossible, failure is predestined. Nowadays, we often hear, "If you can think something, you can achieve it," but this statement is ridiculous. Life is full of limitations, and ignoring them merely increases one's chances of catastrophe.

Nevertheless, phase four of I.A.M., namely, letting go of what has been lost, is no fun. It can be devastating. Although people may recognize the wisdom of pursuing what works and avoiding what doesn't, the process of cutting their losses can feel like death. It begins, after all, with a recognition of how much has been lost and proceeds through the anguish of mourning. Relinquishing impossible attachments is not an intellectual procedure; it is a raw emotional one. Consider also that problem anger does not originate in petty squabbles. It is persistent and energetic precisely because what has been frustrated represents a vital interest. A person's very existence may seem at stake.

As we learned in chapter 6, the motivation underlying thwarted goals often entails a need for safety, love, and respect. When people become intensely angry, they are likely to be trying to avoid serious physical injury, abject loneliness, and/or a grave insult to their self-esteem. Their place in the world, even their continued survival, will seem at issue. This threat may induce them to confuse their goals with their needs. They may, for instance, identify a need for love with the goal of being loved by a particular person. If so, they may refuse to abandon the latter on the grounds that, if they do, they will never be loved. This conviction will electrify their struggle not to lose and will make it difficult for them to recognize that alternative goals may make it more likely that they will meet their needs.

It sometimes seems that people become enraged over trivia, but this is rarely the case. A closer examination generally reveals that they are resisting what appears to them to be a terrible consequence. Often they are right; their genuine needs are being threatened. Physical danger, for instance, is more widespread in civilized society than our beliefs would seem to allow. In recent decades it has become evident that abusive relationships are relatively common. Whereas Freud once dismissed the hypothesis that his clients had been subjected to sexual assault by their parents, today we know that children are frequently exploited by those closest to them. Moreover, when abuse occurs during the formative years, the battle against it can rage into adulthood. The upshot is that for adults, the origins of their anger may be obscure. Thanks to the defense mechanisms they have used to ward off the menace emanating from childhood attackers, it may not be clear to them that they are fighting for safety. Ironically, the greater the danger, the less able they will be to perceive it correctly.

Similarly battles fought in behalf of self-respect can appear misguided. To those not intimately involved, social status may seem ephemeral and of little real import. In truth, however, it can be tantamount to life itself. Everyone wants and needs to be special, that is, to have the positive regard of others. That we all hate to be "losers" is no accidental happenstance, for we know that without respect, we would be treated like dishrags. Our opinions would be disregarded and we would be assigned society's leftovers. For better or worse, respect and social status are correlated with the resources to which one has access. Being a nobody means getting next to nothing; it means having a poorer job, a more shabby residence, ill health, and a less desirable mate. As importantly, the life chances of one's children are adversely effected. It is because social status matters so much that it is fought for so tenaciously.

Love too is of vital import. As children, we forge emotional ties to those who care for us. During our interactions with them, attachments are formed that bind us to life itself. A child who is severely neglected, who has no opportunity to participate in a loving relationship, can lose the will to live. In the past, when orphaned children were shunted into loveless foundling hospitals, over 80 percent of them languished and died. Their failure to thrive, sometimes referred to as "marasmus," was the result of insufficient contact with their caretakers. Though the children were fed enough to survive, their nurses did not have the time or patience to hold and fondle them. Children seem to acquire a desire to live only when love convinces them that life is worth living. When children's emotional deprivation is less profound, the results are not so dramatic. They survive, but with an ache in the heart that won't go away. They may then fight for love with a fervor that appears bizarre to anyone who does not recognize what is involved. Moreover, such people will probably continue to seek love in barren soil. Were they to relax their efforts and accurately assess the hopelessness of their situation, they might be confronted with an internal emptiness that would look very like their own demise. Unloved people often fear that they will perish from loneliness.

Is it any wonder then that anger dedicated to obtaining love, safety, or respect does not want to hear that these are unobtainable? If an evaluation reveals that success is questionable, this conclusion will not be blandly accepted. Since it implies the acceptance of some-thing very like death, it usually invites a renewed battle. Rather than shift their objectives or alter their strategies, people will plunge into their accustomed arguments, brawling with revitalized zeal for what they have wanted all along. In short, failure alone is unlikely to ex-tinguish anger; more probably, failure will reinvigorate it.

People in danger of losing crucial battles generally continue to struggle valiantly. They refuse to acknowledge defeat and propose to fight it out on the same line forever. No matter how lost the cause, they take pride in their faithfulness. If asked why they persist, they might cite "honor" as a prime motive. To them, only the spineless and unworthy yield. Strangers may dismiss them as bitter and ridic-ulous figures, but in their own eyes they can do no other. In fact, they dread defeat more than they value honor. Their fury is more a defense against total loss than it is a matter of principle. Unremitting anger is typically a sign that a prospective loss is reckoned unendur-able. Better then to go down in flames. The alternative of relinquish-ing one's anger will be perceived as a self-inflicted lobotomy, as a kind of "soul-ectomy." To stop being angry will be seen as tanta-mount to embracing nothingness. Therefore, rather than perceive the possibility of other goals, their present objectives will be elevated to the status of continued survival; and the anger dedicated to preserv-ing them will be conceived of as a carbon-steel link to the universe. As long as the anger remains intact, there is hope.

Nevertheless, persistence in failure means additional failure. If an-ger is one's sole possession, one doesn't possess much. Conse-quently, when love, respect, or safety are at issue, pursuing them with interminable, unproductive anger translates into a loveless, val-ueless, and insecure existence. To a person in this situation, giving up and moving on may seem unimaginable, but the status quo is obviously no better. One must understand that, contrary to appear-ances, defeat is not the equivalent of death. It is persisting on a fruit-less course that is stultifying; loosening one's grip on an unsatisfying goal can actually free one's hands for other endeavors.

LETTING GO

Letting go of an unattainable goal entails a kind of mourning. To relinquish goals, people have to grieve over what they cannot have. The same applies to a means of achieving satisfaction when it is treated as a goal. If people's attachments to the strategies they have been using to overcome their frustrations become adamantine, abandoning them will also feel like a loss. In such a case, mourning will be required to break these bonds too. But what is this mourning, and how does it work? How can grief prepare the ground for new objectives and/or for new ways of being angry?

Mourning is a multistage enterprise designed to allow people to relinquish what has been lost. In its most familiar manifestation, it is a mechanism for adjusting to the death of loved ones. When someone we care about dies, we do not just hitch up our trousers and forget them. The death of a loved one stops us in our tracks, and it will take some time before we are prepared to resume our journey. Though the person who has died is physically gone, it will require emotional labor before we can sever our psychological ties to him. The same is true of critical goals. We commit to them just as we do to loved ones. They become a part of our lives and provide us with a framework for living. Indeed, without them, we would be cut adrift. If people are emotionally committed to obtaining love from a particular source, this commitment ties them to this source even when their objective of being loved is not achievable. In this case, not love, but the attempt to obtain love, cements their bond. In fact, a frustrated objective often has the power to bind people very tightly. The very act of fighting for the unattainable can mobilize more energy than would consummating the goal. Breaking an imperfect attachment can therefore be as traumatic as breaking a viable one.

In the event of death, mourning begins with a perception of loss. The death of a loved one is seen as a blow. This final passing is usually unanticipated, even when it has been long expected. Those people who form a part of our universe seem as if they will always be a part of it. We may know that our parents will eventually die; but, when they do, we still feel like orphans. When death is less predictable, as it is with a very young child, it can be more shattering and less fathomable. Because we are unprepared for it, the death seems unreal. Nevertheless, no matter how much we may anticipate a loss, its reality will be unwelcome. To the extent that a bond exists, we will try to hold fast. We may resent and even hate the other person, but, with clenched fists, we try to maintain his place in our life. When someone important is involuntarily torn away, we resist indefatigably. The rupture represents coercion, and we will resent it. Had we been allowed to loosen our grasp voluntarily, the situation might have been acceptable; but when a loss occurs at the behest of an implacable fate, we balk.

It is natural to fight against uninvited losses. Elisabeth Kubler-Ross has described how people first deny, then get angry at, and then try to reverse their effects. Death mobilizes energies to nullify its decision. People refuse to see or accept it. If they can, they will suppress their awareness of it; if they can't, they will work to undo it. In this, anger is a central player. Because a loss violates a person's plans, it is treated as a frustration; something fit only to be overcome. A loved one who dies will be entreated to return; if this fails, we will try bullying. Should the person still choose to remain dead, the same strategy may be turned against God. Only when this larger protest fails will we decide that our loss is irreversible.

The protest phase of mourning can be very protracted. Ironically, the less visible a loss, the greater the energy that will be invested in challenging it. Thus, because frustrations are often less tangible than is death, people may try harder to rescind them. Even when there are few visible signs that they are attempting to undo history, they may brood about what has gone wrong and try to figure out how they can make things right. It may be months or years before they relent and are satisfied that the loss is irrevocable. Only when it becomes plain that no amount of rage will have the desired effect will sadness set in. When it does, people become melancholy, and they may remain so for a considerable period of time. Grief can be inconsolable; indeed they may wish themselves dead. Nevertheless, grief is central to mourning. It is the mechanism that severs a person's ties with what is gone. What is lost may be objectively irretrievable, but it will not be psychologically gone until sadness certifies that it is.

To be sad is to withdraw into one's own private world. There may be tears; there will certainly be lethargy. Grieving people feel sorry for themselves. They are in agony over what has been denied them. Real sadness is like a black glob that expands until it encompasses all of life; it feels like a dark and bottomless pit from which the sad person can never extricate himself. In the depths of a depression, people's eyes hurt, their bodies are wracked with pain, and their brains feel numb. It will seem to them and to those who care about them that they are virtually dead.

Yet appearances are deceiving, for grief can be productive. Sadness is not the black emptiness it seems to be. In its midst, people's minds are tirelessly, reviewing their attachments to the lost person in their myriad of details. Letting go of someone is not an all or nothing proposition; it takes time because many small bonds need to be examined and disconnected. When depressed people stare with unseeing eyes out a window, in their mind's eye they are usually recalling an aspect of their relationship with the deceased. Only after having done so can they come to terms with the fact that this too is gone. If her husband has died, a woman may imagine the feel of his hand in hers or the sound of his voice greeting her at the end of the day. Each such memory will evoke a twinge of pain that must be dealt with. No, she will never touch his hand again. It is in the grave far beyond her reach. And then the tears will well up and her sadness will become palpable. She may feel that she will cry forever, but she won't. Eventually, her sadness will do its work; and, though chastened, she will lift her head prepared to see the world once more. Her eyes no longer gaze out the window and instead will settle on the living.

In the normal course of mourning, grief gives way to acceptance. One's loss is thoroughly digested and its consequences internalized. No longer will it be necessary to protest or to feel pain. The situation will still not be enjoyable, but the person will have reconciled to it. With this, attention will shift from the past to the future. Breaking what were strong attachments leaves room for new ones. A person coming out of mourning is ready to pursue untried relationships with renewed energy and a reawakened desire for human contact. Although not throbbing with happiness, the person will no longer be trapped in a corner by her sadness.

This model of mourning has been successfully applied to death and dying for some time. It has also proven useful when dealing with other obvious losses, such as those that occur in divorce or other life transitions. It has not, however, been much applied to anger management, apparently because anger does not involve an obvious loss. It is usually conceived of as an explosive emotion, not as a reaction to frustrations. But to be frustrated is to lose, to have one's cherished goals stomped on. It may seem odd to talk about losing something one has never had, but a frustrated person has had hopes. There is no corporeal body to testify to the finality of the loss, but a history of thwarted effort affirms that winning was not possible. Though ordinary mourning begins with what appears to be an external provocation (a death occurs, thrust upon us from the outside), with anger the situation seems different. Usually anger has a long history of bitterness and recrimination. It may seem to have no clearcut starting point or obvious point of loss, because these may have occurred years ago. Moreover, as anger apparently originates inside people, it may seem to be their own, not a reaction to something exterior.

Yet anger does incorporate a core of loss. Frustrated people clearly fail. As with death, when a goal cannot be retrieved, mourning may be the only option. People's sadness may be delayed by the vigor of their protests, but it cannot be put off forever. Their anger may try to cheat fate or seek to deny failures by keeping their eyes firmly closed, but eventually the battle with destiny ends and a defeat is recorded. Though it may be a searing, painful defeat, its reality must reluctantly be acknowledged. As with death, when people's obsolete goals die, part of them ceases to exist. Because their commitments have no existence apart from their holders' endorsement of them, admitting their demise consigns them to nothingness. The pain of such a loss can be excruciating. This is why so much anger is never resolved, why many people who become aware of the agony of letting go of important goals elect to remain angry. They simply find continuing to choke down their bitterness preferable to experiencing the torment and emptiness of grief.

What many people fail to realize is that grief is not a boundless misery. They imagine that embracing it will mean remaining lost in its labyrinths forever and judge it better to be actively frustrated than to be endlessly despondent. Having tasted the bitter powerlessness of mournful tears, they fear getting caught in the swirls of a depression that may sweep them to their death. In this, they are not altogether wrong. It is not that they will die, but that grief does have the strength to catch people up and move them in directions they can not consciously control. Sadness happens to people; it is not something they do. Thus, if permitted to occur, it may, for all a person knows, lead to his extinction.

Certainly it feels this way to those who have been resisting a loss for a long time. They have already had experience with intractable foes who wished them no good. Sadness will therefore appear to be a new enemy. What they must somehow discover is that the pain of sadness is actually a portal to freedom. Grief does not last forever; unless people are foolish enough to commit suicide, grief will not cause their death. Its true destination is an acceptance of losses and an ability to embrace other unexplored goals. Should these turn out to be more achievable than the old, their needs may even be met. Thus, by allowing mourning to run its course, they can escape their nagging frustrations and surmount the springs of their anger.

GETTING HELP IN LETTING GO

As with the preceding stages of I.A.M., relinquishing the unattainable can be difficult and may require help in achieving. Even for people who have the intelligence to recognize when they are trapped, emotional commitments may preclude grief. Acknowledging that they have failed and enduring the rigors of their sadness may be beyond their unaided strength. However, with the active support of friends, relatives, or professional helpers, they may be able to break through these barriers and reorganize their underlying objectives. A shoulder to cry on or a hand extended in friendship can make all the difference.

Sometimes support can be supplied quite unconsciously by those concerned with the welfare of angry people. Others' continued devotion can give them the courage to endure. The presence of individuals who are on one's side provides a moral boost. Even when no material comfort is involved, their physical accessibility assures us that we are not alone. This security, in turn, can provide the impetus for engaging in a risky venture such as mourning. Unfortunately, intense grief and violent anger can be threatening even to those not experiencing them and can discourage outsiders from remaining in the vicinity of unhappy people. Providing comfort takes fidelity and boldness, requiring that helpers weather gales of disturbing emotions while remaining constant in their patronage. It also requires an understanding of how anger and sadness work. In guiding people to work these emotions through, their intricacies must be understood.

Now we must examine what it is like to be with a depressed person. Extreme sadness creates a pall over everything it touches. Its black hand spreads pessimism and lethargy wherever it reaches. To be with a grieving person is to be surrounded by a web of misery that feels as if it will drag one down. It is very difficult to sit by a despondent person without feeling depressed. No wonder then that the normal impulse is to flee and/or banish the emotion. Sad people will be told to "cheer up," and even be encouraged to laugh. Certainly, others will assure them that "there is nothing to worry about." Apparently the belief is that if their sadness can be replaced by something else, it will be gone and that everyone will benefit.

But grief is a necessary step in breaking attachments. Interfering with it only maintains bonds that need to be severed. Thus helpers whose misplaced reassurances discourage mourning inadvertently perpetuate the very misery they intend to dispel. Their ignorance of the mechanics of sadness induces them to gum up the works. The most important form of assistance that helpers can render is simply to encourage unhappy people to feel sad. The best way to do this is to allow them to feel sad. Grief is something that happens when a person has the confidence to permit it. It doesn't have to be plotted and controlled; it need only to be freed to pursue its instinctive patterns. Several decades ago, treatment for people experiencing an epileptic seizure included holding them down and inserting a rigid object between their teeth. Nowadays it is recognized that such interference creates further damage. Consequently, today we allow epileptics in seizure to move around freely and merely remove surrounding items with which they might collide. Responding to grief is quite similar.

Grieving people know without instruction what they need to do to work through their sadness. Although they may not consciously understand what must happen, they are capable of working things through when ready. Once they muster the courage to confront their loss, the process of severing ties will begin. As this can be a terrifying experience, at times they will want physical and emotional reassurance. At other times they will want to be alone—the most important item on their agenda being to ruminate about their loss without distraction. In other words, sometimes grieving people want a shoulder to cry on and sometimes they want to be alone. These sufferers are best situated to know what is appropriate and should call the signals. It is the task of helpers merely to be responsive to changing moods; to allow closeness when it is requested and to permit distance when it is indicated. This role is probably more passive than the one most helpers would prefer, but it is far more effective than attempting to dictate the pace of change.

In particular, helpers must allow time for grief to unfold, which it typically does at a rate far slower than any participant likes. Most people want to be finished with their sadness as quickly as possible. Yet it is an agonizingly slow emotion. Grief over serious losses can take years to complete. Urging people onward only retards this process because it upsets the sequencing of their needs for closeness and distance. Instead of being allowed to respond to an inner clock, they are told to do what the helpers think they should, which is usually wrong. This is not to say that helpers should never provide advice or encouragement. It may be useful to spur a person to "hang in there." Likewise, explaining that sadness takes time, but will not endure forever, can provide solace when someone becomes discouraged. It can even help to explain that a particular objective is unattainable. When the answer is given in response to a person's desire to test reality, this too can move the grieving process forward.

For angry people who have discovered that they can never attain the love denied them in childhood, the presence of helpers can reassure them that they have not lost all their ties to life. Warm, concerned others can serve as transitional objects, as a kind of security blanket, bridging the gap between entangling disputes derived from the past and more hopeful future attachments. As people let go of what they cannot have, they must traverse a patch of barren ground where they have virtually nothing. Here it will be too soon to have refashioned a meaningful love relationship, but not too soon to experience the oblivion of feeling unloved. The accessibility of helpers can take the terror out of this emptiness, and their visible humanity can be a warrant of better things in store.

After the worst of grief has passed, people must reorient themselves toward the future. New goals, ones that are attainable, must be able to elicit a renewed allegiance. Alternate strategies of pursuing vital needs must be devised and implemented. As essential as it is to disengage from lost battles, it is equally vital for people to reenter the fray and fight for what they need. Shucking the bands of a destructive anger must not terminate in a retirement from life. If the outcome of a period of mourning is a featureless plateau that stretches endlessly toward the grave, nothing will have been gained.

Of course, this scenario implies that there will be additional failures. Disengaging from problem anger does not mean never being angry again, nor does it mean that one's anger will always be successful. In life we have to take our chances. The best we can hope for is a skillful performance that improves our prospects, never one that guarantees them. Having extricated ourselves from an awkward position, it will be necessary to learn how to use our anger more effectively. As there will be new battles to fight, it is better that these be fought with shiny new weapons. Among the things that people may need to learn is how to choose between alternatives, how to decide on compelling influence strategies, and how to plan with flexibility. Because there is no surefire avenue to success, it is imperative that people keep their needs in mind and make adjustments as necessary.

8

Using Anger

NO SINGLE BEST WAY

At last we come to the final stage of integrated anger management. The other four stages have all aimed at laying a foundation for this, the implementation phase. Ultimately, for problem anger to reach a conclusion, it must realize its objective, that is, it must overcome the frustrations that set it in motion. The energy of anger must be directed toward effectively attaining what is desired. Assuring safety, developing tolerance, and achieving an accurate assessment are all but a prelude to using the emotion to make things happen. Without this final breakthrough all else is dust and ashes, a mere invitation to further frustration.

Yet using anger effectively is no snap. There exists no fail-safe formula pointing toward infallible success. Anger can go wrong. Despite being tolerated or understood and despite the best of intentions, anger can create chaos. Thus, its effective implementation requires skill, effort, and some luck. Planning, self-control, and appropriate external circumstances are all needed. As we have already learned, anger both communicates and motivates. The self and one's role partners are both informed and moved by it. Effective anger depends on influencing the self and the other so that specified goals are attained. In particular, its energy must culminate in a situation in which others no longer constitute a barrier to one's ends. It is when anger suitably communicates what is desired and induces compliance with this purpose that it promotes personal satisfaction.

Still there is no one best way to communicate and no one best way

to motivate. Anger is not the perfect tool that has optimum parame-
ters in all situations. How it should be used depends on a myriad of
factors; and even in favorable circumstances, it is uncertain that it
will have the predicted consequences. In particular, it is rarely possible to be certain that an expression of anger is the best one possible. When implementing the emotion, people make an educated
guess, then must be prepared to alter their actions as events indicate.
What will work depends on their goals, the individuals with whom
they are interacting, and the resources available to all concerned.

Anger is dynamic. It typically arises during the interactions of two
or more people and is subject to the vicissitudes of their relationship.
It is also sensitive to shifts in their internal and external environment. Changes in their respective need structures or demands made
by third parties can exert a powerful impact on them. Factors such
as their relative social status dramatically affect who will be willing
to do what with whom. In consequence, anger must be flexible and
responsive. Although planning is essential, it must not be rigid and
should be pragmatic. People who are absolutely certain that their
way is *the* correct way will usually fail. No matter how glittering a
person's record, life has a way of moving on and leaving the obsti-
nate in its wake. Success is more likely to come to those who can
recognize change and adjust to it. This requires that they have the
capacity to be sensitive to others and that they possess a broad repertoire of potential responses. Those tethered to stereotyped observations and/or reactions are less able to meet new situations appropriately.

The touchstone of effective anger is what works. Failure must not
be denied, nor success minimized. Those who are enslaved by what
they were once taught hasten the day when they will lose. Instead,
they must monitor the actual responses of others. Their antennae must
be out on an ongoing basis to alert them when predicted reactions
don't materialize. Results matter. They are more important than as-
surances from a trusted authority that a particular form of anger is
best. To use anger well, people must trust themselves. They must
have confidence in their ability to recognize the facts and to act on
them.

No one, however, is born with such certitude. It takes experience
to perceive how and when anger works. A slow and incremental process of socialization underlies competent performances. If primitive
anger is to be surmounted, there must be a readiness to learn. Techniques for implementing the emotion can, and do, evolve throughout

a person's life. One must learn the right words, ascertain the proper level of force, and choose the best tactical situation. This is especially true for those grappling with problem anger. During the final phases of I.A.M., it is imperative to be open to new ideas and to innovative forms of action. Those who have a history of failed anger need to develop alternative ways of communicating and motivating; otherwise, their ability to influence their role partners will prove as negligible as it has before.

People who want to become more proficient in using anger should begin with the feeling itself. Having discovered how to tolerate wrath, they must now allow themselves to experience it. This will enable them to evaluate it before, during, and after they swing into action. Determining whether a particular instance of anger is feasible entails observing its actuality. As we noted in chapter 6, suppressing even problem anger shuts out irreplaceable information. Because anger is the surest avenue toward understanding what people really want and how they are attempting to get it, it can provide essential insights as to what has gone wrong and what must change.

A NEGOTIATION PERSPECTIVE

As we have seen, one way to understand how people interact is to perceive them as engaged in a form of social negotiation. Anger can then be interpreted as a bargaining tool. It assists them in coming to agreements that can help attain their wants or conversely can stalemate them in individual or joint misery. When the emotion permits people to work out their differences, they will benefit; when it precipitates interminable, injurious discord, they will suffer. Since anger specializes in interpersonal influence, it is safe to assume that its application involves at least two parties. And because each party has interests that may or may not be compatible with the others, when they mesh, the two can collaborate in mutual problem-solving. When they do not, they have the option of engaging in either shared recriminations or joint attempts at resolving their disagreements.

As may be recalled, the psychologist Dean Pruitt (1981) elaborated a dual concern model of negotiations that is useful in comprehending the range of possibilities available to two disputants. He indicated that, in striving to reach a decision, they can consider the interests of both, the interests of neither, or the interests of one rather than of the other. This exhausts their alternatives. If neither cares who wins, neither has an incentive to fight and the outcome will be left to chance.

For them, anger will not be a problem for neither will feel frustrated. In the case where the participants care only about their own interests, both will be motivated to battle ferociously and may be convinced that any tactic is acceptable as long as it succeeds. Here anger is liable to be vicious and capable of inflicting appreciable damage. In the case where one person doesn't care about his or her own interests but does value those of the other, he or she may simply capitulate, not arguing on his or her own behalf, but yielding willingly to the other's demands and possibly enlisting his or her own anger in the other's behalf. Finally, if both parties value their own and the other's interests, they will be motivated to find a mutually acceptable solution that honors the needs of both. They will logically engage in problem-solving to discover common ground. For them, it is crucial that their anger be an effective instrument in achieving collective agreements.

When anger is used selfishly, it is a deadly weapon that escalates to levels that overwhelm its target. Because the weaker parties are coerced, they feel defeated. Their anger will not be assuaged; and if they are presented with an opportunity to rekindle the dispute, they will seize it. The victors, however, may revel in their success, no longer feeling goaded by frustration or alert to the other's grievance. This reduced vigilance may provide the opening the victim has been hoping for, and their fight will blaze forth anew. When, however, both protagonists are committed to respecting their respective interests, the story is different. Each will be motivated to listen to the other in order to ascertain what is causing distress. That the other's interests are frustrated will be of concern because each needs to know what the other wants if they hope to discover a mutually acceptable outcome. Problem-solving necessitates having a clear perspective on where both parties stand. Although both may passionately argue in favor of a preferred solution, neither can afford to be indifferent to the reactions of the other. Even when their levels of power are not equivalent, the stronger person will find it profitable to refrain from exploiting his advantage and to act as if they were equal.

When such a pair enters a negotiation, they will need to know a great deal about themselves and the other. They have to understand their own and the other's goals, any underlying needs that these serve, the negotiation strategies to which each is prone, and the resources available to both. Their respective strengths have to be visible to both, as do their respective weaknesses. Because it is in their mutual interest to collaborate, they must try to exploit their individual talents while declining to take advantage of their respective limitations. This does not imply that their dialogue will be totally free of acrimony. The negotiating posture that Pruitt recommends, namely, firm flexibility, suggests that the parties pursue their own interests with vigor, while remaining adaptable regarding the means employed. Since a person's basic needs are unalterable, they can not be readily sacrificed. Means, however, are multifarious and can afford to be plastic. If, for instance, one's partner suggests a better way of satisfying shared needs, this should not be mindlessly rejected just because it differs from one's initial proposal. Only pragmatic problem-solving truly solves problems.

Still, in firm flexibility there must be some firmness, which is generally supplied by anger. A willingness to consider other positions does not preclude an energetic defense of one's own. Anger rises in support of meaningful objectives. It is a marker that particular issues matter and that people are prepared to pursue them forcefully. To do less would imply that they didn't care. Those who hope to spare their partners the distress of being confronted with their anger are laboring under a delusion. The result would be that in suppressing their indignation they would mislead their partners about what was at stake. As importantly, no one is better equipped to defend an individual's interests than is a person himself. He knows best what is wanted and cares most about success. Giving up is therefore no favor to any caring role partner. It would specifically make no sense for a person to depend on the mercies of an uncaring person. While others may resent having to deal with the individual's anger, it will be useful for them to understand that they can't get their way without a fight. This may jolt them into a recognition that others too have rights.

Perhaps the worst mistake made by those who renounce the use of their anger is the assumption that anger is inevitably coercive. Because they want to be fair, they hold their tongues and wind up being unfair to themselves. No doubt, anger is forceful. It does command attention and it does press for compliance. It may even hurt people, but it need not extinguish their rights. Coercion brooks no opposition, while legitimate anger is perfectly capable of pausing when it encounters a persuasive counter-argument. It is rage that is deaf. Persons who can tolerate their anger are generally clear-headed enough to realize that it is to their advantage to listen. Because theirs is socialized anger, they know that provoking uncontrolled counter-anger will not advance their cause. Nor are they so terrified of the other's response that they feel compelled to evade it. While they may recognize that the other's anger is able to inflict injury, they also know that it is not ineluctable. One of the central skills of anger management is learning how to be strong enough to deflect coercion. Usually people who understand the dynamics of their own rage find that of the other less intimidating. When it flares up, they will understand that they are no longer helpless children, unable erect a competent defense. Given an increased confidence and improved strategic abilities, they recognize that they can parry others' blows.

Finally, a negotiation perspective suggests that neither party can have absolute control. Rarely are people able to dictate a solution. In the beginning, they may not even be able to discern the outlines of a compromise, let alone impose it unilaterally. This uncertainty may be disquieting, but it is the price we pay for accommodating to the needs of others. Were this world an illusion projected on the insides of our craniums, we would not have to worry about competing desires. But then again, like the inhabitants of Plato's cave, we would be absolutely alone. The fact that our anger is not instantly or totally triumphant means that our dreams can never be completely realized. Yet this is amply compensated for by our ability to share our successes with others about whom we care and who care about us. Though they may from time to time frustrate our intentions, their companionship will satisfy many other vital needs.

EFFECTIVE AND INEFFECTIVE ANGER

Effective anger must be competently applied within a negotiating framework. It must communicate with the self and the other and must motivate the self and other, in ways that promote productive agreements. The person whose anger sends suitable messages and exercises persuasive influence stands a better chance of advancing fair compacts. But to communicate and motivate well, people must (1) know what objectives are capable of meeting their needs, (2) recognize who can assist in obtaining these, and (3) understand what kinds of pressures will enlist others' aid or neutralize their resistance. To put the matter more concisely, angry people must understand what they want, whom they want to obtain it from, and how they intend to get it. Without a delimited *what*, their efforts will be too unfocused to make concrete demands. Without a specific *who*, they will not recognize those causing their frustrations or those possessing an ability to remove them. Without a definite *how*, they will be without relevant skills or plans of action. Anger that contents itself with raw instinct is hardly ever persuasive.

People must also be clear that there are some applications of anger best done without. Misused anger tends to be mean spirited, intemperate, and inflexible. It settles on negativistic goals, unfair victims, and abusive expressions. It thus gets its *what, who,* and *how* wrong. Furthermore, because it tends to be coercive, it usually generates counter-anger. Rather than influencing others in favorable directions, it induces them to retaliate. When these others fight back, they then become more concerned with denying their adversaries what they want than with helping themselves.

Among the goals that herald a malignant use of anger are those that are selfish, mean, or negativistic. The kind of *what* they promote violates the dual-concern prototype and unnecessarily risks alienating others. The fulfillment of one's needs does not automatically have to be at the expense of others. Despite the fact that life is often a zero-sum game (i.e., a game where there can be only one winner), for the most part it is possible to pursue goals that are compatible with those of our role partners. Gratuitously alienating them by flouting their interests is usually a stupid policy.

Extreme *selfishness* is an overt commitment to only one's own needs. Others are totally excluded; they are not perceived as human beings who have aspirations, but relegated to the status of a piece of furniture. Although a certain amount of selfishness is mandatory for firm flexibility, as people need to care about their own interests to defend them, a one-sided concern for the self is self-defeating. What is more, it is usually the product of a deprived history. Unduly selfish people do not contemplate making deals because they are so frustrated that they only want to extract concessions. In consequence, they are off-putting. Their anger is so obviously at odds with the interests of others that it is usually dismissed out of hand.

Meanness substitutes a proclivity to cause harm for a desire to help. Its selfishness is expressed in the pleasure it obtains at seeing others fail. Others' pain becomes the cynosure of a mean person's actions, replacing the pursuit of his or her own interests. Mean people insensitively tread on the vulnerabilities of others and smile at their complaints. Their wrath has an edge on it over and above any justifiable quest for satisfaction, which understandably alienates others because it represents a danger to them.

Negativity is less malignant. Indeed, it can be downright silly, even childish. Its desire is to erect a barrier against the unfairness of others. Negative people are more intent on denying the goals of others than on achieving their own. They feel so weak that their attention shifts from their own needs to others'. When their role partners assert their personal interests as part of a dual concern strategy, rather than perceive this as an opportunity for a mutually satisfying bargain, negative people feel overwhelmed and rigidly oppose the others' interests. In consequence, their anger seems peevish and beside the point. Negativity is often a part of a passive-aggressive strategy. This type of response, though very aggressive, is generally more reactive than passive. A passive-aggressive person does not do nothing, but actively resists others. If asked to take out the garbage, this type of person sits watching television. This sitting may be perceived as passive, but it is actually a form of defiance that takes energy and commitment to maintain. What really characterizes passive aggression is its choice of goals and tactics, namely, those that are in opposition to a more powerful other. While it can be relatively difficult to discern, this sort of strategy is quite adamant. When confronted by an angry partner, the response of a passive-aggressive person is likely to be a firm "What, me? I didn't do anything."

Needless to say such tactics are inimical to the achievement of needs. First, they offend others with their mindless opposition. It is infuriating to know that one is being resisted just for the sake of being resisted. When a two-year-old asserts independence by saying "no," we try to be tolerant, but when apparently competent adults are similarly obstructive, we want to reciprocate. This means that we will be prepared to oppose their goals once we can ascertain them. Second, passive-aggressive people will probably anticipate the reciprocal hostility they arouse in others and will hide their true goals. But this will have the disquieting result of making their goals equally inaccessible to themselves, and therefore more difficult to implement. Third, being reactive diverts energies. Because it is the others' initiatives that are the focus of negativistic people, their efforts to overcome personal unhappiness are relegated to the background. Instead of using their anger to stake out their own case, it is entirely devoted to a rearguard action aimed against others.

The *who* of misused anger can also go wrong, especially when it is inflexible. If anger becomes obsessed with the transgressions of a particular other, it generally misses the mark. When people are firmly convinced that specific others are their nemesis, they can neglect more pertinent others. No matter how accurate their observations about the source of their travail, fixations tend to be counter-productive. If designated others are unwilling to cooperate, no matter how culpable they are, no amount of invective may be able move them. But if no degree of hatred, grudge-holding, or revenge-taking will do the trick, how is a person to succeed? Hatred, which can be defined as an intense, bitter anger directed at a particular other, is constantly in danger of becoming an all-consuming passion. It is a steel-jacketed animosity that lashes out, to the exclusion of all other considerations, whenever a specific foe comes into view. People in the throes of this sort of obsession forget their own happiness or even their personal security and react automatically to the moving red cape that is the enemy. One of the ways hatred manifests itself is in the nursing of a grudge. People with a grudge refuse to excuse injuries for which they hold an adversary responsible. No matter how much time passes or how often the other begs for mercy, this transgression is neither forgotten nor forgiven. In the words of the popular country song, the grudge-holder is constantly "digging up bones."

Finally, the *how* of misused anger has the most complex tale to tell. More things can go wrong with executing the emotion than with what it seeks or from whom it seeks it. Coercion and inflexibility are rampant in the implementation of anger. But we are getting ahead of ourselves. The how of anger is intimately bound up with its ability to communicate and to motivate, and we will be dealing with these shortly. In the meantime suffice it to say that, when the energy of anger is out of proportion to its mission or when it is ineptly applied, it will not fit the person at whom it is directed or the objective at which it aims. Violence, tantrums, insults, sarcasm, and simple loudness transform it into a blunt instrument capable of horrific atrocities or laughable incompetence. Feckless, irresponsible anger is also a menace. While it may not be primitive or even out of control, it usually is obtuse and ill-conceived.

SELF-COMMUNICATION/ESTABLISHING PRIORITIES

Competent anger depends upon many factors, but the first of these is knowing what it wants. Before communicating with or motivating others, people must identify the relative salience of their goals. In other words, before expressing anger, they must prioritize their objectives. No one has enough time or energy to achieve everything. Attempts to "have it all" invariably collapse in disarray. Because overreaching dilutes a person's efforts, it makes it more likely that he will stumble. Fighting everywhere, against any conceivable frustration, means that people must be constantly vigilant and constantly tired. Thus, during moments of crisis, they can not be at their best and will probably lose.

The confederate general Nathan Bedford Forrest is alleged to have recommended that a successful army must "get there furstest, with the mostest"—that instead of being reactive, its officers must be prepared to sally forth when they see an advantage. To do the same, people must know pretty much what they want. Unless focussed on a delimited prize, they will not be able to reach for it when it appears on the horizon. Instead, they will be dependent upon the mistakes and/or ill-fortune of their adversaries. Similarly, a willingness to court every potential battle creates opponents everywhere. If angry people resemble lions constantly on the prowl, others will attempt to drive them off before they have a chance at successful predation. Their pugnacity and greed may attract peremptory strikes, which in turn raise their level of frustration, for their hopes too will be confounded.

Prioritizing goals, as a prelude to guiding actions, is essentially an exercise in self-communication. It is a matter of listening to one's feelings to determine what really counts. At its best, this process of evaluation is ongoing, and not just a reaction to failure. That is, it is prospective as well as retrospective, the object being to prepare a set of options for future use. Listening to one's anger when prioritizing one's goals is not very different from evaluating the emotion when trying to determine what has gone wrong with it. It too entails actually feeling the feeling and placing it in context. People must observe when and where they get angry, then assess what they are aiming for. The purposes that emerge can subsequently be compared with one another to reveal which is the most important. This can be established by measuring their relative strength. The angrier people are at the prospect of being thwarted, that is, the more they want one thing rather than another, the higher its *prima facie* priority.

But unreflective feeling is not enough. The rank that is assigned a particular goal is contingent upon a number of considerations. The first of these is its ability to meet essential needs. Goals that don't lead to satisfactions are not worth having. Second, success must be feasible. No matter how large the potential payoff, if it is unattainable, it can not lead to fulfillment. Third, the impact of the target goal on one's other needs and goals, now, and in the future, must be ascertained. A present success must not be allowed to diminish collateral successes. If a present victory precipitates defeat elsewhere, it may not be advantageous. It is overall success and not immediate gratifications that will decide whether a person is happy.

An act of examining anger to determine its implications can take place both in actuality or in the imagination. The feelings people assess can arise in response to real frustrations or prospective ones. Either way, they can mull over their reactions to see how they fit together. This should not, however, be a forced or time-limited exercise. If it is, they will probably discover only what they think they should. There must be a possibility of uncovering mistakes, which can be achieved only by being alert to the unexpected. When people believe they already understand their priorities, yet find themselves surprised by what they perceive, they can be reasonably certain an error has occurred, that their desires are not quite as they had imagined.

Establishing viable priorities takes foresight and perspective. People must have a clear-sighted understanding of their current and future situation. Despite uncertainties, they must be honest with themselves about their personal limits and those imposed by the world. They cannot afford to believe fashionable pap about being able to achieve anything they want as long as they try hard enough. Nor should present frustrations be given undue weight. Because people are often swayed by propinquity, contemporary failures tend to divert attention from other possibilities. Although failures may cause people to overestimate the value of what was sought, sometimes they must stand back and be dispassionate. They must be able to recognize what is truly important, current setbacks aside.

People must also allow themselves to recognize suppressed messages. They must feel their anger even when they are convinced that they should not be angry. It may turn out that an apparently trivial frustration is actually paramount. If it has been ignored out of a sense of guilt, it may be time to decide whether the goals of those who made them feel guilty in the first place are more important than their own. Perhaps these others were seeking an unfair advantage. Perhaps they claimed that wanting to be loved was selfish because they were unprepared to satisfy such a desire. When setting priorities, the existence of persistent, perpetual frustrations must be considered. These often indicate that, despite appearances, an alluring objective is really impossible. If people keep trying, and failing, despite their most conscientious efforts, then an unrecognized obstacle, for example, the inability of a role partner to provide what is wanted, is probably getting in the way.

A good starting point in assessing one's goals is always one's basic needs. Everyone wants to be loved, respected, and safe. These goals may sound banal, but they cannot be dismissed; they are too consequential. Sadly, however, people rarely achieve them to the degree that they desire. Ironically, individuals often overlook them precisely because their absence is so disquieting. To reiterate our earlier caveat, no one does not want to be loved, no one is indifferent to being respected, and no one does not care about being safe. The search for these needs pervades our lives.

It is also essential that people understand themselves, their values, and their history. They must know, in light of their needs, how their goals have emerged and how, through the agency of their relationships, these objectives have been modified over time. What experiences with success and failure and what influences emanating from important role partners have contributed to the evolution of the kind of people they are? What, for instance, did the attitudes of their parents have to do with their feelings of self-worth? Sometimes seeing where one comes from can illuminate where one is trying to go. It can make it evident whom one is trying to please or how one has been trying to please them. Underlying goals never emerge in isolation. They are always shaped and restructured under the press of actual events and actual persons.

When contemplating one's goals, it is also useful to consider the experiences of others. These can serve as models for the crystallization of objectives not previously envisioned. How others obtain love can, for instance, provide vital clues as to the type of love the world makes available. Whereas one may previously have wanted someone just like one's parent, the observed success of some other may make it evident that love is more attainable from emotionally demonstrative persons.

To conclude our discussion of the prioritizing process, we must note that none of this is exact. The steps one takes to understand the relative importance of goals do not constitute a settled pattern. The reality of goal-setting is that it is an individual and often very private process. Perhaps the best advice one can be given is to be honest with oneself, to care about one's needs, and to make adjustments as necessary. Following these guidelines, people will learn by doing. But if they are still having difficulty discovering what is really meaningful, they should discuss their feelings with trusted others and use the resultant feedback to clarify what they already know.

COMMUNICATING WITH OTHERS/SHARING PRIORITIES

After the self-communication inherent in prioritization comes an external communication of what one has learned. If others are to co-operate in terminating our frustrations, they need to know what is being asked of them. Angry people must therefore send messages that include a "what" and a "how important." This information will enable others to prioritize their responses. Usually they will want to know how likely it is that angry people will persist in their entreaties. Is what they are demanding today as important to them as what they will be demanding tomorrow? Others will also want to compare the relative importance of these goals with those they are being asked to abjure. These latter also need to be prioritized.

Generally, clear messages are helpful to others in their attempts to classify relative value. Open, focused, and direct communications make it evident what is wanted. They say what they mean to the person who needs to hear it. Their goals are not obscured by ornate language or irrelevant claims; and the words, tone of voice, and manner of their expression are such that they are understandable. Thus, the other is not distracted by diversionary tactics or misled by arcane allusions. Often people who are afraid that they will not get what they want hedge their bets by stating their requirements in a manner that is open to interpretation. This way, if they are refused, they can salvage their pride by ascribing their rejection to a misunderstanding. But theirs may become a self-fulfilling prophesy. Because success is often dependent on specificity, as opposed to abstraction, they can create serious confusions.

One of the factors that makes anger effective is its ability to call attention to its wants. This is possible because the emotion is usually very visible. It virtually jumps up and down and cries out for what it desires to have noticed. Persuasive anger takes advantage of this fact. Knowing what it means to say, it surrounds this meaning with an aura of consequence. Emphatic and compelling, it stands out from the crowd and appeals for immediate action. This it accomplishes, not necessarily through loudness or stridency, but via a controlled release of palpable energy. Anger is like electricity coursing through the space between two people and joining them in a common experience. Sometimes it is discerned in the hard edge of people's voices or in the brittle stiffness of their bodies; at other times it is hammered home by the repetitiveness of their commands or the gusto with which they pound a table. When all is said and done, however, it is the eyes that are the most compelling. They are difficult to cloak and when properly mobilized are very penetrating. Angry eyes burn through another person and are not easily dismissed.

A potent expression of anger also depends on having a complaisant listener. No matter how clear or energetic a message, some people won't hear it. If they are more intent on concocting a response than on determining what they are supposed to do, it may pass right by them. Effective communications are therefore contingent on the careful selection of a recipient. Because anger is interpersonal, its ability to achieve its ends requires two people who want to make it work. While it may be helpful to tailor a message to a given listener, much depends on predispositions the speaker cannot alter.

Even when the purpose of anger is understood, it may not have the intended effects. That a message is perceived does not ensure it will be accepted. Receivers may disagree or even be offended. Sometimes they will launch a counterattack because they prefer to have their own interests pursued. Nowadays, thanks largely to the growth of marital counseling, it is widely assumed that any difficulty can be corrected through straightforward communication—that if two people can only learn talk to one another, their enhanced understanding will inevitably lead to a resolution. But this may not be what happens if they truly disagree. If a wife asks her husband for something he doesn't want to give, what then? What if their honest and open communication makes it plain that he no longer loves her? In this case, their communication will exacerbate rather than resolve their problem. Often the interests of people do conflict. This world may not always be a zero-sum game, but sometimes it is. There are times when the only way people can collaborate is by fooling themselves about what they are doing. Indeed, some proclaim this to be the central truth of politics; that persuading the public depends more on fudge, than authenticity. It certainly seems to be true that plain-spoken candidates tend to lose.

What is worse, and what offends delicate sensibilities, is that sometimes blatant dishonesty works. All of our lives we are told that truth-telling is the best policy; and we, in turn, probably resent being lied to. Because we hate deceit in others, we would rather avoid it in ourselves. Still, if we are to be honest, we must admit that secrecy and deceit have a place in our relationships; indeed, that they are sometimes mandatory. This is particularly so for the weak. Consider what would happen if an employee were candidly to tell his employer exactly what about the boss was repugnant. Should the subordinate stare into his superior's eyes, with a baleful gaze, and launch into a recitation of the idiocy of a recent management decision, we know the likely denouement. The employee might be demoted or fired and would at least land in the doghouse.

Were this person to come to us for advice, would we recommend straightforward, energetic communication? The answer for most of us is: in some ideal world, but not in this one. What we would probably endorse is tact. We would say: "Get your message across in a way that will not offend your boss. Tone your anger down and make it more palatable. If necessary, work around the boss. If your employer can't stand to be contradicted, don't contradict him. Do what you must." We would recognize that tact needs to be in the survival kit of anyone who has to brave the disapproval of more powerful others; but while tact is polite and moderate, it is not necessarily open or honest.

When dealing with stalwart opponents who may not be friendly, caution and indirection are often advisable. Sometimes this will entail secrecy, and sometimes downright deception. The fury of anger may prompt people to blurt out exactly what they think, but if they do, they will tip their hand and may sabotage their cause. Rather than engage in this sort of self-destruction, it is frequently necessary to be discreet. What people communicate should depend upon how it will be used. If they have reason to believe that unequivocal communication will be used against them, they are wise to keep still. Supplying an enemy with the means of one's own downfall may be noble, but it is also stupid.

And it is unnecessary. The rules requiring complete honesty are childhood rules, spouted reflexively by many adults but not honored in their actions. As adults we learn that what we share with others varies with the person and the circumstance. We may not be able to put the criteria we use into words, but they are second nature to us. Thus, we know that in the best of marriages, even in the heat of battle, rules of discretion remain in force. Despite the provocation, a caring spouse does not laud the virtues of past lovers or lament the homeliness of the current partner.

Neither, as we have seen, do we always abstain from manipulation. There are times when we get people to do what we want because we have maneuvered them into position. We tell them that we have one objective, when in reality we are pursuing another. If we fear their reaction to the truth, we arrange things so that they react to different truth. This covert control, were it exposed, would be resented, but then again we do not intend to expose it. Manipulation is understandably hated. None of us likes to be made the fool, and manipulation lays its victims open to this charge. It also bespeaks a lack of trust and may bring about circumstances people would forestall if they could. Yet in the real world people manipulate and are manipulated with monotonous regularity. We all implement veiled strategies aimed at furthering hidden agendas. As with deceit, this is usually a consequence of our weaknesses. Manipulation is the refuge of those who would otherwise be defeated. They may fully realize the risks of disclosure, but brave them because they perceive no alternative.

Not surprisingly, manipulation is typically execrated by those who have the power to exercise control. Because they are its natural targets, they would outlaw it by fiat if they could. As it is, they declare manipulation deplorable, immoral, and "sick." But what else are the weak to do? If the strong do not honor their demands, should they supinely abandon their own interests? This would surely make them angrier and more unhappy. Or are we to believe that their interests don't count because their methods are repugnant? If so, many children, women, and economically deprived persons might live desperately impoverished lives. This is not to say that manipulation, secrecy, and deceit are recommended. Empowerment and equality are much better options. If the powerful are willing to be fair or if the powerless can be become stronger, it may be possible for them to arrange mutually satisfying outcomes. When anger is heard and honored, frank and sincere communications assist the bargaining process. There will exist a collaboration in which an access to the truth advances the interests of all. But when unfairness prevails and weakness provides an opportunity for exploitation, indirection is excusable.

9

The Motivation Dimension

MOTIVATING THE SELF

Now we arrive at the heart of the matter. The bottom line in anger management is motivation. The self must be mobilized to remove frustrations, while others must be induced to provide what is needed or at least to step aside. Without this final stage, communication is pointless. As has been suggested, motivating others is a complex and problematic task, which requires close attention. Nevertheless, angry people must begin with themselves. They must regulate the energy of their indignation so that it works for them. Anger automatically motivates people to work toward their goals, and the angrier, the more motivated. Whether this energy will be used well is an open question. The major hazards people face are that they will be tempted to suppress their energies because they are intimidated by them and/or that they may liberate them profligately and dangerously.

When anger is perceived as dangerous, it is often throttled before it can act. Instead of actuating an effort toward change, it turns inward. In a sense, it tries to commit suicide and force itself out of existence. In such a case, a person may not even be conscious of his frustration and will merely feel exhausted or oppressed. The result will be that his energy is not concentrated where it can do the most good. In essence, suppressed anger is at war with itself and thus cancels itself out. It can become available for work only when it rises to the level of consciousness. The first rule in managing the motivation dimension of anger is therefore to be able to "feel the feeling." It must, as it were, be at one's finger tips ready to be called upon as needed. For this to happen people need not coach or cultivate their emotion, but merely allow it. In allowing it, however, they must not sanction its going wild. Thus, the second rule of self-motivation is to experience one's anger in a controlled, disciplined way.

Control enables people to exercise their anger with moderation. It will not be liberated in a blinding flash that will fatigue them or overwhelm their interlocutors. Nor will they give up at the first sign of resistance. Although disciplined anger recognizes the possibility of failure, it persists until it is certain it cannot prevail. The successful navigation of the incremental tolerance phase of I.A.M. should prepare people for both of these eventualities. Learning to feel their anger despite its discomfort will permit them to press ahead regardless of the lure of becoming numb or of going ballistic.

People's capacity to regulate their motivation also depends on their self-confidence. The more optimistic they are about their ability to cope, the more ready they will be to move into action. Only someone who can conceive of victory may be prepared to fight long and hard. Those who are easily intimidated can refrain from pulling the trigger. While their frustration is just as unbearable and their desire to win is as intense, they engage in self-suppression because they feel endangered. When lack of proficiency in using anger has persuaded people that their emotion is a burden, they may need to learn how to be more forceful. Learning to motivate others will have the paradoxical effect of enabling them to manage their own impulses better. When people are confident that they can unnerve potential foes, they become less fearful of themselves.

The above applies especially to people who never feel angry. They may be described by themselves and others as sweet and gentle, but often are disguising a deepseated problem. Knowing that everyone gets angry, if they appear not to, their efforts at self-suppression must be working too well. They therefore need to understand why they cannot tolerate experiencing their frustrations and what it is that is frightening them into self-paralysis. If necessary, they may have to return to the incremental tolerance stage of I.A.M. to become more comfortable with what they are feeling.

MOTIVATING OTHERS

What does it take to motivate others? How can anger persuade them to comply? At the risk of sounding tedious, it must be observed that effective anger is complex. As we begin unpacking its use, it is prudent to recognize it as encompassing many variables. For starters, we must recall that it employs the services of *fear, guilt,* and *sympathy.* Of these, fear is central. While it may not be pleasant to admit, without an ability to arouse fear, anger is feeble. It becomes feckless and incapable of motivating anyone.

Anger generates *fear* primarily through bluster. It is a specialist in threatening displays. Despite those who characterize aggression as intent on inflicting injury, to the extent that it involves anger, it really aims at overawing others. It is "fighting behavior," much like that seen among baboons. These creatures compete for status by trying to demonstrate who is stronger. They bare their teeth and flash their eyelids in the hope that their rivals will back down. We human beings do something very similar; we just have more symbols at our disposal. Like the mandrils', our displays may include violence, but this is ancillary. We are really engaged in elaborate arm-wrestling competitions, the purpose of which is to determine who is tougher. Sometimes arms do get broken, but this is not intentional. Typically, protagonists desist as soon as a winner becomes clear. If we observe our peers closely, we will notice that victors usually do not press their advantage, or losers dispute their failure indefinitely. Like dueling baboons, they withdraw before real blood is spilled.

The central function of anger is to demonstrate strength and thereby induce an acceptance of defeat. It succeeds when sufficient fear has been aroused to achieve this end. The elevated voice and the penetrating stare of an angry person are only so many lizard frills and lion roars. They hint at bared teeth and say, in effect, Do as I demand or I'll bite you. Some claim that anger is uncivilized; that its tactics should be relegated to prehistory, where they originated. Their hope is that we human beings become reasonable and rational. The paradox inherent in this is that apparent rationality often grows out of fear. Although we say that "might does not make right," in fact, often it does. People find power attractive, authoritative, and even sexy. Instead of perceiving it as vicious, frequently it is compelling. When people succeed in intimidating us and we accept their victory, we thereby validate their anger and acknowledge its legitimacy. That these other people have been able to frighten us is taken as a sign of their ingrained superiority, and we respect them for it. Their fearfulness is thus interpreted as a form of strength, and their desires are surrounded by an aura of moral inevitability.

Like fear, *guilt* too is often dismissed out of hand. It seems manipulative and hence unsuitable for influencing others. But guilt plays an essential role in enforcing anger. It does so by inducing others to frighten themselves into compliance. When anger arouses guilt, it counts on the others' internalized wrath to force them into submission. We may begin by screaming at them externally, but soon they are screaming at themselves sotto voce, saying what wretches they are for opposing us. The trick to making this work is to know what will get others to feel culpable. If they can be stimulated into acting on prior commitments, such as their belief that "good" people do as they are told, they may furnish us with a cheap victory.

An appeal for *sympathy*, while more acceptable than fear or guilt, can also promote the success of anger. It may seem incompatible with the other two, but actually all can coexist quite nicely and may even depend upon one another. When angry people are perceived as friends, their role partners generally try to remove the barriers frustrating them, not in fear of their wrath, but from agony over their pain. Their anger makes their partners aware of their suffering, and the partners comply to satisfy their needs. Such fear and guilt as their partners do experience only heighten their awareness of the situation.

But no matter what the mechanism through which anger influences others, whether it be fear, guilt, or sympathy, it should not be so robust that it generates a counterreaction. If it is too terrifying, too remorse provoking, or insufficiently sympathetic, it may pass through an invisible boundary and precipitate resistance. When this occurs, an opponent's desire not to lose swamps his motivation to cooperate. Once such a battle has commenced, the focus will then shift from achieving goals to minimizing the damages.

USING FEAR

Anger is an instrument of power and a surrogate for power. It both influences people directly and warns them of dire consequences if they do not submit. In its first incarnation, that is, as an instrument of power, it has the capacity to arouse fear just by being what it is. Quite apart from whatever else may happen, the emotion is biologically unsettling. Its appearance sets the skin to tingling and can make people feel distinctly insecure. But anger also utilizes other mechanisms for enforcing compliance. It signals that an angry person has the desire and ability to compel obedience, perhaps by imposing severe punishments. In other words, it is a threat. When people display anger, they are warning their targets that this is only an opening salvo and that it would be wise to go along, lest they be seriously injured.

Perhaps something dear to them will be stripped away. Certainly others are in danger of losing the love and protection of angry persons. When anger is effective, this warning is adequate and no further damage need be adduced. The target is sufficiently frightened and reacts as desired. If he does not, however, the emotion can escalate until it creates difficulties out of proportion to its cause.

The direct effects of anger and its signal function are not unrelated. When implemented by powerless people, anger soon loses its ability to intimidate. It quickly becomes evident that all they can do is jump up and down or scream. However energetic the performance, it eventually becomes laughable. When people's pretensions exceed their ability to back them up, they are like children having tantrums, and in the long term their displeasure is treated as irrelevant nonsense.

Often it is when individuals are trying to avoid such a fate that they become most destructive. Because a reputation for impotence is a sentence to social superfluity, it is worth resisting. Ironically, those facing it generally don't know how to exercise power and so tend to overreact, reaching for a hammer when civilized forms of influence would serve better. Unfortunately for them, effective anger is attributed to those who have clout, not to those who merely want it. In interpersonal conflicts, it is the displeasure of the powerful that has consequences. Thus when two people who are equally angry and equally committed to their own ends square off, it is usually the less-compelling party who experiences fear first. The weaker person is apt to lose and knows it. Although he or she has the option of ratcheting up the conflict, he or she is likely to back down rather than precipitate a debacle.

These effects of inequality are not often considered when people discuss the fine points of anger management. More attention is generally paid to the justice of competing causes than to disparities in power. In America, with our ideals of equality and due process for all, we tend to deny the existence of inequality. Nonetheless power counts, whether we like it or not and whether it is fair or not. There is no changing this, and an effective use of anger demands that it be taken into account.

Category Power

Among the factors affecting people's proficiency with power are the social categories to which they belong. Often helping professionals act as if their clients were isolated individuals, bereft of a social environment. They are treated like solitary creatures whose prospects depend totally on what is inside their own psyches. Yet all people are enmeshed in a very real web of enduring social relationships. Much of our power depends upon how we are regarded by our fellows. Moreover, many of these perceptions are not created by us and are beyond our ability to modify. Factors such as social class and gender form a framework defining our actions, regardless of our intentions or talents.

Let us take social class. It conditions the way we perceive the inherent capacities of others. Despite ourselves, we tend to regard those having higher social status as being more worthy. They seem somehow to be more intelligent and more effective. When we encounter people who are rich and famous, we often stand back and treat them deferentially. Approaching a door together, we will become uncannily polite and let them go first. In private conversation, of course, we deny this proclivity. In fact, the whole point of social class is that some people are different and therefore entitled to superior benefits. It is a mechanism for distributing social resources, especially power. People who are born to parents listed in the social register are accorded priority without having to work for it. Because their demands for privilege are reckoned legitimate, when they issue instructions, they are more likely to be obeyed. In particular, when they get angry, all that may be necessary is a raised eyebrow. As a secular nobility, their wish creates ripples of fear that become the command of less fortunate peers. Related to social class but not necessarily coextensive with it are personal wealth and organizational position. These too command respect. Those with money can buy compliance, while high-level executives have subordinates whose job it is to do their bidding. When these people get angry, others look beyond the immediate situation and calculate what their defiance might cost. Fear is generated by the possibility that their subordinates might have to sacrifice strongly desired objectives. Even if no specific reward is at issue, they will worry.

Yet social class, wealth, and organizational position are not stamped on our foreheads at birth. Because they are not immediately visible, society has invented symbols to advertise their presence. The way people dress, the cars they drive, and the accents with which they speak, all serve to communicate their status. When confronted with these indicators, we tend to pay the requisite deference. Thus, the well-dressed person who becomes angry will probably get a more respectful hearing than one arrayed in rags. Understanding this can enable people to elicit more favorable reactions than might otherwise be possible. If they recognize that how they are clothed or how they phrase their demands can determine how their anger will be received, they can decide to manipulate these rather than their decibel level. Similarly, social status is not irrevocably fixed. It is subject to manipulation and hence can be used to enhance the legitimacy of one's anger. Increasing one's wealth or organizational position may require years of dedicated effort, but when achieved it will have a huge payoff.

Less subject to personal control are other social variables. They tend to be ascribed, rather than achieved. In particular, factors such as gender, age, race, ethnic affiliation, physical stature, and physical attractiveness influence how anger is received, yet are relatively impervious to individual manipulation. Being born a woman has enormous implications for how a person will be treated when she gets upset. Whether because of biology, the socialization of gender roles, or a combination of the two, her anger may not be considered ladylike. Thus when a woman engages in anger too freely or too loudly, she may be dismissed rather than considered a person to be reckoned with. The same words, issued in the same tone of voice, may gain respect when emanating from a man, but she and her wishes will be discounted, and she will lose. For better or worse, gender is associated with power, and men are believed both to possess and to deserve more of it. A woman who visibly violates this convention risks being "put in her place." She may then have to fight this tendency, as well as any resistance her specific demands incite.

By the same token, men are expected to be more vocal and forthright. When a man is coy, or excessively deferential, he forfeits the advantage of being male. Instead of being attributed power because of his masculinity, others will wonder if he is "queer" and may require him to prove his entitlement. Fair or not, inevitable or not, the world today is so constituted. Though some people may be tempted to challenge this, most find that they can obtain a greater return by taking account of how things are presently organized.

Nowadays gender is the hot topic, but equally resistant to manipulation are age, race, and physical appearance. The very young, for instance, are usually viewed as less powerful than the fully mature. A face or body that bespeaks extreme youth signals inexperience, a lack of viable social connections, and undeveloped talents. The natural implication is that the young are less capable of inflicting painful sanctions. Likewise, the very old generally lose valuable social connections. When they retire, are no longer raising a family, or are distracted by progressive enfeeblement, they are less able to bring pressures to bear. This is an unfortunate fact of life that people must consider when judging relative power. As distasteful as it may be, it is preferable to asking the elderly to get into physical fights to determine who is stronger.

Ethnicity and race, while more controllable than age, are also a given. If the norms of a society sanction discrimination on the basis of these presumably biological categories, those judged to belong to them will be degraded. No matter that the boundaries between them are arbitrary and imprecise, the victims will be thought less intelligent, less cultured, and less moral. Because they are prejudged to be less legitimate, so will their anger. To be black or Hispanic in contemporary America is to bear the onus of being criminal, uneducated, and poor. Although people may be none of these, what they appear to be will influence how powerful and worthy they are thought to be. Consequently, when they become enraged, these assessments may determine whether they arouse trepidation. If their anger is seen as impotent "street" anger, their listeners may be more inclined to call the police than to hear what they say.

Overcoming the disabilities imposed by the vicissitudes of racial/ethnic stratification is a daunting challenge. Although social change may be in order, such change is a long-range strategy; in the meantime, people may need to manipulate the symbols that society already makes available. Despite people's social categories, the way they dress or speak, the jobs they hold, the schooling they have achieved, and the place they live all affect, if marginally, the esteem in which they are held. The unfairness of prejudice need not be taken as an excuse for repudiating these other advantages.

Some social categories are even more intractable than is race. Physical stature, body weight, and facial configuration too can cause people to be written off as inconsequential. Moreover these are often beyond modification, except through the most radical of procedures. A person may not ask to be short, fat, or ugly, but will be regarded as inferior anyway. A tall man, for instance, is typically thought more intelligent and energetic than is a short one, and on this assumption his anger will be accorded more weight. Still, should those at a physiological disadvantage meekly accept this situation, their destiny is sealed. Rather, they may need to rely more on individual sources of power than on corporate ones.

Individual Power

In addition to the muscle bestowed by membership in a social category, power emanates from personal qualities. These too can provide the sting needed to make anger formidable. Fortunately, each of us has the possibility of becoming the kind of person who can command the respect of others. Despite the disparity in our talents, we can elect to become more competent, dependable, and well-connected, albeit in different ways. Being good at something, developing a reputation for consistency, and/or cultivating powerful allies can increase the repute in which we are held and hence the degree to which we can be intimidating.

Perhaps the place to begin cultivating personal power is with one's individual confidence. Self-confidence almost magically presages success. People convinced they are able to do something can by their very bearing persuade others that they can. And because others think so, it will be easier for them to do. Self-assurance, once established, spirals upward toward greater achievement. Yet, contrary to many self-help books, confidence is not manufactured from thin air. People will not judge themselves to be powerful just because they repeatedly tell themselves they are. Nor will a chorus of flatterers persuade them that they are wonderful, when the world teaches them they are not. Confidence is born of success, and success only. Words deceive, but performances have solidity. It is when people actually do something, and do it well, that they learn what they are capable of.

In other words, central to confidence is competence. Being skillful at a task others find difficult assures people that they have a special capacity. To be more precise, superior confidence grows out of superior achievement. Being visibly better will intimidate others, who may respect their accomplishments but will also be frightened by them. People who realize that in comparison they are less adroit will understand that more competent people can make them look foolish if they so choose. This is why it is uncomfortable for a novice tennis player to be matched against an expert; the prospect of losing is too great. Superior skills empower people by making them appear formidable. Because others will calculate that they can win, they are likely to be awarded priority. As with social status, they will be treated as having authority, which in turn will boost their self-confidence. Thus, they will learn that they need no longer literally frighten others to have their claims honored. With their superiority established, a mere allusion to it can induce others to be more attentive. This, of course, places a premium on developing competence. People who locate a specialty in which they have an advantage thereby make themselves and their anger more impressive.

Intimately connected with the notion of competence is that of reputation. For competence to influence others, it must both be real and perceived to be real. A reputation is a settled opinion as to a person's ability. To have a favorable reputation is to be consistently judged favorably. When they have established a positive reputation, people do not have to continue proving themselves, at least not as often. Conversely, when a negative reputation has been put in place, it is difficult to overturn. Often a reputation for competence is earned early in life. People growing up in families that encourage success, accumulate a string of achievements that can convince them and others of their potency. In adulthood, this will give them a degree of confidence that can inoculate them against life's unavoidable setbacks. Those without this advantage have to struggle to carve out a desirable niche. They must engage in tests of strength with others to create an affirmative record in the here and now. This will take determination, courage, and talent, none of which comes easily. Enviable reputations aren't cheap; they are too valuable.

Those who feel weak often err in thinking that they can acquire respect through bluff. They reckon that if they appear tough, others will tremble at their approach. In fact, this strategy sometimes does work. As long as they are not challenged, they may be able to get away with it. Sadly for them, however, because competition for priority is rampant, sooner or later someone is bound to test their mettle. If they are then found wanting, their carefully crafted charade will collapse. Similarly, vain threats have a way of being found out. People who promise punishment without being able to deliver it will soon be accounted frauds and judged to have less power than they actually have. It is when dealing with strangers that bluff has the greatest chance of succeeding. Many a con man has persuaded his mark that he is invulnerable. Once familiarity develops, however, the truth will come out. This is especially true between intimates. A wife comes to recognize her husband's weaknesses no matter how hard he tries to cover them up, and a new boss loses the awe of her colleagues after they have seen her blow a deal. A "don't mess with me" attitude can take people only so far. If they want their anger to retain its authority, their claims need substance. When asked, "Where's the beef?" they must have an answer.

Finally, the power attributed to individuals can be altered by their alliances. No one is more powerful than a collection of persons. When we coordinate our efforts, we human beings become supercompetent and therefore superintimidating. If I speak for an organization or even a loose affinity group and, more particularly, am perceived as being able to enlist its support, I magnify my own voice and command greater attention. To contradict me would be to hazard the wrath of too many others. Such alliances may be made with specific others, as when a person engages in networking or is hired by a powerful corporation, or they can be made with anonymous others, as when we appeal to moral rules in the expectation that those with similar commitments will rush to our aid. Allies cultivated in either way assist in contests for reputation, emboldening people when they confront competitors. When other members of our social set, religious community, or professional fraternity are literally or spiritually available to us, we gain courage in excess of that justified by our personal resources. Moreover, if our opponents know we are well-connected, their confidence will be diminished.

On the other side of the alliance phenomenon is the fact that isolating people makes them less threatening. This is one of the most important functions of ridicule. If we can succeed in making someone look foolish, others may be persuaded to join us in ostracizing him. They will renounce their allegiance to him and instead take our side. Thus people who can be made to appear morally inept lose face and become weakened. Once they are shamed, they may even conspire in further weakening themselves. Because of their humiliation, they will want to disappear and will no longer be as energetic in their self-defense.

Furthermore, appearing powerful and well-connected makes us desirable allies, which in turn can give us another advantage vis-à-vis the less well connected. If these others are motivated to beg for our support, we are in a position to disable them through indifference. In this case, they can be intimidated by threats of approval withheld. Often this sort of sanction is very subtle, involving a *not* doing, rather than a doing. (We call the phenomenon "neglect.") Because the prospect of being isolated can be devastating, excluded people may be willing to do practically anything to get back into the good graces of angry people who have allies.

All in all, the power people are perceived to have and are prepared to exercise determines their ability to unnerve others. The bigger they appear to be and the better able to enforce their claims, the wider the berth they and their anger will be given. Regardless of the merits of their case, they will be positioned to overcome frustrations because others will be motivated to avoid a confrontation.

The Tactics of Invoking Fear

Still, anger backed by power is not always efficient. How the emotion is applied also counts. When and where it is displayed help determine if it will be respected. Anger exercised at the wrong moment or with an inappropriate amount of energy can be as inept as that devoid of force. Thus words that in one context elicit cooperation in another will incite an armed rebellion. What is necessary is *tactical* skill. Anger must be intelligently guided so that it produces the greatest effect with the least effort. Its power must be arrayed so that it both intimidates and achieves its object.

The first and most important tactical fact to be considered is the amount of energy that a person should employ in a particular situation. Another way to express this is to ask: How angry is *appropriately* angry? There exist, especially among the young and the weak, what might be called the "myth of loudness" and the collateral "myth of heat." These hold that the only variable determining the effectiveness of anger is its intensity, that the greater the energy applied, the greater the impact. This suggests that the best course to take to convincingly influence people, is to out-shout them. Thus, anger is viewed as a battering ram which is always and everywhere more effective when it is direct and brutal.

The only drawback to this theory is that it almost never works. Sometimes voluble anger can surprise and overcome its victims before they have an opportunity to mobilize their defenses. For the moment, at least, they will have to capitulate. More usually, people see loud and overheated anger coming. In which case, if they can avoid being seduced into a shouting match, all they must do to deflect the storm is to close their ears and ride it out. Shouted anger is not as overpowering as many people suppose; certainly it does not invariably carry the day. The weak and inexperienced may be impressed, but the self-confident usually find it overdone.

Indeed, excessively loud anger can be entertaining. Unless it is coming from someone whose power is grounded in other resources (perhaps one's immediate boss), it is "sound and fury signifying nothing." When children raise their voices, it is because they don't know better; adults generally do so because they are impotent. In fact, experience should persuade us that quiet anger is typically far more effective than the loud variety. Certainly it can be more unnerving. When someone looks at us through squinty eyes and with a hushed intensity warns us to desist, we take notice. Imagine a Mafia don whispering in your ear that he is unhappy with you. Thoughts of sleeping with the fishes immediately leap to mind. Now think of a mother screaming at her children, cursing their very being and promising to visit mayhem on them. Her first shrieks may demand their attention, but if there is no follow through, her sputterings can become a grating distraction. Though her children may have to live with her wrath, they will be inclined to roll their eyes and tell themselves: There she goes again.

Loudness is not necessary to call attention to a demand, nor is it essential for intimidation. Whispered rage can actually be more terrifying. It not only informs us that speakers are deeply frustrated but also says that they have sufficient self-command to do something about it. If they intend to inflict punishment, they have the mental composure to make it stick. We may not know what they are thinking, but whatever it is, we will fear that it is unwelcome. Quietness is chilling precisely because its largely unseen sting is potentially devastating. As an indicator of controlled anger, it signals that its promulgator is accustomed to winning. Loudness, by comparison, displays all of its wares and opens itself to evasion.

Intelligent anger regulates its energy to suit its purposes. It knows that neither loudness nor quietness, neither heat nor coolness, is always appropriate to the situation. A particular expression of anger must be calculated to elicit the desired response, which depends on its message, the circumstance in which it is delivered, and the mindset of the listener. Hence, when dealing with sensitive or tenderminded people, a low level of intensity may be best. Coming on too strong may only overpower them and make it more difficult for them to perceive what is wanted. Instead of rushing to comply, they will be immobilized by dread. By way of contrast, argumentative types may be impressed by someone who appears equally combative. For them it is tangible energy that carries weight. Because of these differences a certain degree foresight and flexibility is critical. Without an ability to make adjustments in the intensity of one's anger, the emotion is only a reflex action that benefits from neither socialization nor intelligence.

Many factors must be considered when formulating a strategy for anger. Among these are the appropriateness of the target, the suitability of one's timing, the correctness of the locale, the desirability of the cause, and the fittingness of the emotion's level of visibility. Let us begin by inspecting some of the facets that go into choosing an appropriate target. The people at whom one gets angry should not be selected arbitrarily. They must be such that influencing them will make a difference in the light of what is wanted. Although they do not have to be the same people who have caused our difficulty, they must be able to do something about it. If they cannot, getting mad at them will be pointless.

Consider what may happen if people aim their rage at others who are unable to satisfy them. These second parties will certainly be dismayed by the demands made. But though properly intimidated, they can offer no response that will be deemed satisfactory. Unable to reduce the anger directed their way, they will feel trapped. Sooner or later they will want to retaliate. Meanwhile their attackers will remain frustrated because they still have not obtained what they desire. All in all, this is a prescription for stalemate or worse. Nor should targets be selected for their utility as scapegoats. That they are too weak to resist will not justify the imposition of our displaced anger. Scapegoating is at best a temporary diversion that can bring a momentary release. Unfortunately, it also deflects us from pursuing what we truly need. Just as important, it is unfair; and unfairness is bad policy. Aside from its moral repugnance, it breeds ill will and creates superfluous enemies.

Also important is settling on a single target. When anger is diffuse, it loses its potency. Those who get angry at the whole world influence no one. As no specific other is being spotlighted, no one will feel responsible. Furthermore, because no particular other bears the full brunt of their rage, it is unlikely that anyone will feel especially intimidated. One of the mistakes that student teachers frequently make is trying to maintain discipline by loudly demanding that their classes instantly behave. The more strident they become, the less inclined are their pupils to obey. Experienced teachers, in contrast, select individual students as the focus of their fury. They ask one child what he thinks he is doing and then watch as he cringes back into his seat. The other students, having observed this interchange, will get the message and soon quiet down. They will realize that their turn may be next and will understand that in a one-on-one contest with the teacher they will lose. The point is that to be awed by anger, a person must be isolated from others and not inadvertently grouped with potential allies. Treating someone as a representative of a group allows that individual psychologically to fend off an attack and not to feel personally accountable. Should a baleful glance be directed his way, all he has do is point a finger at another member of the group and he is off the hook.

Another factor that must be taken into account in strategizing the use of anger is appropriate *timing*. For anger to be frightening, it makes a great deal of difference when it is employed. Specifically, the receptivity of others is not constant. If targets are distracted by private concerns, they will be less inclined to be attentive and more likely to feel frustrated by new demands. Preoccupied people are short on patience and long on irritability. Because they are not geared to listening intently or responding energetically, it is better to wait and catch them in a more sympathetic mood. This, however, requires self-control. A person must be able to tolerate anger sufficiently to delay its implementation.

Proper timing also involves measuring one's resources against those of others and moving into action when the advantages are running one's own way. Any competent general knows that a battle should be fought when the odds are favorable. Just because enemies present themselves at one's front, does not mean they should be attacked at this moment. It is usually wiser to wait until they offer a flank or divide their forces. Then one can hit them hard and decisively. Power is always relative and will not be intimidating unless it is perceived as superior.

Tactically related to proper timing is finding a suitable *locale* for one's anger. A battle fought on another person's turf favors her cause. It makes it probable that she will have more resources at her disposal and will be better prepared psychologically. For instance, it is usually unwise to confront people where they have allies immediately available. Surrounded by friends, they feel emboldened. What would scare them when confronted in unfamiliar surroundings will now seem trivial. Thus challenging people in their own home or office risks a much stiffer rejoinder than does catching them alone in someone else's office. In unaccustomed territories, beleaguered by alien faces, people feel vulnerable. Like Siamese fighting fish who have wandered into another fish's waters, they become more concerned with defending themselves than with being aggressive.

Nor is the *subject* of a conflict irrelevant. People give themselves a tactical advantage when they choose to do battle over issues where they have a good and specifiable case. This entails having a grievance for which others (including the target person) have sympathy and upon which their attention can be focused. People who angrily demand satisfaction over matters that are perceived to be frivolous or ill-considered risk alienating supporters. Instead of siding with them, others will judge them mean-spirited and abstain. A cause perceived as fair and well balanced draws upon the commitments of others. If they can be made to feel that what is at stake threatens their integrity, they too will be motivated to fight. If, however, they believe the injury they are being asked to inflict is out of proportion to the cause, they may become angry at the aggressor. It is therefore wise to choose causes that are in accord with social norms and for which evidence is readily at hand. A visible murder gets everyone incensed at the murderer, while a fancied killing elicits yawns.

As important as the quality of the subject at issue is its quantity. This is perhaps an awkward way of saying that it is not a good idea to fight too many battles at once. The propositions a person chooses to contest should not be so numerous as to dilute her resources or divide her attention. It is to be hoped that she will prioritize her goals and tackle them separately, in order of importance. But even if opportunity, not importance, decides when a particular demand is made, concentrating on just one goal will bring someone's emotions to bear more forcefully than otherwise. The issue joined will be seen more clearly, and her power will be more obvious and frightening. In consequence, others' responses are more apt to address the matter at hand in a positive fashion.

Another tactical consideration involves the *visibility* of one's anger. Common wisdom has it that all is fair in love and war, which implies that deception is sometimes allowable. The general who telegraphs his plans to an enemy may be cashiered for treason. His superiors will realize that being too open enables the foe to erect a stouter defense. Maintaining secrecy keeps adversaries in doubt and multiplies one's own power by making it uncertain where it will be applied. Fear is enhanced by uncertainty. Generals therefore expend considerable resources on concealing their objectives. They camouflage their formations, promulgate false messages, and order tactical feints, all to confuse and mislead their opponents. Despite the danger of being caught in a bluff, effective anger also depends on manipulating appearances. When it comes to intimidation, boasts and puffery coexist with secrecy and misdirection. For example, sometimes angry people must pretend less interest in an issue than they really have if they want to gain the time needed to prepare their case. If opponents can be led to believe something is unimportant, they may be slow to mobilize their own resources. Also, angry people must recognize that quiet anger obtains much of its power by being inscrutable and that it is frequently better to present an enemy with a fait accompli than to offer a chance to bargain. This latter might provide the other an unnecessary opportunity to be unfair.

Perhaps all of this sounds cynical. Given the current stress on directness, it may be supposed that people should always abjure secrecy and deceit and that they should never be manipulative or misleading. Yet consider that we sometimes treat secrecy as sacred. The very people who tell us to be open and honest in our relationships also extol privacy. But what is privacy if not secrecy about personal matters? It is keeping our exact income to ourselves, or not revealing that we love someone who does not love us. Why else do we do this if not to maintain control over issues that are of vital concern to us, but about which we feel vulnerable? It may even be admirable for a victimized person to deceive a persecutor (e.g., a wife beater). An ability to conceal terror and to present an unintimidated front may save her from a terrible trouncing or even enable her to go on the offensive.

A further tactical consideration involves people's awareness of their *limits*. However skillful their timing, targeting, or concealment, it is important that they not overextend themselves. No matter how strong or clever they are, a more powerful and better prepared adversary will always be lurking somewhere. Even Clint Eastwood's Dirty Harry character was able to articulate that "A man's got to know his limitations." Even he knew that a false and uninformed bravado can be the prelude to a route. In the case of anger, an imperious exploitation of a present tactical advantage can pave the way for a subsequent debacle. What is needed is modesty and perspective. Play to win, but not as if one were an invincible God.

One way in which this need for modesty manifests itself is in the requirement that angry people not ask too much of others, or ask it too tactlessly. First, asking too much gives others an incentive to demur. Whereas a modest demand might arouse antipathy, outrageous claims require people to lose more than is comfortable. When the stakes are raised and vital needs are threatened, the power they channel into their defiance increases exponentially. Fear is pushed aside, and they fight energetically and passionately. Second, tactless insensitivity is an unnecessary inducement to resistance. People who are sure that they are strong enough to be obnoxious underestimate the reactiveness of their opponents. Few others are so weak that their sensibilities can be ignored with impunity. Slapping a person in the face is an affront that even the most timid will want to challenge. In fact, most of us understand this and become tactless only under duress. We then overlook potential reactions, not because we discount the power of our adversaries, but because we are trying to deny our own failings. It is our desire to pretend to be stronger than we are that prompts us to disregard the evidence that they are worthy of respect.

Angry people must retain an awareness that even the apparently weak can become stronger and tactically more adroit in time. After all, they too are human beings who can learn and who can hold a grudge. Being too smug and too confident only allows them space to regroup without having to fear scrutiny. In essence, people's own obliviousness, predicated on a false sense of omnipotence, can provide such adversaries with the concealment they need to prepare for a later victory. One may win at Pearl Harbor, but lose at Midway.

The fact that we all have limitations also suggests that people should use the full panoply of resources available to them. For anger to be threatening, it may have to be more than just threatening. It may need to exploit emotions other than raw fear. An elicitation of sympathy and guilt should also come into play. These can prepare opponents to accept angry demands by inducing them to lower their guard. If others know that only fear will be deployed against them, they may never reveal the chinks in their armor. This is actually just the old story of the carrot and the stick. All that is implied is that it may be necessary both to threaten and to seduce. Johnny-one-notes who are unable to ease off when they see that an opponent is not flinching magnify their difficulties through their own intransigence. Anger that seeks only to intimidate soon wears out its welcome and in the process loses its ability to frighten.

Lastly, anger should be applied in such a way that it admits of success. Many times people snatch defeat from the jaws of victory. They are so certain that they will lose that when confronted with success they fail to recognize it. Perhaps because of a history of weakness, they grossly underestimate their power and do not perceive when they have succeeded in intimidating others. Instead of accepting that they have made their point, they continue to fight with unabated vigor. This often leaves their adversaries with no recourse but to maintain a fighting posture; and in the end it is they who conquer.

Furthermore, an adversary must be allowed to lose. Failure can be galling and, if not cushioned by sportsmanlike conduct, is especially difficult to accept. When victors rub in a defeat by gratuitously celebrating their victory or when they advertise another's embarrassment to third parties, they can provoke renewed hostilities at the very moment of triumph. They may then have to ask whether the additional pleasure of humiliating their adversary is worth the possibility of negating their success. Sometimes it can happen that people capitulate only when they have reason to believe they will not be humiliated. They may be prepared to make concessions in private that they would not begin to consider were they being observed by their peers. Because they value their reputation, they would rather keep fighting than confirm others' perception of them as losers. Thus if we want to win, we must allow them to salve their wounds. As the late Erving Goffman (1952) observed, sometimes people must be allowed to "cool out" before they can become comfortable with failure.

An unnecessary reversal of fortune can also be precipitated by a refusal to accept an incomplete victory. People who must have everything they want before they are willing to lay down their arms discourage others from making concessions. If they are unwilling to compromise, why should others? An all-or-nothing mentality is an excellent prescription for interminable battle. People who genuinely wish to terminate their frustrations are therefore well advised to relinquish fantasies of total satisfaction. In this world we have to live with others who have needs of their own, and so we must allow them satisfactions. Perhaps the best way to describe this attitude is to call it "maturity."

10

Cooperation/Confrontation

EXPLOITING MORALITY

Effective anger does more than force people into compliance. However well it is plotted and executed, if it only intimidates, it risks spawning alienation. Anger is not a nice emotion, but people don't always want to be reminded of this fact. Sometimes they prefer to perceive it as a sword of justice, that is, as legitimately claiming cooperation, rather than extorting it. If anger is viewed only as a matter of power, the temptation is to seek a countervailing power. If, on the other hand, it is regarded as advancing God's work, it is more likely to be perceived as deserving respect. In particular, if anger is used to elicit guilt, others' prior commitments can be used to extract their assent. Their own fears and internalized anger will be manipulated to achieve what a frontal assault can not. When this maneuver is successful, they will feel that they have proffered agreement voluntarily, which will greatly diminish the possibility of their becoming indignant and contradicting the angry person.

If this sounds strange, perhaps it is because the process is usually presented as a matter of upholding moral rules. The peculiar jujitsu of guilt works, in part, because the role of anger in it is rarely noted. Rather, the penance offered is perceived to flow from an appeal to a greater good. The fact that intimidation is involved is lost, and people feel that they are giving consent to an obvious truth. Guilt, like anger, is unpleasant but, when aroused in the name of morality, is not discerned as an external threat.

Morality, of course, is agreeable in a way that anger isn't. Whereas anger has a snarling visage, morality wears a halo. By drawing a curtain over its mechanics, it disguises the fact that it can be arbitrary and unfair and persuades people that they are the source of their own difficulties. If they would only be "good," if they would only listen to and obey the dictates of their consciences, they might receive absolution. Guilt, exercised in the name of morality, is regarded as unchallengeable, in part because it appears beneficial. It promises us help, presenting itself as upholding virtue, rather than as being a self-punitive reaction that follows upon the angry demands of others.

If we are to penetrate this veneer, it is necessary to examine the connections between anger and guilt and to observe how they operate. It must be understood that morality institutionalizes both of these emotions. By organizing them socially, it makes them predicable and relatively genteel. Almost from the moment we are born, we are enveloped in a miasma of moral rules. We are barraged by a blizzard of demands telling us how to behave. These may be necessary for the maintenance of communal living, but are not always fair or without pain. Nor are they beyond questioning. Moral rules may seem inevitable, but they too are fallible human creations.

Morality usually enforces shared social standards. During the course of growing up, these come to seem so natural that they are unconsciously accepted. Lying is wrong, and that's that. When asked why we believe this, we generally don't know; it is enough that the rule feels right. Nevertheless, moral commitments have tangible origins that, when examined, can be seen to vary in their validity. While some are beyond reproach, others are of doubtful authenticity. When guilt derives from unfair dictums, though enforced internally, it remains unjust. Thus some people learn to be totally giving and come to believe it wicked to desire anything for themselves. In this case, their personal morality can become the ally of unfair role partners. Even when it compels fair rules, guilt can induce people to neglect their vital interests. By tapping into prior commitments, it can persuade them to neglect current needs.

But how can this happen? How can guilt conspire to weaken people's resolve when they are challenged by an angry other? To find out, we must travel back to their early childhood. It is here that morality is established and that the groundwork for subsequent guilt is laid. From our youngest years, we are surrounded by socially enforced rules. Proscriptions against lying, cheating, and stealing are ingested along with our mother's milk. Our parents deem these sufficiently important to compel our obedience. Thus, when we are caught lying, they do not smile benignly or marvel at our skill; far from it, they become agitated and/or grumpy. They then angrily inform us that such behavior is unacceptable and, if repeated, may trigger a serious penalty.

Now consider our likely reaction. This parental anger will be profoundly persuasive. Backed as it is by a credible threat of punishment, it will capture our attention and demand compliance. Since it is doubtful that we can alter their mandates, our options are narrowed. If father and mother won't change, we must do the adjusting or risk a jarring confrontation. Because the ramifications of their anger are so frightening, most of us learn not to direct our counter-anger toward them. Instead, we bite our tongues and desist from the prohibited behavior. Although we may want to continue, an internal voice warns us to conform. This inner protector, which we label guilt, backs its recommendations with anger. It promises to conduct a peremptory strike against us anytime we are motivated to defy parental prescriptions and can actually be more frightening than they are. What is more, it is always present and always ready to act.

Internal prescriptions thus established seem absolute, almost divine. As children, we are biologically primed to perceive strongly enforced demands as immutable and unbounded. When parents insist that lying is wrong, this does not sound arbitrary or negotiable. Quite the contrary, their words are taken as implying that lying is wrong now and forever. Much as children assume that the form of a favorite story is immutable, so too will they conclude that moral rules are fixed in the form in which they were originally taught. Another way to describe this phenomenon is to say that moral rules appear "categorical." Children may not fully understand the implications of these dictums, but once accepted they are perceived as universal and unchanging. The more adamant the parents' insistence (that is, the more emphatically the rules are backed by parental anger), the more unequivocal they seem.

When the dynamics of morality are set in motion, the result is an internal commitment to what seems to be a crystalline truth. Lying is wrong, with no exceptions. The consequence is that such rules tend to persist virtually forever in a primeval, unrevised form. The very intensity of people's guilt interferes with their reconsidering the rules, which therefore become very conservative and are available to be invoked at virtually any time. When this mechanism is directed toward maintaining guidelines against murder, it is to be applauded. We can all be grateful that such prescriptions are difficult to revise, for their conservatism provides an assurance that they will not be easily flouted. That guilt makes moral rules categorical decreases the probability that others will even consider infringing upon them.

When, however, the mechanisms used to institute moral principles are implemented unfairly, they can trap people in commitments that are inimical to their interests. Intense external anger can force them to feel guilty about things that are arbitrary and inequitable. Though they may feel put upon, their internal anger will be so powerful that they will attack themselves for even questioning the fairness of their situation. An example of this predicament is to be found in the lives of children who are regularly accused of "selfishness." Whenever they want something, they find themselves confronted by self-righteous parents who demand that they focus on parental needs. Therefore they never realize that they have a right to be selfish and that, although limits must be placed on their demands, they cannot afford to neglect themselves. Parents who prevent this realization are usually so needy that any request emanating from their children seems too threatening to them. As a result, their children feel guilty when asking for anything. Their own hungers seem like a species of insurrection that must be ruthlessly suppressed. As adults such persons have difficulty asserting themselves. When anyone tells them that they are overreaching, they rush to agree and hastily back off.

It is this sort of predisposition to which anger appeals. Whether people feel bound by a valid moral principle or a bogus family substitute, when someone accuses them of an infraction, their guilt springs into action. At the merest hint of displeasure, they get angry at themselves and demand that they change their own course. To know what it is that makes such people feel culpable is to know how to enlist their energies against themselves. It is to magnify one's own power by augmenting it with a fifth column that was implanted in another's soul years ago.

While this strategy is very potent, it must not be supposed to be all-prevailing. Guilt may be difficult to resist, but mature people learn to cope with it. As the years pass, they become more utilitarian and weigh their choices in terms of their own, and other's, interests. By loosening their ties to simplistic canons interjected when they were too young to comprehend them, they free themselves to negotiate new rules. Those who are most vulnerable to the old patterns are the ones forced to labor under unfair standards. If, in their youth, they were made to feel excessively guilty, they can become rigid and unable to perceive their actual situation. The irony is that those who were treated most unjustly are the ones who have the greatest difficulty rectifying their situation. As the victims of coercion, they remain susceptible to self-manipulation long after others have developed the strength to plot their own destinies.

Like intimidation, guilt can be fair or unfair, effective or ineffective. Some people are moralists who revel in playing a blame game. They regularly disguise their anger as righteous indignation and whenever thwarted resort to a pose of injured innocence, which places their adversaries at a moral disadvantage. To hear them tell it, they are on the side of the angels, while others are callous and insensitive. If the latter have a moderate sense of imperfection, it will be unmercifully exploited. The merest admission of a deficiency will be used to leverage them into acknowledging responsibility for countless fantasized wrongs. This unfortunately can create more problems than it solves, even for moralists. Though they get to ventilate some of their anger, they foreclose the possibility of collaborative problem-solving.

Some unfair moralists specialize in playing the part of the martyr. Instead of directly expressing their anger, they represent themselves as the victims of an injustice. By inflating their own contributions and minimizing those of their opponents, they claim that they are the target of gross unfairness. The others are persuaded that they ought to feel guilty for being unprincipled. In contrast, martyrs portray themselves as especially deserving, if for no other reason than that they have had to endure extreme suffering during most of their lifetime. This sort of person specializes not only in guilt, but indirection. They exploit others' weak spots by trying to fool them into believing their situation is other than it is. Martyrs are decidedly not fair or open. But happily, even guilty people grow tired of them. Certainly others will not enjoy their company. The assistance these others provide is grudging at best and not of the same quality as when their own interests and sympathies are engaged. Therefore it is improbable that exploiters will get what they truly want. Their frustrations will remain largely unaddressed because in manipulating others they destroy the dialogue between them.

Also, it is best not to forget that anger is part of a social negotiation and that other parties, whoever they are, have some power. This suggests that, if only from enlightened self-interest, the latter's long-term needs should be figured into the equation. For this reason, an appropriate use of guilt should tap into shared social commitments. Guilt works better when it appeals to widely held cultural norms because these have generally been constructed to reflect social fairness. Time-tested moral principles are widely acknowledged precisely because they have been found to meet the needs of a broad spectrum of people. Thus, social rules having to do with selfishness generally reflect established decisions about what is equitable. A person who accuses another of being self-involved appeals to the latter's sense of fairness. The hope is that this other, or any passing third party, will agree that justice demands rough equality and hence will be motivated to make concessions.

People who arouse guilt in another should feel as great an allegiance to the principles they invoke as does the one to whom they try to apply them. When a rule can be turned around, the odds are that neither party will feel exploited. This, of course, is the principle behind the Golden Rule. It works because it enables people to barter with each other on what amounts to a level playing field. Likewise, Aristotle's Golden Mean suggests that moderate demands are more effective than exorbitant ones, moderation generally being correlated with fairness. Finally, effective guilt should not be wholly negative. If it works exclusively by denying individuals things they want, it loses its persuasiveness. A set of rules based only on "shall nots" deprives people of one of guilt's greatest benefits, namely, its ability to foster cooperation in effecting satisfying goals. Human beings need a personal return for participating in dual-concern negotiations; otherwise, it might pay them to embrace their selfishness and exult in their guilt.

GAINING SYMPATHY

So far the reader may be forgiven for suspecting that using anger sounds suspiciously like engaging in a military campaign. The object seems to be to scare people into compliance or to trick them into doing the same. Certainly it has been described as saturated with intimidation and deceit. Although there has been some talk of eliciting cooperation, this has been submerged in a discussion of power, tactics, guilt, and manipulation. Where, one might legitimately ask, is human kindness? Where is freely given assistance or heartfelt concern? Do these not exist? Is life just a matter of bludgeoning other people into submission before they get a chance to do the same to you?

Let us hope not. Life would be barren indeed if it incorporated neither compassion nor warmth. Fortunately people do care about one another and frequently are altruistic. We sympathize when someone we care about is forced to endure the misery of a lingering frustration, and are motivated to help, not because we are frightened or are feeling guilty, but because we are concerned. We gladly cooperate in making him feel better because we wish him well. In short, as friends, we have no desire to thrash him about the head and shoulders.

Moreover, anger works best when oriented toward the future. Though our sympathy for others may soften our attitude toward them, so too should our long-term concern for ourselves. No one has only one frustration whose termination will convert his life into a never-ending idyll. Further problems invariably crop up. Therefore, the people who help us with a difficulty today may be positioned to help with another one tomorrow. Should our initial interaction with them convert them into resentful foes who begrudge us our success, they are not likely to be inclined to be cooperative later on. In all probability, their previous experience with us, having left them familiar with our tactics, will make them formidable opponents. If, however, we cultivate their friendship, their disposition will be different. In this case, they may sympathize with us and seek ways to be supportive.

Intimidation and guilt are best at gaining a temporary advantage. They are primarily here-and-now levers toward cooperation. Sympathy, on the other hand, is a relationship variable. It bespeaks an ongoing inclination to be helpful. When it exists, it predisposes people to accept and to understand the bitterness of their role partners' anger. Though the latter's words may not be honeyed, they won't be interpreted as an attempt to create injury. Nowadays the term "sympathy" has fallen into disrepute. It carries with it a distinct aroma of condescension and arrogance. No one wants to be so weak as to merit it. Perhaps empathy will be acceptable, for it is a draught fit for equals, but sympathy smacks of inferiority. Its recipients must acknowledge that their situation is worse than other people's and that others are doing the giving while they are only receiving. Yet sympathy can mean caring. It does not have to imply that a benefactor is feeling superior. It can also reflect a concern with the interests of a friend.

Ironically, the sympathy aroused in response to anger can be less off-putting than that proffered for a demonstrated weakness. Its recipients, having first roared out their might, can more easily claim moral equality.

Effective anger takes account of the big picture, including the potential presence of sympathy. When plotting a way to influence others, it calculates their willingness to cooperate. Indeed, the emotion works best when it knocks on a partially open door. Angry people who do not promote sympathy where it is possible deprive themselves of half their strength. At least as much energy ought to be directed into cultivating the concern of others as into overpowering them. There are three primary considerations involved in gaining such sympathy. The first is not to be too threatening, the second is to foster a positive relationship, and the third is to present one's case favorably. When anger does not intend a war, when it is able to draw upon friendship, and when it invokes a responsive purpose, it allows others to listen and join one's cause.

People who are afraid that another's anger will injure them must think first of their own defense. They cannot permit themselves to be too open to the other's point of view, for this may steal the precious energy needed to erect an adequate shield. In consequence, anger that hopes to be sympathetic must eschew connotations of violence. Though it may be dynamic, it can not be bloodthirsty. If it arouses panic, it destroys its appeal. This means that angry people must be aware of the effects of their anger. They must gauge when their fury goes overboard and be capable of ratcheting it back to more acceptable levels. By taking care not to be excessively threatening, they assure their role partners that it is safe to be sympathetic.

One vital aspect of a nonthreatening stance is allowing another person time to agree. Often angry people want immediate satisfaction. Because they are impatient for results, they adopt a strategy of constant and escalating pressure that, even if it starts out being tolerable, is ultimately transformed into a menace. It must be understood that even the most sympathetic others need leeway. Because the ordinary reaction to anger is resistance, they must be allowed space for this response to subside and room to contemplate the consequences of their compliance. Only when they are permitted to work things through at their own pace will they come around. Otherwise their internal equilibrium, indeed their very freedom, will feel under attack and they will become defensive. People rightly guard themselves when they feel vulnerable. Being belligerent at such occasions will violate their personhood and, as it were, stab them in their sleep.

Avoiding gratuitous threats is also a good first step toward establishing a sound relationship. Friends do not threaten friends. On the contrary, they are supposed to support one another. As presumably they possess a long-term allegiance to one another's interests, in times of need they should be able to depend on each other. With a friend, one can let down one's guard. One can say what one thinks because one is certain that it will not be turned against one. In short, friendship is based upon trust. Absent this abiding faith, it is no more than a pretense; it is just an empty shell ready to shatter at the first sign of trouble.

Trustworthiness, however, is not easily established. Certainly proclaiming that it exists is a reliable indicator that it doesn't. The problem arises because trust entails proving a negative. It requires demonstrating that one will not inflict harm, now or in the future. But the future is unavailable for examination. People cannot provide incontrovertible evidence about what they will do at some future date. We all know that a placid surface and good intentions may conceal a wealth of mischief. In consequence, we test one another. Before we extend our credence, a multitude of occasions must pass in which harm was possible, and perhaps to the advantage of the other, but did not occur. Ordinary life provides many such circumstances, but they are so central to establishing trust that we manufacture additional ones. Because we want to be certain about our potential friends, we intentionally, if unconsciously, throw temptation in their path. We flaunt our vulnerability or ask something of them that is not to their benefit and then observe what happens. If they are unfair or insensitive, they fail. Much as a wife will lose confidence in her husband when she discovers him cheating on her, the relationship will never be the same.

Beyond trust, a sound relationship is also grounded on bonding. We human beings do not treat others as interchangeable. We do not ask help of whoever happens to be available, for we wouldn't know what to expect; after all, they are strangers with whom we have forged no lasting attachments. Friends are not only trusted; they are known. They are a part of our universe in predictable and cared about ways. In a sense, they are part of our being. Their successes are our successes, and vice versa. When they lose, our own world is diminished, for central to our purposes is the advancement of their purposes. Another way to say this is that there exists a "relationship" between us.

We are not merely standing side by side; we are travelling together along a shared pathway. The best example of this, of course, is love. Whether between a parent and a child or between two adults, love is a commitment, it is hoped a joint commitment, to a common fate. It is not a statement of intent, but an emotional reorientation that changes one's world-view and values.

To love someone is to honestly care, but this caring does not come about just by wishing it to be so. When a baby is born or a couple is courting, the previous world of those involved is torn asunder and an emotional disequilibrium created that can be rectified only by re-organizing their priorities. Their commitments change, their feelings change, and their activities change. In essence, their lives become different. After a period of infatuation in which the loved one seems perfect, each is incorporated into the other's world. When this process is complete, their relationship acquires a reality that cannot be easily renounced. In the case of a strong bond, it will take an extended period of mourning to break.

Though not all bonds are equally strong, even simple friendships create allegiances. A true friendship establishes an inclination to be helpful that can be drawn upon in times of stress. Even when summoned by anger, friends are prepared to listen and be sympathetic. They recognize that the other's vital interests have been threatened and want to be protective. As many philosophers have affirmed, such bonds are of inestimable value, undoubtedly worth the pain and uncertainty that go into creating them. The implication is that it pays anyone who contemplates being angry to have friends. Such relationships are sound investments whose existence will make it more probable that when something goes wrong, there will be someone prepared to be patient, compassionate, and receptive.

Fortunately, being angry does not preclude the establishment of friendship. Despite the fact that anger can alienate others, it is compatible with love. Indeed, the energy animating anger can be attractive. As long as it is not destructive, its fierceness may be admired. True, others will be cautious; but they will also be stimulated. Angry people are likely to be perceived as exciting, forceful, and capable of leadership. Nevertheless, it is also important that they be animated by issues worth getting upset about. Even the most patient friend will be repulsed by too many summons to assist in problematic endeavors. Ultimately sympathy depends upon being aroused by a sympathetic case. A sound relationship will get a person listened to, but even the best of friends are swayed by what someone has to say. If anger demands the impossible or the outrageously unfair, it increases its probability of being rejected. Also, if expressed in terms that are too obscure or unpersuasive, it may be dismissed, despite the significance of its message.

A good case is generally one that furthers vital interests. It must be perceived as removing important frustrations. Those of the person, his or her role partners, or significant third parties all count. At the very least, someone must seem to receive a benefit. If the only result of emotional outbursts is that they allow people to express themselves, they are apt to be considered self-indulgent. How an individual's needs are evaluated also depends on their salience to others. Do they hear them? If they don't, if they are more concerned about their own interests, their sympathies may not be engaged. Instead of being intent on assuaging another's unhappiness, their attention will lie elsewhere. Anger never occurs in a vacuum; the presence of other's concerns is therefore not irrelevant.

Being persuasive is another factor in this mix. No matter what the relative merits of a case, if it is not presented as valid, it is unlikely to elicit compliance. Thus, angry people may have to support their assertions with compelling, often culturally acceptable, reasons. They will have to depict the connections between their needs and those of others in ways that are dramatic. Unless they can make others aware of where the advantages lie, they may not realize what is at stake. But outlining such connections takes intelligence and linguistic skill. Usually people must recognize and mentally rehearse what is at issue before they can adequately express themselves. All too often it is not the person with the best case, but the one best prepared to articulate it who prevails. This places a premium on intellectual clarity. It is a mind unclouded by rage that contributes most to a person's ability to plan strategies and to implement them.

AVOIDING COUNTER-ANGER

As has already been pointed out, it can be essential to consider the presence of counter-anger. When intimidation and guilt are pushed too far, they can generate resistance. Indeed, anger hangs on a knife edge. It is an exceedingly powerful motivator, but one that, when overdone, creates its own opposition. On one side of the knife people may feel like irresistible conquerors, but just an inch farther and they are on the defensive. Instead of finding others trying to placate them, they find themselves beset by the others' fury. This reverse anger can be enormous, for often it is a mark of desperation.

Let us take the case of intimidation pushed too far. People who are apprehensive about another's anger may be incapacitated by fear, but if further threatened, they can be impelled to fight, no matter what. Either because they feel they have nothing to lose or because they just can't take it any more, they may lash out regardless of the consequences. Suddenly they will have the energy of the possessed. Like that of a cornered animal, their anger will rise to heroic, if primitive, proportions; and they will slash back with fists, words, and vitriol. Because they have little concern with rationality, they will not calculate their interests or seek profit. On the contrary, they pursue total victory, the goal being the removal of the tormentor, if necessary through his utter destruction. Given this potential, counter-anger must not be lightly dismissed. No matter how focused people are on obtaining their goals, they cannot afford to disregard the fact that they are dealing with other human beings whose sensitivities give them the potential for violence. One of the functions of civilization is to control human ferocity, but sometimes it does such a good job that we forget how destructive we can be. Yet no one, except perhaps for the most profoundly disabled, is incapable of demolishing others.

It is essential that angry people know when to quit. If they are not to obviate their effectiveness, they must estimate the other's breaking point and act accordingly. To the extent that they are able, they must avoid foreseeable problems. As we have learned, this can be achieved by being alert to others' reactions, by not debasing them, and by allowing them the possibility of compliance. Should these precautions fail, angry people must be ready to engage in damage control. They may need to remove themselves as a provocation and temporarily placate the others. Or, if they realize that a future engagement can present better odds, they may decide to withdraw the present challenge and await events.

When people get angry, they must be in sufficient control of themselves to monitor their opponent's response. If, instead of cooperating, fire begins to rise in the other's eyes, it may be time to lower the temperature. When adversaries begin to push back, automatically pushing harder against them can be the wrong move. Though sometimes others can be overpowered, often they cannot. A strategic withdrawal may be in order to allow the angry person time to reevaluate his tactics and his rival time to cool down. In any event, it is essential to refrain from unnecessary provocations. In particular, it is unwise to debase others. Too often enraged people feel compelled to insult those who stand in their way. In their haste to extirpate an obstacle, they take aim at the other's social status. They know that if others can be branded "nerds" or "bumpkins," their ability to resist will be lowered; that, this apparently childish name-calling can prompt them to draw back rather than risk being treated as defective by third parties.

But fighting words sometimes do lead to fights. Verbal provocations can precipitate bloodletting. It is therefore prudent to consider how far one wants to proceed. Angry people must reflect on whether the results of a potential battle are worth the pleasure of getting things off their chest right now. Will what at first flush seems like a cheap victory really end badly?

Counter-anger can also be generated by preventing others from being agreeable. While few people actually intend to foreclose compliance, their demands can be couched in terms that have this effect. Because they require total conformity, they force others to rebel. It is almost never the case that people do precisely what is asked of them at the moment they are asked. To do so would be tantamount to surrendering control of their destiny. It would involve becoming an automaton, who makes no choices and hence whose needs are irrelevant. This is why even toddlers delay when asked to come for lunch. They use a minute more of television-watching to establish that the decision to eat is their own. Adults can afford to do no less. Consequently it is imperative to allow them to do things their own way, even if they don't get them quite right or are a little slow. An angry person must recognize that others need latitude, despite their sympathy for him. Because their interests are being transgressed, they have to make internal adjustments before they can proceed. The upshot is that angry people cannot afford to be too desperate. If they are so heavily invested in a goal that a momentary delay seems intolerable, they may obviate others' good-will.

Nonetheless, if a mistake has been made and it is not possible to forestall counter-anger, the game is not over. People can still salvage victory, or at least limit the damage. Because the other person's anger is no more irresistible than their own and because it too tends to be self-limiting, conflicts can be resolved even after an explosion. Since the purpose of counter-anger is to defend against the aggressor's own anger, when this is achieved, it will usually diminish. Unless its fires are fed by some strong underlying frustration, it will generally subside when the provocation that caused it has been turned aside.

Yet counter-anger must be taken seriously. When it arises, it cannot be derogated as a passing fancy. Its lifespan may be short, but in that period it can inflict considerable harm. In fact, when it appears, it must take precedence. Whatever the personal agendas of angry people, their implementation will have to be delayed so that they can answer this new challenge. However, they must not be intimidated by counter-anger. They must not be provoked into heedless fight or flight or paralyzed by internal guilt. Only if they keep their wits about them will they be able to evaluate their situation and respond appropriately. The strategy for neutralizing counter-anger should be obvious. Just as with ordinary anger, the goal is the removal of a source of provocation. When others are no longer confronted by forces they feel impelled to resist, they will calm down. This will occur even after they have lost control, for even wild anger loses its energies when it is without purpose. Thus, angry people will find it advisable to stop demanding what the other finds intolerable and, if necessary, leave the scene. If they can't win just now, there is no point to continuing the campaign.

It may also be useful to placate others. If they are making counter-demands, it may be wise to accede to these, at least temporarily. It may even be prudent to assume a submissive demeanor. To do otherwise might be interpreted as a threat that can call forth further anger. On the other hand, a soothing voice, a body drawn into itself, and congenial words signal an absence of malice, which may induce a person to back off. But needless to say, this temporary cessation of hostilities does not mean the war is over. Successfully placating another is not equivalent to abandoning one's own interests. After a truce, it is usually possible for people to renew their quest, albeit from a different direction. Assuming that their frustration is still intolerable, they can continue, but with a revised strategy. This time, however, they will have the advantage of an expanded awareness that should enable them to plan more insightfully.

COPING WITH OTHER PEOPLE'S ANGER

Not all anger directed toward us is counter-anger. Others too have frustrations, quite apart from any provocations we may produce. But no matter the reason, when these others launch an attack, we will have to respond. Unless we are in complete agreement with them, their wrath will constitute a problem for us, and we will have to decide whether to comply or resist. Can we, for instance, achieve a mutually satisfying bargain or must we stand our ground? When the other's anger is forceful or primitive, will we have to disarm it? If we do not, will we be swept away in a tide of external influence, or even of physical injury? Fortunately, others' anger can be managed much as is our own. Since it too is driven by frustration, it will respond to achieving its underlying goals. Therefore, the same steps utilized in making our own anger safe, tolerable, and effective can be applied to theirs. If they can master the intensity of their emotion, learn to make cogent demands, and settle for realistic bargains, they too will calm down, and we will be out of danger.

What we must not do is react reflexively. If other people become belligerent, responding in kind can make us every bit as irrational as they are. What is worse, it will ensure that we are ineffective. Although it may be okay for us to get angry, the feeling should not be so intense that we cannot use our heads to concoct a suitable rejoinder. One of the best ways to achieve such equanimity is to refuse to take others' anger personally. Even though it is directed at us and may be meant quite spitefully, if we perceive it not from our point of view but from theirs, it will be easier for us to see how they can be placated. As difficult as it may be, we must try to be objective, otherwise we can get so caught up in our own goals that we are unable to assist them in achieving theirs.

We must not forget that the ultimate objective is to help other people use their anger effectively, that is, to communicate and motivate more competently. The clearer their messages and the more tactically sophisticated their use of intimidation, guilt, and sympathy, the less likely we are to be injured or overwhelmed, and the more responsive they will be to us. At the very least, they may come to appreciate that arousing our wrath is not in their interest. Instead, they may endeavor to facilitate a mutually beneficial bargain from which we can both gain.

The best way to forestall an ill-advised response is by understanding others' anger. Even though they may neither understand it nor be able to control it, we can inquire into their frustrations, their underlying goals, the targets of their anger, their tactics, and so forth. If we listen carefully and observe the context of their sentiments, we may be able to recognize patterns they don't. Just as well-intentioned helpers can use role-taking to penetrate our motives and methods, so too can we place ourselves in their shoes. Because we are all human beings, we can understand their situation and respond to its realities. Indeed, the better we are at mastering our own anger, the easier it will be to assess theirs.

Once we understand what they are doing and why, we can decide how to respond. If we know what they want, we can determine what we are in a position to give. If they are asking for the impossible, we may realize we have a problem. But if their wants are in accord with our aspirations, we may decide to go along. Even if they do want the impossible, there are options. We can, for instance, try to make them aware of the futility of their demands, in which case they may reassess their goals. Ideally, we should help them understand that they are engaged in a negotiation with us. When they do, we can then talk about our individual and joint interests and engage in problem-solving with an eye to producing a mutually agreeable compact. If we both treat our anger not as a primordial passion that must be expressed as energetically as possible but as a tool for interpersonal influence, we can evolve mechanisms for swaying each other.

The degree to which we can help angry people depends, in large part, on our relationship with them. No matter how correct or compassionate we are, we may not automatically be able to get them to listen or to move in a positive direction. Our ability to persuade or to instruct is also contingent upon our relative power and upon the bonds between us. If we are not strong enough to command attention or if they are unsympathetic to us, we may be dismissed out of hand. Thus, it is not unusual for irrational bosses to run roughshod over innocent and well-meaning subordinates. Even if employees want to help their bosses reform, they will have to make their first goal protecting themselves. When bosses feel that their power is being challenged by subordinates, attempts to assist them will often be perceived as further frustrations. Similarly a spouse's ability to provide aid or comfort is limited by the degree to which good will exists in the marriage. If a husband hates or is intimidated by women, his wife's honeyed words will sound like an affront. When she correctly points out the self-defeating nature of his actions, he will take this as an effort to undermine his masculinity. Her best recourse, perhaps her only recourse, will be an appeal to a third party. If she cannot avoid being provocative, it may be necessary to bring in someone who is not so perceived.

Indeed, this circumstance is so common that there are professionals who specialize in being nonprovocative. We call them mediators.

These middlemen intervene when parties cannot negotiate fairly among themselves. They help facilitate communications and protect against an excessive use of power. Mediators serve as referees and interpreters who separate antagonists and regulate their interactions so that no one becomes irrationally hostile. Marriage counselors, group therapists, lawyers, arbitrators, politicians, business executives, and even friends and relatives can assume this role. Ideally they can intercede before anger becomes primitive and smooth out the playing field so that the parties can hear their respective needs.

Fair, nonconfrontational anger is one of the most important competencies any person can possess. An ability to use the emotion in social negotiations is absolutely central to the creation of a satisfying life. Without it, people succeed in neither their personal nor their professional careers. If a mediator is indispensable for achieving such negotiations, one should be employed, but it is far better for people to learn how to engage in fair negotiations themselves. In the next chapter we will talk about the use of anger in the context of the family. How husbands and wives, parents and children, use anger to negotiate their differences is crucial to the development of their respective social roles. Yet fair anger is a delicate matter, especially in intimate relationships. It does not come automatically and certainly is not universal.

11

Anger and the Family

THE UNIQUENESS OF THE FAMILY

Families provide a unique context for human interaction. Within the family, people live more closely together, for longer periods of time, than virtually anyplace else. When a family is working as it should, its members bond tightly and cooperate more intimately than elsewhere. Sociologists would say that they form a primary group in which face-to-face contacts predominate and where emotions are actively engaged. One of these emotions, of course, is anger. Indeed, it is one of the elements that enables families to be families.

A family engages in many tasks. It both structures and sanctions sexual liaisons; it provides a safe haven within which individuals share love and companionship; it enables people to nurture their children while converting them into full human beings. Families are also economic units, in which people can pool their resources and participate in the consumption of social goods. Finally, families help establish social status. The family helps determine many of its members' enduring relationships, including those outside the family. Thus, to belong to an upper-class family is to be granted special privileges just for having been born into it, while membership in a lower-class family is fraught with liabilities.

Given the family's functions and face-to-face nature, anger takes on added significance within its confines. When the emotion is used well within its context, it facilitates intimacy and personal growth. When it is not, it can create anguished loneliness and utter despair. Since it is in families that males and females have their closest contact, it is here that they collaborate most effectively or destructively. Within the family, they can utilize their anger to cement honest, supportive alliances or to destroy a mortal enemy. Nor should we forget that families provide a framework for the interaction of parents and children. Here too anger can be both positive and negative. It can be an instrument for teaching crucial social lessons or for instituting an oppressive tyranny. In the end, it may enable the young to become stronger, more resilient adults, or it can rob them of their dignity and leave them with scars that never heal.

Hence it is that family anger presents both opportunities and hazards, that it can be used to negotiate bargains in which everyone wins or blatantly abused in such a way that all lose. Because of the closeness of the family, intimidation and guilt are especially liable to abuse. Since intimacy engenders knowledge of another's weaknesses, while simultaneously providing access to them, it provides an occasion for exploitation. The uncaring and the insensitive can bore into the soul of a trusting other and convert what otherwise might be a modest reproach into a source of eternal damnation. Consequently, within the family, appeals to sympathy are more prudent than is the use of intimidation. Anger that enlists cooperation is much safer than that which extorts an unfair advantage. All in all, because people living in families have to put up with one another, they can not afford to allow their grievances to accumulate or injuries to fester.

THE WAR BETWEEN THE SEXES

In this age of feminism, it is difficult to ignore the sometimes contentious relationships that exist between men and women. While millions of couples forge lasting partnerships, there seems to be an edge to many cross-gender interactions. Often men and women seem to be at odds over relative trivia, appearing almost to relish battle with one another. Indeed, a continuing, perhaps sexualized, tension forms the leitmotif of many intimate relationships. It is no mistake that we speak of a "war between the sexes."

Assuming that this friction is not merely a function of an inherent male "brutality" (as is sometimes alleged), can it be understood in terms of the contrasting biological natures of men and women, the exigencies of social structure, or arbitrary patterns of socialization? Although these questions are too deep to be explored here in their entirety, it may be possible to discern some outlines of important truths. We have already noted that there are gender-based differences in how anger is expressed and received—that men, for instance, are encouraged to be more overt than are women. But what are the underpinnings of these differences, and what is their impact on intimacy? Can variations in gender style be reconciled and, more to the point, can men and women learn to be fair with one another? If they cannot, can or should their styles be altered?

Historically men have been thought more action-oriented and women more emotional. Sociologists have described them as respectively "instrumental" and "expressive." By this they have meant that men tend to specialize in getting things done, while women concentrate in maintaining the stability of relationships. These dispositions can manifest themselves in men being direct and forceful and women being self-effacing and supportive. Such a depiction has, to be sure, been challenged: many feminists assert that it is unfair and inaccurate and advocate reforms to help women attain more power and enable men to curb their propensities toward barbarism. Nonetheless, social science research continues to show gender differences. Thus, the real argument seems to be over the etiology and potential alteration of these disparities, not their existence.

Two of the more fashionable theses put forward to explain gender differences entail physiology and social structure. Some would say that men are genetically more aggressive, while women are organically more nurturing. So far the evidence is equivocal, but there may well exist temperamental differences derived from factors such as hormonal disparities, for instance, in testosterone levels. Those favoring structural explanations point out that men and women confront different social tasks. Men are still expected to provide financial support for their families, while women continue to be held responsible for rearing the young. Fair or not, these obligations have an enormous impact on the strategies with which many men and women tackle life.

Certainly men are raised to participate in male hierarchies. In their childhood games and adult work patterns they pit themselves against other males and compete for dominance. In this, they learn to wield their anger as a weapon to keep others at bay. The ability of one man to intimidate another is matched against the corresponding ability of the other to intimidate him, and the two observe to see who is strongest. The winner is then accorded the respect due a superordinate animal. Women, however, are raised to be more sympathetic and supportive. When, as girls, they play with their friends, they rarely

indulge in the competitive group struggles of boys. Instead their pastimes are used to demonstrate physical and verbal agility in such a
way that all can win. Not for them games like football and hockey,
but rather jump rope and hopscotch. Girls also spend more time talking about their friends and relationships. (Boys meanwhile are arguing about sports figures and politics.) Women care far more about
feelings than do men, having social permission both to cry and to
commiserate with the pain of others. Males, in contrast, are required
to be strong. In their world, a show of emotionality is an admission
of weakness and hence an invitation to defeat in contests with their
peers. It might point out where they are vulnerable and tempt others
to take advantage.

Men must especially not show fear. One of the reasons they may
favor an open expression of anger is that it is an excellent vehicle for
disguising the presence of this less acceptable emotion. Women,
however, are allowed to be victims. They are encouraged to high-
light their weaknesses and even to use them as weapons. For them,
there can be strength in weakness for they know that dominant males
are taught not to attack defenseless females. Rather, they are supposed to treat them like ladies. Historically men have been urged to
open doors and to abstain from coarse language in their presence.
This enables girls and women to manipulate signs of vulnerability in
ways that can forestall a male attack, for example, through tears.

Although these differences may be learned, most parents are aware
that their children often act out primordial patterns despite their injunctions to do otherwise. Boys like to play with toy guns and spontaneously draw pictures of death and destruction, while a majority of
girls continue to ask for dolls and are fascinated by the latest trends
in clothing styles. Perhaps socialization has its greatest impact in
sharpening preexisting differences and providing a vocabulary for their
expression. In any event, whatever their origin, there are differences,
and couples must find a way to cope with them. It is conceivable
that a solution might be found in androgyny or gender-based segre-
gation, but most people elect for a more traditional arrangement. They
enter marriages and create families and, when they do, typically engage in interactions in which their anger is used in traditional ways.

But what are the traditional male/female modes of getting angry?
To some, what follows may sound stereotyped (and it definitely is a
simplification), yet it is meant only as a typification of a broad range
of individual differences. First, men tend to be louder, more physical, and more direct. When they get angry, their first reaction is a

frontal assault in which they attempt to overpower their adversary. Secrecy and finesse are often repudiated as effeminate and weak. Women, in contrast, are more verbal and submissive. Even when angry, they are more likely to placate others than are men. For them, the long way around is often the safest. Most women are acutely aware that, in a fight with a man, they are generally engaging a physically more powerful opponent whom they cannot afford to provoke into violence. This puts a premium on indirection, which may, however, be perceived as "sneaky." From a man's point of view, a woman will try to talk him to death and manipulate him into doing what she wants. Yet from the woman's perspective, men are simply obtuse. Because they are given to irrational bluntness, they must be handled with caution. Dealing with insensitive, often immature, brutes with no concern for the feelings of others, it is the woman's responsibility to do the caring. The implication is clear; when it comes to anger, the two sexes don't communicate. Or so it seems.

It may well be, however, that these differences actually facilitate intimacy. If—and this is an assumption that not everyone is prepared to make—a close relationship is fostered by the existence of an unambiguous division of labor, then differences in anger may reflect a stable pattern of collaboration. A man's bold energy may be the mark of his status as the family's representative to the outside world, while a woman's tactful indirection will enable her to hold her family together. The man's style will make him a more successful breadwinner, and the woman's style make her a better nest-builder. In the modern world, as formulated above, this division is a caricature, but it may still underline a genuine distinction in the tasks of men and women. If so, both may need and cherish the contributions of the other. Their differences may, in fact, permit them to respect each other and to maintain their separate identities. Intimacy, as we shall see, is advanced by the possibility of both partners being successful, and a division of labor, including of their anger, can facilitate this.

ESTABLISHING INTIMACY

The fundamental prerequisite of intimacy is equality: emotional equality and equality of worth. Two people cannot live with one another and love each other if they do not meet on a comparable footing. If the needs or humanity of either goes unrecognized, sooner or later one or both will resent the situation. The subordinate partner will feel cheated and demeaned, while the dominant one will feel bored or patronized. In the modern collaborative marriage, each partner must be able to contribute to the joint venture or a sense of unfairness will develop. Unless both bring something to the table, something recognized and respected by the other, one or both will feel exploited and/or insignificant. Either way, intimacy will fail, for in their inability to share, someone is bound to feel unhappy and opt out.

To share with the other, each party must have strengths. Each must be able to stand up to the other, while at the same time understanding him or her. Social scientists have found that successful couples tend to have similar values and similar levels of intelligence. Many of their other strengths may not match point for point—one may, for example, be rich while the other is physically more attractive—but on balance they will bring equivalent resources to the relationship. If they do not, if one feels superior and the other inferior, either or both will be reticent with the others. The inferior one may fear sounding stupid, while the superior will be worried about causing injury. Similarly, the subordinate may use indirection in the belief that a straightforward confrontation will spell defeat, while the dominant one will feel too unchallenged to say anything to his or her "dishrag" mate. One of the best indicators that equity exists in a relationship is that the two feel comfortable with one another. In an equitable arrangement, neither feels self-conscious, nor is either motivated to impress the other. Each will have taken the measure of his partner and be convinced that they are evenly matched. And because both have nothing to prove, they can relax.

The problem then becomes how to establish emotional equality when two people are different. How do partners who vary in gender find a way to argue in which both can be heard and in which both have a reasonably good opportunity to succeed? This dilemma is exacerbated by the fact that intimacy breeds vulnerability. Because intimates come to know each other exceedingly well, they have the possibility of attacking precisely where the other is incapable of defence. This is most visible in divorce, where the parties often seek revenge rather than compromise. As even the movies make plain, it is common for a "wronged" party to go for the jugular, thereby further estranging the other. The question then is: How can this sort of bloodletting be avoided when people want to stay together? If inflicting pain is so easy and if differences in style make misunderstandings so likely, how can they become angry without causing irreparable damage?

As we all know, often they don't. But when they do it is generally because they have learned to negotiate fairly. Instead of engaging in unbridled competition, they strive to maintain equity. In particular, the two engage in dual-concern negotiations in which each respects the underlying goals of the other. When they have disagreements, their means of expression are restrained, and they remain responsive to each other's counter-demands. Most particularly, they continue to be sympathetic, despite their differences and their passions. Because they truly care for one another, the fulfillment of each other's goals is important to them. This sympathy then enables them to recognize their respective difficulties and to see past their dissimilarities in style to the substance of what is required.

An ability to disagree is vital to all intimate relationships. It enables people to communicate what they really want and to do so with a level of intensity commensurate with their desires. This enables them to estimate the respective priorities they give their individual demands and to settle on a solution that optimizes their personal and joint satisfactions. As long as they are honest with one another, as long as they are not trying to win for the sake of winning, they should be able to find common ground. Utterly divisive is fighting for improved status. In a marriage this destroys equality. Hence the partners must show moderation. They cannot afford to forget that maintaining long-term stability is more valuable than any temporary advantage that might accrue. Nor should it need saying that love and disagreement are compatible. Often the most reliable sign that two people really care about one another, that they are truly bonded, is that they feel free to disagree. Their arguments may generate heat but not be divisive because each knows how the other feels and both are flexible enough to repair inadvertent wrongs.

Understanding and remaining in communication with an intimate partner takes commitment. Since men and women typically live in different worlds, it may not be immediately apparent to each why the other is reacting as he or she is. Understanding a partner's goals and the pressures he or she is under takes effort. The desire to make this effort is usually contingent on the existence of a deep sense of attachment. If men and women are not to be chauvinists, if they are to look past their individual situation and appreciate that of a very different sort of person, both must be willing to exercise empathy and imaginatively put themselves in the other's place. To achieve this, they must bring their partners into their world and consider their mates' point of view as they would their own. Commitment also en-

ables people to stay put despite the unpleasantness of angry disagreements. Anger is not fun, not even when emanating from a loved
one, not even when one believes that it is a prelude to personal growth
or renewed intimacy. To stay and fight it out, a person needs to be
convinced that the pain and uncertainty are worthwhile. A commitment provides this assurance by creating a bond, the loss of which
feels worse than the pain of battle.

An ability to negotiate equitably is also an integral part of the establishment of an intimate relationship. After a courting couple get
past their initial infatuation, they must work out a modus vivendi.
Living with someone entails recognizing his or her limitations and
tolerating them. It especially means crafting a division of labor in
which each knows where the boundaries lie and where each respects
the other's space. If a woman is given custody of the kitchen, a man
must learn to ask her permission before he upsets her organization
of it; if a man reigns supreme in the garage, his mate may want to
consult him before taking the car in for routine maintenance. Such
divisions can be arbitrary, but once established will prevent many
fights.

Anger then is an instrument for creating and maintaining peace.
Within the family it helps to generate and guard turf, the existence
of which will warn the other to back off before he goes too far. Despite its potential for violence and for unfairness, if implemented with
caution and sympathy, anger is a warrant that a bond is real, that two
people care enough about each other to be honest. As the old saw
has it, when a man and women fight, outsiders had best watch out.
If they interfere, they may soon discover that they have become the
target. Intrafamilial fighting, when well controlled and well managed, enables people to expand their horizons. By permitting them
to overcome burdensome frustrations (even frustrations with one another), it deepens their satisfactions and makes their alliance more
fruitful. No wonder trespassers must take care.

FAMILY VIOLENCE AND ABUSE

Nevertheless, family anger can get out of control. Spouses can and
do abuse one another. Men, in particular, have a proclivity for visiting violence on their wives. Nowadays this has become such a widespread social phenomenon that we cannot fail to mention it. The
questions that must be raised are these: Why do so many men treat
women like enemies? And why do they not stop before they produce

so much sorrow? The short answer is that some of them are too weak to use their anger wisely. They lose control and resort to primitive rage, not because they are dominant creatures who are taking advantage of their dominance but because in their impotence they become so frustrated they cannot calculate what is in their interest. Abuse is a token not of strength, but of failure. It is the refuge of men who cannot compete successfully with other men and who, because of this, salve their wounds by savaging their wives and girlfriends.

As has been noted, men are competitive creatures. They are always in a race with other men for relative status. Although they may not be in active fights, they are acutely aware of their respective positions and alert for signs of weakness. Among the worst things that can happen to a man is for him to be a loser in these tests of strength. It means that he is not a "real" man and will make him vulnerable to the ridicule of others. They might, for example, taunt him about his failures, thereby diminishing his status further. Even if they say nothing, the fact that they could will eat at his innards, and he will revile himself for his inability to prevent them from doing so.

To women, all of this may sound silly. Women often can't understand why men don't just relax and enjoy the solace of their love and acceptance. Many do not realize the extent to which even they judge men by their hierarchical success. As Henry Kissinger once observed, power is a compelling aphrodisiac. Women may say they want sensitive men, and perhaps they do, but they certainly don't want "wimps." Men perceived to be weak lose in contests for their love. Men, therefore, strive to prevail. They work hard at their jobs, often neglecting their families; they play equally hard at sports in which they believe they have an advantage; they even engage in illicit activities if they fear they can't succeed in more socially acceptable ones. For a man, to be incompetent, ineffective, or unlucky is virtually a sin, which he will use all of his energies to forestall.

What then is man to do should he fail? Must he sit back and relish his situation, or can he do something about it? If he is in an intimate relationship, what ramifications will his dilemma have for that relationship? When a husband and wife argue, he will usually assume that he should be dominant. As the man, he will believe that he is supposed to be the stronger one and he would like his wife to acknowledge this. She, however, quite rightly seeks moral parity. She knows that if she fails to uphold her side of the disagreement, not only will she lose, but their relationship will suffer. When a man is in fact strong, her energy and anger will remind him that she is a person to be reckoned with and will induce him to treat her as an equal who has valid interests of her own. If, however, he is not powerful, the situation is quite the reverse. For such a man, his wife's demonstrable vigor is a reminder of his impotence. The specter of her victory will haunt him, for it might confirm that he is a failure. What better proof could there be of his inability to compete with other men than that he loses to a woman? In consequence, his anger will escalate beyond measure. Unlike his more successful peers, he will have difficulty controlling his passions and may explode in an orgy of violence. If he subsequently beats his wife, it is not because he has harnessed the power of his anger, but because it has escaped and gone berserk.

Unfortunately there are many losers in this world. Many men do fail. By their standards and those of the people they care about, they are misfits, and worse. For them, life is a series of galling frustrations. It is a slow-motion horror show that they are incapable of interrupting. Somehow, somewhere, they must gain power, so why not with a woman? Husbands who are hierarchical failures do not need the excuse of shrewish wives to unleash their anger. When they arrive home after a day of exasperating setbacks, they are ready to displace their rage on the closest available target. Intimacy, of course, furnishes this closeness; and the fact that their partner is a woman, who is probably physically weaker than they are, will make her a safe victim. (The same, we must note, is true of children.) The physicality of much intrafamilial abuse is a direct result of this male advantage in size and strength. Abusive men may be out of control, but they are usually sufficiently aware of their situation to recognize where they have the upper hand. What they fail to realize is that they might be more successful if they were less violent.

Ironically, the very incompetence of these men in implementing their anger makes them ineffective even with the women they are close to. Though they may want to be respected, their primitive ferocity only gets them feared. Because they don't understand and/or are unable to act on their understanding that intimidation is detrimental to long-term relationships—that it, for instance, undermines their ability to generate sympathy—they alienate rather than influence their partners. This, in turn, exacerbates their frustrations, and they become more primitive and less effective. For them, anger is a descending spiral of loud explosions punctuated by exhausted impotence. For their partners, it is a painful wall of irrationality that cannot be penetrated or evaded.

How then to interrupt this cycle of misery? Should such men be thrown in jail or subjected to aversive conditioning? Should their wives be advised to leave them and seek court orders of protection? Perhaps they should. Since safety must always be the primary consideration when dealing with out-of-control anger, some form of protection must be initiated. The secret to managing rage, however, is to recognize its origins and purposes. As long as violently abusive men are treated as if they were possessed by the devil and subjected to exorcism and incarceration, they can only be contained, not changed. Requiring them to express their anger, or punishing them for doing so, may be viable means of interdicting their violence, but not for disarming it. Anything short of removing their frustrations is a stop-gap strategy. Only when a person, including an abusive husband, gets what he wants or changes his underlying goals will his rage subside. Only when he wins, does he cease being a loser.

This should immediately suggest a more effective strategy for helping abusive men. Rather than rob them of their anger, we must assist them in learning how to use it more efficaciously. If they are too weak to win, they must become stronger. This may seem paradoxical, but they will not be kinder to the women in their lives unless they can become more competent as men. When one looks only at the battles between a particular man and woman, it may seem as if the husband's demands are absurd and that he should simply learn to be more reasonable. When it is recognized, however, that his underlying frustrations have to do with his failures as a man, it becomes clear that he needs more success rather than further punishment. What he requires is a way of utilizing his abilities so that he can stand up to other men and claim his place in the sun. Only then will he lose his motivation to displace his wrath maliciously on a woman.

Merely blaming violent men for what is admittedly unacceptable behavior may satisfy a need to express oneself, but it does not obtain what is really wanted, namely, more harmonious male/female relations. Yes, a man who is violent must be stopped. I.A.M. makes it plain that safety comes first. Yet some have come to consider that the real object is to exact revenge. This, however, would lead to an alienation between the sexes that most people would not find attractive. Better to teach an impotent man the rudiments of effective anger so that he can utilize his energies more efficiently. If he can be assisted in keeping his eye on his goals and in understanding that he is engaged in influencing a person whose good will is important to him, perhaps he can get where he wants to go in a kinder, gentler manner.

SOCIALIZING CHILDREN

Similar considerations apply when contemplating the socialization of children. If women are vulnerable to abuse, obviously children are more so. They are considerably weaker than either of their parents, and as members of the family, they too are readily accessible to attack. Children do not have the resources, the insights, or the social supports of adults. They are thus quintessential victims who are easily subjected to the whims of unscrupulous parents. If the latter are too weak to control their anger or if they use it exclusively for their own advantage, their offspring can suffer to the point of death.

Some have thought to avoid this dilemma by advocating permissive parenting. They would have parents withhold their anger and allow their children to make decisions on their own. Rather than threaten the young, it is suggested that they be offered "unconditional positive regard." "Don't put your child down," a parent is told, "merely dispute what he does." The notion is that adults should reason with their children, not knock them down with a blast of fury. Anger, especially intense anger, is alleged to be a primitive instrument that can only damage a child's vulnerable self-esteem. Because it is unnecessarily frightening, it will convince him that he is perverse, depraved, and unloved. Better to share a hug and a offer a gentle nudge in the right direction.

Yet this can be a horrendous mistake. Abuse is, to be sure, a menace. And gentle love is far more protective. Nevertheless, effective anger cannot be left out of the parent/child relationship. Its absence would prevent parents from energetically informing or motivating their young regarding essential issues. How else would the latter learn the importance of some lessons? How else could they to be moved into speedy action when this is urgently needed?

First, anger sets limits. It warns children about dangers and provides a barrier against disaster. No matter how wise or perceptive children are, they do not begin life understanding where all the land mines are buried, nor can they independently determine where the social boundaries are drawn. Thus, they will not realize that running into the street to retrieve a ball may end in forfeiting their lives or appreciate that telling an aunt that her dress is ugly will offend her. It is, therefore, incumbent upon parents, who have already learned these lessons, to share them with their children. It is the least they can do. But they must also do more. They cannot just share this information as an assemblage of neutral facts. Children must be made to understand that there is a penalty for some transgressions. This is the purpose of parental anger. It grabs children by the collar and threatens them so that they will recognize when something meaningful has happened. They are told in no uncertain terms that they *must* not dash out into the roadway—*or else!* Of course, this will be frightening; it is meant to be. If parental anger were not sometimes intimidating, it would not be worthy of notice. Nor would it motivate compliance. But because it is, and does, it can be protective. Children will come to respect valid limits and be less likely to inflict injury on themselves or others. Though they may have had to endure pain in the process of acquiring this knowledge, they, and not merely their parents, will benefit. With more permissive parents who let children do whatever they please, it is hard to tell what the outcome might be.

It should be noted that in being taught limits, children also learn character and morality. Children who understand and respect the rules of social engagements are easier to live with and easier to love. Although it may be honest to tell Aunt Helen about her dress, it is decidedly not endearing. Children who are allowed to bumble along oblivious to the interests and sensitivities of others eventually become a pariah. If they do not realize or make allowances for the frustrations they inflict, in the end they make people so angry that few will tolerate them. Much better for their parents emphatically to warn them that some forms of selfishness are inadmissible. It is when parental fury makes them aware that adjustments are necessary that they begin on the path toward civilization. For better or worse, compromises and self-discipline are necessary for us to live among our fellow human beings; and the angry negotiations of children and parents are the place where these lessons are first taught.

Among the things that a child must learn is morality itself. We have already briefly explored how anger initiates guilt; it remains only to remark that much of this guilt is essential for the survival of society. In explaining how anger can be used to arouse internal controls, the impression may have been given that the mechanism is usually unfair. Perhaps in some families it is, but in a great many others it, in fact, facilitates fairness. When guilt is used to enforce truly moral rules, it advances the cause of cooperation and of mutual satisfaction. Another way to put this is to say that parental anger can establish a conscience and that a fair conscience promotes fair interactions. (Freud called this the development of a "super-ego.")

Moreover, the limits and rules imposed by angry parents tend to last. If they are indeed important, then it is essential that they not fade. They have to remain in the memory and continue to influence people as they grow older. It will not do for children to refrain from chasing a ball today, only unthinkingly to dash out into traffic next week. The fear imparted by a parental remonstrance has to remain active so that it will cause them to pause before reaching the tarmac. This can occur because the lesson involves emotional learning. It is precisely because children have been frightened by their parents' anger and not merely subjected to bland rationality that they internalize protective injunctions.

Earlier we noted that lessons learned in emotional contexts are remembered. Now we can see that such memories constitute a central aspect of childhood socialization. No children would learn to be human beings if parental anger did not capture their attention and pound its messages home. Were these not made indelible, every one of us would continuously have to reinvent the world. If we had to depend only upon our own cognitive memories, we would always need to pause to consider whether a particular action was right before we acted; and by the time we were sure, the moment would have passed.

Nevertheless, because of the enduring character of emotional lessons, anger must be used carefully. While it cannot be abjured, it must be employed fairly. Parents have to impose it, not merely at their own convenience, but in the interests of their children. As the balance of power between a parent and a child is grossly unequal, this places the burden on the parent. Parents must not take advantage, but rather compensate for their children's relative weakness. This means not only recognizing their interests even when they do not but also reinforcing their childrens' ability to assert themselves. The situation that should prevail may best be described as a "moving equilibrium." At any given age, a child will be less powerful than his parents, but more powerful than he was the year before. In turn, the relative disparity between the two will gradually narrow so that the ratio of their power eventually approaches one. Presumably there will come a moment when they will find themselves evenly matched. Meanwhile, they can be equal only if the parent compensates for the child's deficiencies. Just as a parent can even out a footrace by giving a child a head start, so too can their fights be made more symmetrical by the parent's refraining from using anger at full force or from attributing a forcefulness to the child's anger that it does not possess.

Obviously, the younger a child, the more allowances have to be made. Yet, as long as the object is to maintain a rough parity, the two can talk to each other with each being heard.

When parents do not try to overawe their children, when they allow themselves to be moved by their children's anger, parents and children can engage in honest disagreements and enter into negotiations grounded in the interests of both. Children will be permitted to advocate their priorities in a way that is noticed, while parents can take care not to be so intimidating that their children are afraid to hear their side. Remember that anger provides information about priorities largely through its intensity. Since a parent's anger is capable of being more robust, precautions do no more than elevate a child's anger to an equivalent level, thereby enabling both to obtain a more accurate sounding of the relative importance of their respective concerns. Were these adjustments not made, children would have few choices beyond engaging in tantrums or withdrawing their demands. Either way, it would be difficult to effect an appropriate bargain. If a child's demands were not made, her parents might be oblivious of them; but if these demands are expressed primitively, the child's anger might become the focus of their interaction and controlling it would take precedence. Therefore, artificially leveling the playing field permits the sharing of vital details.

Clearly, children are not experts at getting angry. They make appalling mistakes in expressing themselves and in attempting to exert influence. Sometimes they seek to be intimidating when they do not have the means of doing so; sometimes they try to be manipulative by utilizing concealments that are laughably transparent. This is to be expected of those who are only discovering how to be angry. But because they are also in the midst of their emotional socialization, their parents can obstruct the learning process if they overreact.

Among the mistakes that children make is misbehaving. When they are upset, they can become extremely provocative. As intimates of their parents, they have an opportunity to observe what frustrates them; and in their impotence, they may decide to exact revenge by visiting an injury just where it is most unsettling. Children may refuse to go to bed on time or to complete their homework for the very reason that their parents want them to do these things. Sophisticated parents will recognize what is going on and respond accordingly. Rather than protect their turf, they will try to understand what is frustrating their children and help them obtain what they want, assuming it is within reason. This can be achieved either by directly providing what the children want or by helping them to develop the skills needed to attain it themselves.

Children are also notorious for footdragging and indirection. They dawdle when they are asked to do things, and when they comply do "almost" what is asked. This can be infuriating to a parent, for whatever the demand, the child arranges to not quite accede. It is such behaviors that give children a reputation for being perverse. Yet upon closer inspection, theirs is a natural reaction to the strains of childhood. Adults ought never discount the powerlessness of their children. The latter are often more vulnerable to neglect and abuse than is commonly realized. Because they are so dependant, they cannot effectively assert themselves. Though they may want to tell their parents precisely where to go, they know the consequences of doing so. When they review their alternatives, they note that running away could lead to starvation, while fighting back could result in a hospitalization. Given this choice, passivity and indirection can seem attractive. If a person doesn't agree, but isn't allowed to disagree openly, then the only viable option may be an appearance of agreement. Such indirection at least allows for the possibility that the other will change his mind or forget. Passive aggression is as sensible a refuge for an oppressed child as it is for an oppressed adult. (And what child does not sometimes feel oppressed?) It enables the child to do something, which will be far less destructive to self-esteem than would be an abject capitulation.

One of the most important factors in teaching children how to get angry is allowing them to pit themselves against their parents. Though this strategy is obviously grating to parents, it enables children to test their growing strength in relative safety. As long as intrafamilial disagreements are kept honest and fair, children will see how others react to their indignation and learn to make accommodations. Thus, the toddler can take note of how others react to a barrage of "no's" while the teenager can research the merits of staying out late or hanging around with obnoxious friends. Gradually what will evolve is a complex picture of who can influence whom. Because there are few guidebooks to the intricacies of anger, we all learn by doing. Indeed, practice is essential, for using anger is a skill, not a piece of academic information.

Of course, all of this presupposes that sympathy exists within a family. The little contests that occur in all families become effective lessons only when parents and children care enough about each other not to abuse their advantages. Otherwise all that occurs is a desperate melee in which everyone is more concerned with self-protection than with a negotiated settlement. It is also helpful if parents are themselves effective users of anger. If they are not, it is unlikely that they can provide useful models for their children. Often children acquire influence strategies not by independent invention, but from observing what works for others. Also presupposed is that children are allowed to learn about anger in contests with their peers, for example, their siblings. As they engage in jousts with these relative equals, they can evaluate their respective strengths and weaknesses. Both in their games and in their schooling they can take each other's measure to determine the kinds of pressure that succeed. Sometimes they will win and sometimes lose; and though no one likes losing, failures can be instructive. In the end, such trials vastly widen the area in which children can successfully assert themselves.

Children who don't acquire these lessons within their families and/ or aren't permitted learn them from their peers fall behind in the race to become competent adults. This world is not for the timid or the fastidious. It is frequently a hostile place where we must be ready to defend ourselves. Consequently, parents who try to shield their children from the bruises of growing up do them no favor. The best defense against irrational, unfair anger is a certain knowledge of how to use the emotion effectively. It will enable children to assert their own rights and to parry the assaults of others. They will also come to understand the limits of their ability to influence others and therefore will not engage in as much wasted motion. In sum, they will learn that, though anger is not nice, if properly managed, it can come in handy.

12

Anger and Organizational Leadership

THE RATIONAL ORGANIZATION

If the ideal in family relationships is egalitarian, in organizations it is traditionally hierarchical. Where the marital couple is supposed to form a partnership, in business and government, the model is of the superior and subordinate. One person is designated the leader, while others are assigned the role of follower. This has profound implications for the use of anger. The dual concern model of social negotiations, which channels the emotion symmetrically, is less applicable, and so tyranny becomes a distinct possibility. When one person's decisions are accorded more weight than that of others, as is the case in hierarchy, the consequences can be devastating.

The patron saint of organizational theory, Max Weber (1947), sought to explain how bureaucracies inhibit excessive, irrational power. His writings indicate that while the main purpose of this sort of organization is unambiguous control, it works best when structured and limited. Apparently the efforts of large numbers of people cannot be effectively coordinated unless they are subject to discipline. They seem to need shared goals and synchronized patterns of behavior to integrate their contributions. Yet the power used to enforce such guidelines must itself be carefully delimited lest it generate unintended side-effects. Since the energy needed to maintain discipline can be quite substantial, it is especially important that it be regulated and determinate.

Weber, a close student of history, was aware that many early forms of social organization depended on terror. Primitive empires, such as the Assyrian, maintained their authority by erecting pyramids of skulls to intimidate subject peoples. As recently as a century ago, slavery was widely practiced as a means of keeping subordinates in their place. Indeed, in the United States we continue to suffer from the legacy of the violence used to deny slaves control over their destinies. Fortunately, today most people are aware that terror can be counterproductive. Though it can force people in desired directions, they do not go willingly or enthusiastically. Indeed, if it is to remain effective, those imposing terror are compelled to maintain the pressure and must divert their energies from more constructive endeavors. Conflict, not cooperation, becomes the theme of their existence, and everyone's condition is thereby diminished. Specifically, unfairness and violence are perpetuated, with those at the top becoming as brutalized as those under the lash.

Modern bureaucracies, by contrast, aspire to equity and voluntary participation. Many of their rules are specifically designed to maintain control without having to resort to brute force. This is apparent in the motto: *Sine ira et studio* (Without fear or favor). Special privilege and terror are renounced, while rationality and legitimacy are exalted. Bureaucracy endeavors to employ reason as the principal means of achieving its ends. Rather than be directed by whim or fury, it attempts to substitute well-thought-out rules, usually dubbed procedures. These essay to be impersonal and efficient. Because they are drained of arbitrary passion and presumably are known to all, they can provide a standard to which everyone can appeal. Capricious anger is to be held in check by the fact that it is the rule, and not the individual, that is supreme.

The leaders in such organizations are also supposed to be delimited and reasonable. Theoretically no tyrants need apply. According to the Weberian model, the source of a leader's authority should be rational and legal. Subordinates ought to acquiesce in the power of their superiors because they recognize it to have been legitimately bestowed by the organization. In other words, leaders have been hired (or promoted) in compliance with organizational rules and if their orders are consistent with organizational purposes, their subordinates should be ready to obey. This, of course, assumes that leaders' methods are not arbitrary or coercive and that their subordinates are culturally prepared to comply. It is not primarily through any special qualities they may possess, but by a joint subscription to a shared institution that their cooperation is motivated. The relationship between them may be inegalitarian, but shared rules will give everyone some power and rights.

The qualities essential in an organizational leader are very different from those needed by a primitive warrior. There is a much greater premium on self-control than on overweaning physicality. The fact that a boss is able to "beat-up" a subordinate is irrelevant, while knowing what to do is not. Expert power becomes far more significant than coercive power, competence more valuable than charisma, because bureaucratic effectiveness depends on understanding the rules and being able to implement them in ways that work.

All this would seem to suggest that anger has no place in the modern organization. Indeed, if one reads the works by the scientific management school, the emotion should be left at the office door. It is not to be used because it is inefficient, irrational, and unscientific. Nevertheless, anger turns out to be as essential for bureaucracy as it is for the family. Organizations that seem well-conceived on paper grind to a halt when the emotion is drained from them. In fact, anger is crucial to both creating and sustaining organizations. Without it, hierarchies could not exist; they would have no shape or direction. Though primitive anger may be incompatible with rational association, controlled anger is at its very heart. It forms the kernel around which leadership coalesces.

Hierarchy is a mode of imposing what has been called "imperative coordination." This sort of arrangement is organized in a ladder of ascending authority, with those in a superior position being accorded the right to give orders to those below them. There exists a chain of command whereby those at the top assume responsibility for deciding what will be done as well as for motivating those at the bottom to do it. Thus, it is a leader's task to plan joint activities and to make certain that they are carried out. The implication is that if the objectives of a superior are frustrated by a lack of cooperation by his subordinates, the very ability of the collectivity to pursue its goals will be compromised—that it will, for instance, be unable to turn out automobiles if everyone on the assembly line feels empowered to decide when and how to work. Anger, in this case, becomes a tool for enforcing coordinated effort. Presumably, in commanding compliance, a boss advances not a personal agenda, but one calculated to benefit all.

Hierarchy, it must be understood, is a stabilized pattern of orders and compliance, of anger and submission. Its specific ranks are not decided anew every time there is an issue of contention. Rather, once one has been established, there is a propensity for the subordinate to knuckle under to the superior. When the boss gets angry, subordinates generally assume that he or she has more power and hence wishes that carry more weight. In such a circumstance, a knitted eyebrow can be as devastating as a battalion of tanks. The leader and the follower do not come to blows because both acknowledge that in a showdown the leader is bound to prevail. The consequence is that the subordinate abstains from issuing a challenge, while the superior refrains from being brutal. Their interchange is civilized and ordered from top to bottom because, intellectually and emotionally, both believe in the potency of the leader and the leader's anger.

Such a set of beliefs must, however, be socially constructed. Plato may have believed that leaders are born with a trace of gold in their souls, but today we demand that our leaders prove themselves. We want to know that a person's power is real before we acknowledge it. And here is where anger comes in. Hierarchies are in part created by tests of strength that determine who is more forceful. Leaders are supposed to be people who can make their anger stick. In the jockeying for position that is a typical feature of most organizations, people go out of their way to determine how they measure up. Often conflicts are initiated specifically in order to establish who has the greater clout and hence the greater ability to awe others. Once this is educed, members of the organization will know who deserves precedence.

Needless to say, this process is not always fair or straightforward. Nor does it depend exclusively on the power of the individual. Within organizations, coalitions are forever forming and reforming with the intent of furthering the aspirations of their adherents. This means that some people will come along for the ride, that frequently it is connections and/or tradition rather than efficiency that decide the victors. Nevertheless, hierarchies do develop within organizations. And the way they are structured always has profound consequences, including the very existence of the organization, the shape of its activities, and the relative power of individuals. Fair or not, the rules, rewards, and directions of an organization as well as the careers, rank, and prosperity of its members hang in the balance.

Still bureaucracies are more than forums for imperative coordination. They also embrace egalitarian forms of coordination that are equally dependent on the competent use of anger. Though some people may be more powerful than others, successful hierarchies are not unidirectional. Influence not only flows from the top down; sometimes it moves sideways or even from the bottom up. The dual-concern model of negotiations may occasionally be contradicted by the inegalitarian nature of organizations, but it is not completely contravened. Just as functional families make adjustments that allow their children to exercise power, so organizations provide mechanisms for empowering those near the bottom. Once it is recognized that hierarchical precedence does not always coincide with superior wisdom, it becomes critical to gain access to relevant information wherever it may be located in the chain of command. Although leaders may be able to impose their plans, it helps if they are aware that these can be greatly enhanced when modified by input from below.

The difference is really that between democracy and totalitarianism. Both of these systems may be hierarchical, but the latter is far more rigid. In the West, we recognize that a competition of ideas often produces the best solution; therefore, we encourage people to speak up and assert the validity of their perceptions—or at least this is our ideal. Out of this kaleidoscopic contest, we expect creativity and compromise to emerge. When they do, we believe that all will benefit, that the goals and methods which develop will be better suited to our needs because the competition will keep us and our associations fluid and better able to adjust to changing circumstances. Although we realize that mistakes will be made, we hope nevertheless to be spared the thickheaded despotism of an arrangement such as that of the former Soviet Union.

As with family negotiations, this sort of organizational wrangling is contingent on a vigorous use of anger. Often it is only when people are able to speak up in ways that command attention that their contributions become effective. Though the hierarchy of an organization will temper the form in which anger is expressed, the emotion can still have weight. Subordinates can learn to assert their observations in ways that do not flout authority, and their superiors can adopt methods of exercising power that do not overawe. When both avoid excessive intimidation, or counter-anger, it will be possible to establish a productive dialogue.

Some would suggest that simple cooperation can be just as effective as angry coordination, and sometimes it is; but it is no substitute for hierarchy or for firm negotiations. Indeed, cooperation is often possible only because a hierarchical context already exists. Many times it is only after anger has stabilized into a pattern of rank that people feel safe enough to treat each other as equals. In a sense, this is the paradox of anger: on the one hand its potential for violence creates interpersonal danger; on the other, its ability to establish hierarchy and to facilitate negotiations reestablishes security. In any event, it is organizationally indispensable.

From the perspective of the individual, competent anger is mandatory. For the would-be leader, it is essential in establishing position and for enforcing structure among subordinates. For the subordinate, it is a mechanism for maintaining self-respect and achieving a measure of control. Whether used on the offense or on the defense, the emotion establishes the boundaries of interpersonal action and it gets things done. With all its drawbacks, when controlled and intelligently implemented, it is more a creative force than a destructive one.

ORGANIZATIONAL LEADERSHIP

As with any application of anger, anger asserted in the name of leadership can be analyzed in terms of its "what," "who," and "how." It too will have a goal, persons at whom it is directed, and a method of operation. These, however, are subject to different constraints than they would be on a more personal level. Within organizations, not all goals are equally appropriate; nor are all targets or modes of expression equally valid. Rather, they are modified by the purposes and limitations of the organization. First, the goals of organizational leaders are restricted by the goals of the organization. They are not apt to receive support for objectives that are deemed idiosyncratic. Their superiors, their subordinates, and their peers will not respect goals that do not promote the interests of the joint enterprise. Should they demand compliance with an exclusively personal goal, neither their bosses not their peers will back them, which will severely diminish their power. Likewise, subordinates will note that they have exceeded their authority and will not feel bound to conform. The organizational theorist Chester Barnard (1968) once observed that leaders must not give orders that will not be obeyed, for in doing so they lose their legitimacy. Disregarding established organizational goals and substituting obviously personal ones is an excellent vehicle for self-destruction, in that it undermines the predisposition of colleagues to be supportive and followers to be compliant. Instead, everyone resents the would-be leaders' selfishness and band together to deprive them of their jurisdiction.

Similarly, a leader's authority is threatened by efforts to assert power that have no organizational mandate. If the "who" toward whom anger is directed is not someone over whom a leader has command, an argument can be expected. One of the features of hierarchy is that it specifies who is subordinate to whom. This means that bosses can count on only particular others to recognize and be influenced by their wrath. They must not anticipate that everyone will be equally impressed. Clearly their superiors and peers will not react with the same degree of deference as do their inferiors. Nor will all those of a lower rank jump to immediate obedience. If they are subject to the authority of a different chain of command, they will resent what they will perceive as a usurpation of power and may rebel via passive aggression. Rather than being impressed by these leaders' energy, the subordinates will feel put upon and either ignore them or feel impelled by counter-anger to recruit an opposing authority, perhaps their own boss, to resist them.

Moreover, the who and what of a leader's anger must be coordinated. Not all organizational goals work with all subordinates. Organizations generally specify that a superior has authority only within a specified domain. Thus anger used to enforce activities that are not part of a follower's job description will lose its punch. Instead of maintaining discipline, it is apt to elicit resentment. Just as guilt works only when a person has a prior moral commitment that can be evoked by another's anger, so organizational demands must be able to draw upon a target person's agreement that he is being asked to do what is in fact his duty, for instance, that when he is being required to fetch coffee, this is part of his job description, not an effort to demean him. If an employee feels his integrity is being assaulted, the structures previously created in his mind by his hierarchical membership will become irrelevant. He won't be intimated, or comply, because he will not feel it is his function to do so.

Obviously, the "what" and "who" of organizational anger are relatively determinate, while its "how" can be extremely complicated and difficult to implement. As is true of all forms of anger, this aspect of the emotion involves both communications and motivation and utilizes intimidation, guilt and sympathy to achieve its ends. What makes organizational anger particularly challenging is that it must be precisely controlled, appropriate to its task, and coordinated with the efforts of others. Such anger tends not to be spontaneous and can be very complexly choreographed. Since it occurs in an arena of multiple, highly structured relationships, it cannot afford to ignore these. The questions it asks before swinging into action must therefore address not only how a particular person will react but also how others in the vicinity, including those in the chain of command, will react. This complicates the tactics and multiplies the amount of planning necessary.

Let us begin with communications. As with other instances of anger, it is often vital that persons in organizations be clear about what they are demanding. They may need to share their priorities so that others can recognize them. It may also be useful for them to be deceptive upon occasion. The rules of interpersonal influence are not suspended when one joins a bureaucracy. When others are prepared to comply, clarity will facilitate conformity; when they are not, manipulation and secrecy can work better. In recent years there has been a movement toward "Management by Objectives" (MBO). This form of supervision assumes that subordinates are generally prepared to follow instructions as long as they understand them and have input in creating them. Such a belief obviously places a premium on communication. It suggests that a lack of clarity is the central reason why subordinates fail in the tasks assigned them and that therefore the best way to overcome impasses is to be candid and direct. Yet even in organizations, life can be intricate and circuitous. MBO may try to simplify through clarity, but people do not resist anger merely because they don't understand its intent. As with marital communications, bureaucratic functionaries sometimes become stubborn precisely because they do understand. Sometimes they realize full well that a particular order is against their interests, and they react accordingly. Communication is not a panacea, just an attempt at influence, which may stand or fall for other reasons.

Intimidation

Now we come to the issue of motivation. Here again it proves the nexus of anger management. But motivation is at once more problematic than communications and more multifarious. The bottom line for utilizing anger remains successfully influencing others. This means that organizations too require an infusion of intimidation. Despite Weber's renunciation of "fear and favor," an ability to arouse fear is an essential constituent of organizational anger. This may not be pleasant and certainly violates the image of rationality that leaders try to project, but without it, those in authority would appear weak. Leadership implies strength, and competent anger provides the backbone of this strength.

Those who wish to be perceived as worthy of leadership must be able to frighten subordinates. These others must sense that, if they defy the leaders' directives, they will have to pay a penalty. Otherwise the leaders may be ignored. Still, superiors cannot afford to be too intimidating, for this would terrify others and prevent them from responding competently. The objective is to make demands stick without inflicting trauma. One must lead, not inundate. But this requires that anger be used judiciously. If leaders take pleasure in creating consternation, others will be more concerned with defending themselves than with complying. Arousing their fear may be essential, but it is moderate fear that is most effective. The best stance leaders can take is thus one of quiet anger. Because they must be perceived as tough, not bizarre, their anger has to be controlled and purposive. Only then will it be appropriately unsettling. Loud anger, for instance, can indicate that bosses are unsure of themselves. Others will fear their explosions, but these will be regarded almost as passing thunderstorms. Subordinates will take note of them, but they will be too unpredictable and ephemeral to have a lasting impact.

To build a reputation for real toughness, leaders must be able to tolerate anger and frustration. They need to be patient, decent, and above all not mean. Leaders are looked to to keep their heads even in circumstances of stress. If they lose their tempers too easily or react too sharply when exposed to others' anger, their ability to think is impaired. Because intense emotion interferes with reason, those depending upon leaders for guidance would have reason to doubt them. They would justifiably wonder if their confidence was misplaced. This is why subordinates often test their leaders to see if they have what it takes. Thus they will want to know how their bosses are likely to react when they get angry. Will they be vindictive? Do they carry a grudge? When confronted with a problem do they look away or flee down the nearest corridor? If the answer to any of these is yes, they are apt to be distrusted and their anger avoided. If, however, they listen to indignant subordinates without becoming ruffled and maintain their composure during times of crisis, they may well have the strength to lead. Because such leaders are not as easily frightened by anger and frustration as are the subordinates, they will be able to rely on the leaders' good sense to protect them from the inevitable organizational uncertainties.

An ability to tolerate anger provoking situations is so important that new bosses are regularly scrutinized to determine how much they can take. Those newly appointed to positions of authority may be expecting subordinates to defer to them, but will find instead that these employees drag their feet and make continual references to the superior achievements of their predecessors. This may feel like disrespect, but it is actually a first opportunity to prove themselves. Experienced leaders use initial resistance to demonstrate their equanimity. Because they are self-confident, they do not overreact or take things personally. They simply go about their business of making solid decisions and enforcing them fairly. Neophyte leaders, in contrast, often create a fuss. They call special meetings, demand obedience, and appeal to their own superiors for aid. They fail the test of toughness because they are not tough.

In an attempt to forestall a rebellion, many new bosses make a show of strength themselves. They become the new broom that sweeps clean. To ensure that their anger is respected, they try to demonstrate that they are capable of inflicting serious punishments. Therefore, they create an issue that others are likely to resist and, when they do resist, fall upon them like the proverbial ton of bricks. This lets their subordinates know who is in charge and makes them more cautious in subsequent encounters. Though this may sound crude and is often unnecessary, sometimes it is no more than a reversal of the tests inflicted by subordinates on their superiors, that is, it is just a dramatic way of establishing who has superior power.

One of the best ways for bosses to demonstrate that they are tough and that their anger is worthy of respect is to utilize it on behalf of the organization or of their subordinates. The leader who stands up to the belligerence of an irrational customer, or who angrily defies raids on his staff by a colleague, will be respected. Similarly, if he intercedes to prevent one subordinate from taking advantage of another, others will be grateful. Anger that is perceived of as protective is less likely to be resisted. Even though it is intimidating, people will allow themselves to be frightened into doing that which they believe is for their own good. They may not enjoy being pressured into performing an onerous task, for instance, to re-do a job that was previously botched, but they will comply because deep inside they know they will benefit. Thus the perceived legitimacy of bosses' anger will make it more tolerable.

Of particular import for leadership is anger used to control group frictions. Even though organizations are supposed to be rational, the people who inhabit them are often in conflict. Sometimes they are at odds about organizational decisions; sometimes, regarding personal matters. Either way, a quarrel can be inimical to the interests of all concerned, including the organization. If it is not resolved, other more important business can be adversely affected. Here leaders have an opportunity to assume the role of mediator. They can use their anger to prevent a fight, thereby permitting the parties to resolve their differences. If they are perceived as the toughest person around, their anger will be powerful enough to divert the parties from their own agendas, and their suggestions may be accepted because they are viewed as authoritative.

More difficult to determine is when intimidation is valid for maintaining close supervision. Often organizational subordinates are not motivated to perform the jobs for which they were hired. Although they may have agreed to these as conditions of their employment, many try to evade them in practice. Their ideal is to obtain the greatest remuneration for the least effort. In this case, the supervisor's task is to enforce a fair day's work and to keep a close watch so that her subordinates do not slack off. This means that those under her will be wary of her presence. The merest hint of her approach will make them flinch and induce them to knuckle down. They will fear that if they are caught goofing off, she will become angry enough to utilize her ultimate power, namely, that she will get them fired.

The problem that arises with this sort of supervision is that it is not equally effective in all circumstances. With subordinates who are young and/or poorly motivated, there may be no option, but with more experienced and/or skilled employees, it will justly be resented. Professionals, for instance, must be trusted to motivate themselves. If anger is used to enforce their compliance, they are apt to bridle at it. In ordinary circumstances, professionals have internalized motivators and need only to be allowed to implement them. Close supervision is an affront to them because it indicates that they are unprofessional. Their bosses' anger will imply that they are not capable of self-discipline. In such cases, bosses need to use less anger and allow professional guilt to maintain control. Their central chore is thus to determine whether their subordinates really are professional.

Leaders must also employ anger upon occasion with their peers and supervisors. Here it is used to establish their weight in the power game. Much of the work of organizations is done through overt negotiations where goals and strategies are hammered out. Often these negotiations occur at meetings specifically designed for the purpose. At such gatherings leaders must frequently assert positions that can be identified with themselves; otherwise, they will be considered ciphers and may forfeit all hope of being respected or promoted. Consequently, people go out of their way to make themselves heard, and, if need be, will use anger to underline the significance of their proposals.

Typically, at a first meeting called to review a particular issue, there will be a clamor of competing ideas. Because all the contestants want to make sure they are not lost in the shuffle, many use bluff and bluster to make their points. At times these meetings can get quite heated, which means they rarely lead to a quick resolution. More commonly it is at subsequent meetings, after people have had time to calm down and consider their options, that a suitable compromise is achieved. Thus, the successful leader is one who is capable of intimidating peers, but who does not do so interminably and against all odds. An ability to limit one's demands, and to accept some of those made by others, is absolutely requisite.

Guilt/Sympathy

Effective organizational leaders must be exquisitely attuned to the commitments that their followers and peers bring to the work place. Obviously this applies to their professional obligations, but also such factors as their work ethic. People on a job may sometimes dress similarly, but they are not products of the same cookie mold. Each has a separate history and a distinct family and culture that help determine a unique approach to assigned tasks. Some, for instance, are moved by a strong desire to achieve, while others want nothing better than to be left alone. Because of this diversity, superiors must be students of human nature, who understand that their job is not so much to motivate people as to channel the motivation they already possess. Usually subordinates will do what their bosses say not so much because they fear (or love) them, but because they are being asked to do something that is in accord with their own objectives or, at least, something that does not contradict them. Many of these self-actuators have a quasimoral character that derives from early socialization. Thus, it is not unusual for people who grow up on a farm to take hard work for granted. When employed in a factory context, they apply the same standards and bend every effort to complete even unpleasant tasks. Bosses can take advantage of this by using displeasure to indicate when an employee's own standards are not being followed. This will generally be more successful than being coercive.

It must also be recognized that many of the standards that are used to elicit guilt are cultural. In a pluralistic country such as the United States, it is particularly important to understand the ethnic/regional heritage of individuals. Someone with a Scandinavian background may react very differently than a colleague whose ancestry is Chinese, Jewish, or Italian. Each may, for example, respond differently to an open show of emotion. Nor will their sense of responsibility be the same. While it is to some extent a stereotype to say that Jews feel culpable for intellectual failures or that Italians are more burdened by physical incompetence, these reactions are derived from traditions that can be traced deep into their ethnic pasts. Each individual, to be sure, is different, and none of us can be equated with the traditions of our ancestors, but these legacies leave residues that can influence how we behave.

It should not be imagined, however, that only childhood or culture determine a person's unconscious commitments. Someone can be sensitized to guilt through his professional socialization as well. An extensive period of schooling and/or reliance upon a professional community for support and training can internalize a strong set of standards, for example, a code of ethics. Often these mandates are inculcated during periods of stress. It is no accident that potential doctors and priests undergo very demanding periods of learning. During their internship, neophyte doctors are subjected to rigorous hours and even more rigorous discipline. Just when they are most tired and most insecure, they must endure angry demands to perform flawlessly. Because at such moments they are liable to be psychologically unable to resist, this has the effect of instilling the same sort of internal structures as were created by parental demands during childhood. The rules so learned become part of their identity and are available to be called upon by those who know of their presence. For them, the Hippocratic oath will be more than a series of words; it will represent a duty to which their superiors and patients can appeal with measurable effect.

Moreover, powerful, self-enforced norms are not the exclusive domain of professionals. They can be created within the work place itself. Indeed, among blue-collar workers, these are more the rule than the exception. Typically, when a group of people toil together for an extended period of time, they develop a joint approach to their shared task. In particular, they settle upon a particular way to perform the job and an equitable rate at which to perform it. Because the performance of any one person will reflect upon the adequacy of the others, all have an interest in maintaining guidelines with which they can be comfortable. Those who do too much will be perceived as rate-busters, while those who do too little will be seen as slackers. Either way deviants will be a threat to the group and their patterns branded unacceptable. The reaction to such pressures is usually conformity. Most people hate the isolation and harassment that are the lot of the deviant. In consequence, they, like the professional, adopt the guidelines of their reference group and make these their own.

Leaders who do not understand the power of such standards are doomed to impotence. The combined determination of their subordinates will prove much more powerful than they. No matter how intense their anger, it will be dissipated on the shoals of an implacable resistance. Better by far to recognize the existence of group norms and to exploit them for organizational purposes. A boss does not want to destroy group standards, but rather appeal to them to motivate compliance. If these standards are contrary to the interest of the boss or the organization, the question then becomes how to introduce more congenial standards. It may well be possible to negotiate the establishment of norms that are in the interest of both the organization and work group.

Moreover, leaders cannot afford to disregard the commitments of their peers. While the lone cowboy may be a hero in American mythology, he does not fare well in the modern bureaucracy. Because the bureaucracy is the abode of people who must coordinate their efforts toward a common purpose, they need to create stable alliances. This is why loyalty is at a premium in organizations; it is why its denizens often remark about the necessity of "going along to get along." Making waves is one of the cardinal sins of the modern corporation precisely because it disrupts the patterns needed for working together. It is why coalitions are carefully crafted and passionately defended. Doing otherwise would risk impotent isolation.

Contemporary executives are creatures of their relationships. To the degree that others willingly work with them, to this same degree is their power enhanced. Their bosses must be prepared to back them, and their peers must refrain from undercutting them. Without these others' cooperation, it would soon become apparent that their anger had no teeth; that its clout was contingent on others being sympathetic. If these others perceive an executive's anger as irrational or inimical to their own concerns, their patronage will be tepid. As with the executive's own subordinates, their sympathy arises from a consensus of values and/or a perceived harmony of interest. Creating and sustaining these beliefs is therefore one of the main functions of office politics.

It is friends, not enemies, who ratify the authority of individuals vis-à-vis their subordinates. The presence of friends also improves one's prospects in office negotiations. The existence of sympathetic others, including superiors, peers, and subordinates, adds weight to arguments in favor of particular goals. It is not personal loudness, but a visible army at one's back that makes an angry demand worth listening to. In politics this is called having a constituency. In organizations it often entails joining an established faction. Usually organizations contain several preexisting parties, which demand allegiance. When people come on board, they are asked to choose sides. If they don't, they may be ostracized and treated like enemies by all. Often they can gain sympathy only from those who perceive them as aligned with themselves. Because of this, choosing sides must be done with extreme caution. Mistakes may tarnish an entire career. Those with whom people ally themselves need to have the potential for being sympathetic to their causes and the capacity to offer a quid pro quo for their fidelity. A blind, reflexive allegiance to partners who cannot or will not reciprocate enhances no one's stature. This process of modifying, and calling upon, organizational alliances is exacting and arduous. It takes considerable skill, luck, and tenacity, which is why not everyone succeeds in organizational politics.

The single most important thing people must understand about managing their anger in an organizational setting is that counter-anger is a constant threat. Potential enemies lie in wait everywhere. Whether intimidation, guilt, or sympathy is their primary source of influence, they cannot afford to be arrogant. Leaders who are drunk with success are soon called to account. Because they are surrounded by strong, highly motivated people,they must stay in control and act with propriety. Wild fury will undercut them in every direction. It will rob them of allies, destroy the illusion of their superior capacity, negate their appeals to a common purpose, and create unnecessary antipathies. An organizational position is like a long-term love affair. Leadership within a bureaucracy is not a matter of winning individual battles, but of prevailing in its interminable squabbles. This makes it imperative to avoid the temporary disasters that can abrogate future achievements. Because uncontrolled, unplanned anger has precisely the contrary effect, persons prone to it will be considered "loose cannons," best avoided before they self-destruct.

ORGANIZATIONAL FOLLOWERSHIP

Because organizations are inherently unequal, anger takes on a very different cast for followers than for leaders. Hierarchies are inherently unfair, allowing far more discretion for those on top. Subordinates must therefore learn to protect themselves from what may be an irrational assertion of power. Because bosses are liable to use their anger to uphold their own status, those on the receiving end may find their assertiveness quashed. Not only must they brace themselves against the wrath of these more powerful others, they must understand that their own anger can be a provocation that may need to be controlled lest it elicit retaliation.

The primary concern of organizational followers must be self-protection. Because they have less firepower than others with whom they are in regular contact, in a showdown they can come off second-best. This does not mean that they need to give up and abjectly accept any demand aimed their way. If anything, because of their relative weakness, they must develop an area of discretion where their assertions predominate.

This will require that they be acutely aware of their limits so that they are able to perceive their advantages and press them when appropriate. Their anger can be made to matter as long as it is activated prudently and modestly.

Protecting Oneself

Subordinates can be badly hurt. In tests of strength they can find themselves beaten into submission. In many cases, they will lose their jobs, be demoted, or be treated as irrelevant. One way or another, when confronting bosses over issues they do not want to face or in a manner they find offensive, they will be forcibly reminded of who is in charge. It is the rare superior who does not feel threatened by an open demonstration of a subordinate's displeasure. Such a direct confrontation tends not to clear the air, but to invite a reaffirmation of the superior's power, during the course of which any form of intimidation may be utilized to uphold that position. Generally the more effective, or overt, the challenge, the tougher will be the response.

In organizations right does not always make for might. Injustices abound. People will sometimes have to endure galling losses to others who are their inferiors as human beings. Bosses are not always as smart, good, or dedicated as those they supervise. When they angrily demand compliance, they may be imposing actions that are not as desirable as those favored by their underlings. They may know and their subordinates may know that preferable alternatives exist—alternatives more favorable to the interests of all, including the organization—but the bosses' way will still be adopted. In the military, the saying is that "there is a right way, a wrong way, and an army way." In organizations there is also the superior's way, which is likely to prevail.

Subordinates who challenge their bosses just because their bosses are wrong may find themselves in for a surprise. Even though everyone is supposedly serving the interests of the organization, these interests may not be what determine the outcome of a clash. The subject of such a conflict may be as is initially stated, but it will soon devolve into a struggle over power itself. If the bosses' authority is challenged, protecting it will take precedence over all else. In this, bosses usually find they have the support of the hierarchy, for those who compose it will fear that a loss of face by one of their number threatens them too. Consequently, they will close ranks, and challengers will be isolated or crushed.

In a clash over power, subordinates can find themselves stripped of allies. Their rational arguments go unheard, and they stand alone. Even their peers may desert them, for they will not want to be tarred by the same brush. A person may therefore have to devote energy to guarding against attacks that can come from every quarter. No longer will an individual's ideas matter, for the central concern will be simple survival. No more argumentative memos to superiors; no more unsolicited suggestions for improving procedures—these must stop, and the person will have to learn to keep his head down, for it will be perceived as a target. It is for this reason that followers need to assume a more defensive posture than do leaders. They must be especially careful to know their situational limits, which entails understanding their bosses' sensitivities, as well as those of the organization, peers, and the social environment. As subordinates, they cannot afford to be oblivious to these factors, for if they assert their anger without concern for potential repercussions, their condition will become worse. Similarly, they must know their personal limits. If feelings of omnipotence seduce them into making untenable claims or overestimating their relative strength, they can go too far and lose too much.

None of this, however, should be taken to suggest that followers give up their legitimate claims or retreat into impotent isolation. Allies count as much for those at the bottom as for those at the top. They too can participate in groups that cooperate to promote specific agendas. Plugging into the norms of such groups, building friendships, and manipulating serendipitous circumstances, including boss's vulnerabilities, can all be effective strategies for subordinates. Though it may not be possible for them to be as overt with their anger, if they are well connected, their bosses may fear treading upon their sensibilities. As superiors know, they too can lose fights or at least be impaired by them, and this may encourage them to allow their subordinates to exercise delimited areas of power. As long as they themselves retain a sufficient locus of discretion, they may be prepared to relinquish some to their underlings. Subordinates who understand this can negotiate jurisdictions in which their anger is respected.

Professionalism/Decentralization

Among the best ways that subordinates can create discretionary space are through professionalism and decentralization. These are both mechanisms for increasing the power and freedom of those who implement the actions of an organization. In the former case, an actor's enhanced authority derives from a superior expertise and from membership in a community of experts; in the latter, it flows from an organization's decision to delegate power as widely as possible. Either way, increased power in the hands of subordinates will give their anger additional muscle.

Professionals, namely, those whose specialized training certifies them as well qualified to make certain decisions, gain power because their expertise is openly recognized. Their bosses and their bosses' bosses, know that professionals can make a wiser choice than they can. Since one of their goals is the prosperity of the organization, they will be motivated to relinquish a little power in the hope that their position will be bolstered by greater organizational success. Professionals also gain leverage by appealing to sources of power outside the organization. The professional groups to which they belong have an interest in preserving their authority because the status of other professionals belonging to them is also at stake. They will attempt to uphold their expertise, for if it is slighted, so will that of many more.

The result is that professionalism creates an opportunity for individuals to enforce their decisions. This, however, places a responsibility upon them. Since they will often be in a position of leadership, that is, of creating and maintaining organizational structure, they must be competent and prepared to take risks. All of the caveats that apply to authority deriving from hierarchical position apply to them also. They too must worry about upholding the organization's interests, and they too must be concerned about the allegiance of those to whom they issue instructions. To the extent that they have an ability to make their anger stick, to this same extent they must have the courage and wisdom to act wisely.

Decentralized power is more the province of blue-collar or pink-collar workers. Their right to make decisions and to angrily enforce them can result from an organization's conclusion that they are apt to possess superior judgment in certain areas. They too presumably have an expertise, but it derives from their experience on the job and from a firsthand knowledge of the given situation. Usually bureaucratic leaders are of necessity removed from front-line operations. As coordinators of overall policy, their decisions often have an abstract quality. The people on the scene, however, if properly motivated, can be concrete and responsive. Indeed, if allowed power, their enlarged sense of control may increase their motivation and focus their attention. The trouble is that the more successful they are, the more their superiors will feel their own position is undermined. This almost unavoidable source of tension guarantees that forces will be pushing both for decentralization and against it. In the end, an equilibrium will be established, but it may be one with which no one is completely comfortable.

In any event, anger is unlikely to be banished from organizations. There will always be a tug-of-war over who does what. Moreover, mistakes will always be made. The object therefore is to design an organization so that it maximizes an effective distribution of power, while maintaining the integrity of the hierarchy and of the individuals who compose it. Total justice is unattainable, but a meliorist strategy can contribute to a progressive improvement in the lot of a broad majority. No absolute rules apply to this process, but the more good will, the better.

13

Conclusion

Anger has been described as a "misunderstood emotion" (Tavris, 1982), which it certainly is. Even presumed experts have had difficulty in depicting it. Some have reviled and rejected it, while others have romanticized and embraced it. The reality, as we have seen, is more sober and multidimensional. While not a loveable emotion, anger is crucial for the individual and society. As such, it must be used, and used well. If a person can break through the myths and understand its complexities, anger becomes an instrument for survival and well-being. The techniques advocated by most anger management approaches are not incorrect so much as they are out of context. When understood as helping to assure safety, to advance incremental tolerance, to facilitate an evaluation of anger, or to communicate and motivate more effectively, they make a good deal of sense. It must also be borne in mind that sometimes the objectives promoted by anger are unattainable and must be changed.

It turns out that the scope of integrated anger management is very broad and that it can be applied to a multitude of situations, persons, and problems. We have seen its relevance to the family and to organizational leadership, but it also has other institutional and personal applications. Thus it can be employed to address difficulties emanating from social structure, individual limitations, or political stresses. Specifically, it can be used to deal with social-class conflicts, criminal justice problems, mental illness and mental retardation, legal disputes, and international discord. It is even applicable to psychotherapy.

Let us consider psychotherapy. This treatment modality entails letting go of dysfunctional social roles. These, however, are rarely altered without a fight. Part of the process of working them through involves getting angry with those people who have helped to establish them. Thus, individuals trapped in an eating disorder may need to become overtly angry with parents who have discouraged them from growing up. Only then will they be able to begin developing appropriate new roles. Even here, they will need anger to help negotiate satisfying new patterns of behavior.

On a more social scale, understanding and being able to use anger is essential to working out the very real disabilities imposed on some minorities. We have briefly touched on issues having to do with black rage, but it should be obvious that these are particularly salient in contemporary America. While it has often been possible to ignore them, when they erupt, they clamor for attention. And when they do, there are the inevitable calls to solve root causes. Still, there is no consensus about what these are, or how they should be handled.

Although many sources of black frustration are quite evident and there is no dearth of suggestions for removing them, analyses for doing so tend to be simplistic and somewhat detached from the realities of coping with an intense emotion. What must be answered is how the dangers of the black rage can be contained, how individual blacks and their leaders can accurately evaluate their situation, and most important how they and the white community can work together to achieve the achievable. Simply calling attention to a problem or agitating for a utopian solution is an incomplete strategy. If blacks are to use their anger in ways that culminate in success, they must understand that they are trying to influence others, specifically whites, and that, having accomplished this, it may be up to them to use the energies embedded in their rage to perform at a level consonant with their aspirations. If whites are to cope with black rage and their own frustrated ambitions, they must be neither patronizing nor provoked to reflexive counter-anger. For their part, they must be prepared to engage in a dialogue in which both sides use firm flexibility to promote their causes. This may not be polite, but it can cut through the public hypocrisy that has prevented honest, safe, or productive encounters.

Similar considerations apply when dealing with issues of poverty. It too puts people at an unfair disadvantage and can make them angry enough to fight. Thus, more and more individuals have come to realize that social justice is in everyone's interests. By broadening the spectrum of society for whom success is possible, more people can be enabled to get what they want and need. For this to happen, however, the upper classes have to give up something. Fortunately, what they gain in terms of safety and social cooperation will more than compensate. From the point of view of the poor, it is essential that they understand their goal, not as retaliating against the wealthy, but as attaining riches of their own. When they do this, they may discover that expanded welfare benefits are not their best option and that creating and exploiting opportunities are.

Anger management strategies are also applicable to criminal justice populations. While some caught up in this system are victims of inequitable social arrangements, for others anger has become a way of life. Their very identity is tied up in intimidating and bullying the vulnerable. As many helping professionals have found, this means they are not especially susceptible to appeals to be "good." Indeed, criminal justice audiences often find that these appeals sound like pious attempts at robbing them of their strength. In part they are correct. In so far as it is being recommended that they feel guilty, they are in fact being asked to internalize the anger of others and to impose limits on themselves. Though outsiders may understandably see this as necessary, the targets can not be asked enthusiastically to agree. In consequence, a different approach may be warranted. If violent people can be made to understand that their anger is being misused and causing them to lose rather than to win, it may be possible to help them develop more effective forms of self-assertion. Thus, one need not say, "Don't be angry," but rather, "Be angry, but be smart too."

When dealing with a chemically dependent population, a similar approach is indicated. These individuals are bullying themselves even more than are other people. In their hopeless helplessness, they perceive no possibility of ever obtaining what they want, so they take out their frustrations by damaging themselves. This means that if they can be aided in seeing what they truly desire and helped to attain it, they may lose their impetus toward self-abuse. Though this approach would not be easy, it does open up an avenue for treatment.

With a population having even graver personal limitations, such as the mentally retarded or the mentally ill, a different, more active, tactic is advisable. These people may not be able to understand or apply the tenets of I.A.M. themselves. Specifically, mentally retarded people may not have the cognitive skills to comprehend what they want or to understand what they must do to attain it, while mentally ill individuals may be prevented from doing likewise by an inability to cope with strong emotions. In these cases, others may need to do for them what they cannot do for themselves. Thus, helpers may need to be particularly skilled in deciphering the underlying goals of the mentally retarded or in arranging that these be met. This, of course, implies that the helpee may never be fully independent, but this can be an unavoidable consequence of disability.

Moving back toward a larger canvass, I.A.M. is also relevant to the legal system. This infrastructure is obviously concerned in part with conflict resolution, often of ferocious conflict. Indeed, part of its function is to prevent people from going out of control. It therefore needs to assure safety and to facilitate productive negotiations. Often it achieves this through physical restraints, or at least by requiring people to pretend they are rational. Although this is sometimes essential, it can also help to pierce to the emotional core of an issue. Hence, techniques that deal more directly with mechanisms for anger resolution, such as mediation strategies, can be useful to both lawyers and their clients.

I.A.M. even has a place in politics and international affairs. These enterprises, despite the posturing they entail, often have the deadly serious mission of resolving grand-scale social frictions. Anger builds up within polities and between nations and needs to be managed every bit as much as between individuals. Because factions and states have competing interests that they may be unable to reconcile, they generally jostle for position, seeking an advantage. Unfortunately firm flexibility when projected onto a national or international stage can be overwhelmingly powerful and extremely insensitive. Politics, which has been described as the art of the possible, when handled deftly seeks ways to overcome these tensions. Thus, politicians and statesmen may be understood as semihonest brokers whose task it is to keep social frustrations from getting out of hand. For them, a familiarity with anger management means understanding how and why their constituents or their opponents are so hardheaded and recognizing what to do about it; in other words, knowing how to arrange deals whereby the largest number of people can have their frustrations reduced without resorting to war.

Finally, it must not be expected that I.A.M. will convert humanity into a company of saints. Although it may make it possible for them to use their anger more effectively, clearly the emotion will continue to be misused. People will always make mistakes about their goals and about their means of achieving them. Sometimes they will be selfish, sometimes even cruel. To ignore these facts is only to deny oneself an opportunity to cope. Still anger is essential. It is found everywhere: in business, in politics, in the arts, and at home. It occurs between intimates and strangers, the old and the young, the kind and the mean-spirited, the brilliant and the retarded, the friend and the enemy. It is the prerogative of all races, all religions, and all cultures. No one is above it, and no one is beyond its reach. But wherever it appears, it makes things happen. Indeed it structures the very social relations through which we interact and through which we attain happiness.

Selected Bibliography

Adler, A. 1954. *Understanding Human Nature.* Greenwich, Conn.: Fawcett.

Alexander, F. 1948. *Fundamentals of Psychoanalysis.* New York: W. W. Norton.

Aristotle. 1941. *The Basic Works of Aristotle.* Edited by R. McKeon. New York: Random House.

Arnold, M. 1968. *The Nature of Emotion.* Middlesex, England: Penguin Books.

Averill, J. R. 1982. *Anger and Aggression.* New York: Springer.

Bach, G. R., and P. Wyden. 1968. *The Intimate Enemy.* New York: Avon.

Bach, G. R., and H. Goldberg. 1974. *Creative Aggression: The Art of Assertive Living.* New York: Avon Books.

Barlow, D. H. 1988. *Anxiety and Its Disorders: The Nature and Treatment of Anxiety and Panic.* New York: Guilford Press.

Barnard, C. I. 1968. *Functions of the Executive.* Cambridge: Harvard University Press.

Barrish, H. H. and I. J. Barrish. 1989. *Managing and Understanding Parental Anger.* Kansas City, Mo.: Westport Pubs.

Bazerman, M., and R. Lewicki, eds. 1983. *Negotiating in Organizations.* Beverly Hills: Sage Publications.

Beck, A. 1976. *Cognitive Therapy and the Emotional Disorders.* New York: International Universities Press.

Berger, M. M., ed. 1978. *Beyond the Double Bind.* New York: Brunner/Mazel.

Bierstadt, R. 1950. *An Analysis of Social Power.* American Sociological Review, 15: 730–738.

Blau, P. 1963. *The Dynamics of Bureaucracy.* Chicago: University of Chicago Press.

Bloom-Feshbach, J., and S. Bloom-Feshbach, eds. 1987. *The Psychology of Separation and Loss.* San Francisco: Jossey-Bass.

Bowlby, J. 1969. *Attachment.* New York: Basic Books.

———. 1973. *Separation: Anxiety and Anger.* New York: Basic Books.

———. 1980. *Loss: Sadness and Depression.* New York: Basic Books.

Bratter, T. E., and G. G. Forrest. 1985. *Alcoholism and Substance Abuse: Strategies for Clinical Intervention.* New York: Free Press.

Breuer, J., and S. Freud. 1957. *Studies on Hysteria.* New York: Basic Books.

Brim, O., and S. Wheeler. 1966. *Socialization after Childhood.* New York: John Wiley.

Brownell, K. D., and J. P. Foreyt. 1986. *Handbook of Eating Disorders: Physiology, Psychology, and Treatment of Obesity, Anorexia, and Bulimia.* New York: Basic Books.

Bry, A. 1986. *How to Get Angry without Feeling Guilty.* New York: NAL-Dutton.

Cannon, W. B. 1929. *Bodily Changes in Pain, Hunger, Fear and Rage: An Account of Recent Research on the Function of Emotional Excitement.* New York: Appleton-Century-Crofts.

Chomsky, N. 1972. *Language and Mind.* New York: Harcourt, Brace, Jovanovich.

Clausewitz, C. 1908. *On War.* New York: Penguin Books.

Cole, J. 1985. *Thwarting Anger: A View of Anger.* Novato Calif.: Growing Images.

Cotter, S., and J. Guerra. 1976. *Assertion Training.* Chicago: Research Press.

Cranston, M. 1982. *Jean-Jacques.* New York: W. W. Norton.

Dahrendorf, R. 1968. *Essays in the Theory of Society.* Stanford, Calif.: Stanford University Press.

Dalrup, R. J. and D. Gust. 1990. *Freedom from Anger.* New York: Pocket Books.

Darwin, C. 1965. *The Expression of Emotions in Man and Animals.* Chicago: University of Chicago Press.

Davis, M. 1973. *Intimate Relations.* New York: Free Press.

DeFoore, B. 1991. *Anger: Deal with It, Heal with It, Stop It from Killing You.* Deerfield Beach, Fla.: Health Communications.

Denzin, N. R. 1984. *On Understanding Emotion.* San Francisco: Jossey Bass.

Dollard, J. R., L. W. Doob, N. E. Miller, and R. R. Sears. 1939. *Frustration and Aggression.* New Haven, Conn.: Yale University Press.

Dollard, J., and N. E. Miller, 1950. *Personality and Psychotherapy: An Analysis in Terms of Learning, Thinking and Culture.* New York: McGraw-Hill.

Dorpat, T. L. 1985. *Denial and Defense in the Therapeutic Situation.* New York: Jason Aronson.

Doty, B. and P. Rooney. 1990. *Shake the Anger Habit!* Redding, Calif.: Bookery.

Edelson, M. 1970. *Sociotherapy and Psychotherapy.* Chicago: University of Chicago Press.

Elias, N. 1982. *Power and Civility.* New York: Pantheon Books.

Ellis, A. 1962. *Reason and Emotion in Psychotherapy.* Secaucus, N.J.: Lyle Stewart.

———. 1977. *Anger: How to Live with and without It.* New York: Citadel Press.

Erikson, E. 1950. *Childhood and Society.* New York: W. W. Norton.

Fein, M. 1990. *Role Change: A Resocialization Perspective*. New York: Praeger.

———. 1992. *Analyzing Psychotherapy: A Social Role Interpretation*. New York: Praeger.

Fenichel, O. 1941. *Problems of Psychoanalytic Technique*. New York: Psychoanalytic Quarterly.

Fine, R. 1979. *A History of Psychoanalysis*. New York: Columbia University Press.

Fishman, H. C., and B. L. Rossman, eds. 1986. *Evolving Models for Family Change*. New York: Guilford Press.

Forward, S. 1989. *Toxic Parents: Overcoming Their Hurtful Legacy and Reclaiming Your Life*. New York: Bantam Books.

Frank, R. 1988. *Passions with Reasons: The Strategic Role of the Emotions*. New York: W. W. Norton.

Frank, J. 1973. *Persuasion and Healing: A Comparative Study of Psychotherapy*. Baltimore: Johns Hopkins University Press.

Frankel, L. P. 1991. *Women, Anger and Depression: Strategies for Self-Empowerment*. Deerfield Beach, Fla.: Health Communications.

Franks, D., and D. McCarthy, eds. 1989. *Sociology of Emotions*. New York: JAI Press.

Freeman, L. 1990. *Our Inner World of Rage: Understanding and Transforming the Power of Anger*. New York: Continuum.

Freud, A. 1966. *The Ego and the Mechanisms of Defense*. New York: International Universities Press.

Freud, S. 1953–1974. *The Standard Edition of the Complete Psychological Works of Sigmund Freud*. Edited by J. Strachey. London: Hogarth Press and Institute for Psychoanalysis.

———. 1961. *Civilization and Its Discontents*. New York: W. W. Norton.

Frijda, N. H. 1987. *The Emotions*. Cambridge: Cambridge University Press.

Fritz, J. 1985. *The Clinical Sociology Handbook*. New York: Garland.

Garbarino, J., C. J. Schellenbach, and J. Sebes. 1986. *Troubled Youth, Troubled Families*. New York: Aldine de Gruyter.

Gaylin, W. 1981. *The Rage Within: Anger in Modern Life*. New York: Simon and Schuster.

Gelinas, P. J. 1979. *Coping with Anger*. New York: Richards Rosen Press.

Goffman, E. 1952. "On Cooling Out the Mark." *Psychiatry*, 15.

Goldberg, S. 1973. *The Inevitability of Patriarchy*. New York: William Morrow.

Goldstein, A. P. and A. Rosenbaum. 1982. *Agress-Less: How to Turn Anger and Aggression into Positive Action*. Englewood Cliffs, N.J.: Prentice-Hall.

Greenberg, L., and J. Safran. 1987. *Emotion in Psychotherapy*. New York: Guilford Press.

Grusky, O., and G. A. Miller, eds. 1970. *The Sociology of Organizations: Basic Studies*. 2d ed. New York: Free Press.

Gurman, A. S., and D. P. Kniskern, eds. 1981. *Handbook of Family Therapy*. New York: Brunner/Mazel.

Hankins, G. 1988. *Prescription for Anger: Coping with Angry Feelings and Angry People*. Beaverton, Ore.: Princess Pub.

Harre, R., ed. 1986. *The Social Construction of Emotions*. New York: Basil Blackwell.

Heller, D. 1985. *Power in Psychotherapeutic Practice*. New York: Human Services Press.

Hersey, P., and K. H. Blanchard. 1988. *Management of Organizational Behavior: Utilizing Human Resources*. 5th ed. Englewood Cliffs, N.J.: Prentice-Hall.

Hobbes, T. 1956. *Leviathan, Part I*. Chicago: Henry Regnery.

Hochschild, A. R. 1983. *The Managed Heart: Commercialization of Human Feeling*. Berkeley: University of California Press.

Hollingshead, A., and F. Redlich. 1958. *Social Class and Mental Health*. New York: John Wiley.

Izard, C. 1977. *Human Emotions*. New York: Plenum Press.

Jahoda, M., and N. Warren, eds. 1966. *Attitudes*. Baltimore: Penguin Books.

James, W. 1950. *The Principles of Psychology*. New York: Dover.

Janov, A. 1970. *The Primal Scream, Primal Therapy: The Cure for Neurosis*. New York: G. H. Putnam and Sons.

Kemper, T. D. 1978. *A Social Interactionist Theory of Emotions*. New York: John Wiley & Sons.

Klama, J. 1988. *Aggression: The Myth of the Beast Within*. New York: John Wiley & Sons.

Kubler-Ross, E. 1969. *On Death and Dying*. New York: Macmillan.

Kurtines, W. M., and J. L. Gewirtz, eds. 1987. *Moral Development through Social Interaction*. New York: John Wiley & Sons.

Kutash, I., and L. Schlesinger, eds. 1980. *Handbook on Stress and Anxiety*. San Francisco: Jossey-Bass.

Lazarus, R. A. 1991. *Emotion and Adaptation*. New York: Oxford University Press.

Leary, M. 1983. *Understanding Social Anxiety: Social, Personality and Clinical Perspectives*. Beverly Hills: Sage Publications.

Lerner, H. G. 1985. *The Dance of Anger*. New York: Harper and Row.

Lewis, M., and C. Saarni, eds. 1985. *The Socialization of Emotions*. New York: Plenum Press.

Lewontin, R., S. Rose, and L. Kamin. 1984. *Not in Our Genes: Biological Ideologies and Human Nature*. New York: Pantheon Books.

Light, D. 1980. *Becoming Psychiatrists: The Professional Transformation of Self*. New York: W. W. Norton Co.

Lindzey, G., and E. Aronson, eds. 1985. *Handbook of Social Psychology*. 3d ed. New York: Random House.

London, P. 1964. *The Modes and Morals of Psychotherapy*. New York: Holt, Rinehart and Winston.

Lorenz, K. 1966. *On Aggression*. New York: Bantam Books.

McClelland, D. 1975. *Power: The Inner Experience*. New York: Irvington.

Maccoby, E. E., ed. 1966. *The Development of Sex Differences*. Stanford: Stanford University Press.

McGoldrick, M., J. K. Pearce, and J. Giordano, eds. 1982. *Ethnicity and Family Therapy*. New York: Guilford Press.

Madow, L. 1974. *Anger*. New York: Macmillan.

Madsen, K. B. 1959. *Theories of Motivation*. Copenhagen: Munksgaard.

Maslow, A. 1954. *Motivation and Personality*. New York: Harper and Row.

Matthews, A. M., M. G. Gelder, and D. W. Johnston. 1981. *Agoraphobia: Nature and Treatment*. New York: Guilford Press.

Messer, M. H., et al. 1992. *Managing Anger: A Handbook of Proven Techniques*. Niles, Ill.: C.O.P.E. Publications.

Mischel, W. 1968. *Personality and Assessment*. New York: John Wiley & Sons.

Mousner, R. 1973. *Social Hierarchies*. New York: Schocken Books.

Neuman, G. G. 1987. *Origins of Human Aggression: Dynamics and Etiology*. New York: Human Sciences Press.

Norcross, J. C., ed. 1986. *Handbook of Eclectic Psychotherapy*. New York: Brunner/Mazel.

Oatley, K. 1992. *Best-Laid Schemes: A Psychology of Emotions*. Cambridge: Cambridge University Press.

Plato. 1941. *The Republic*. Jowett translation. New York: Modern Library.

Pruitt, D. G. 1981. *Negotiation Behavior*. New York: Academic Press.

Rainwater, L. 1970. *Behind Ghetto Walls: Black Family Life in a Federal Slum*. Chicago: Aldine.

Rebach, H. M., and J. G. Bruhn, eds. 1991. *Handbook of Clinical Sociology*. New York: Plenum Press.

Retzinger, S. M. 1991. *Violent Emotions: Shame and Rage in Marital Quarrels*. Newbury Park, Calif.: Sage Publications.

Rice, L., and L. Greenberg, eds. 1984. *Patterns of Change*. New York: Guilford Press.

Rochin, G. 1973. *Man's Aggression: The Defense of Self*. Boston: Gambit.

Rogers, C. 1951. *Client Centered Therapy*. Boston: Houghton-Mifflin.

———. 1961. *On Becoming a Person*. Boston: Houghton-Mifflin.

Rorty, A. O., ed. 1980. *Explaining Emotions*. Berkeley: University of California Press.

Rubin, T. I. 1969. *The Angry Book*. New York: Collier Books.

Ruesch, J. 1961. *Therapeutic Communication*. New York: W. W. Norton.

Sarton, M. 1982. *Anger*. New York: W. W. Norton.

Scarf, M. 1987. *Intimate Partners: Patterns in Love and Marriage*. New York: Random House.

Scheff, T. 1979. *Catharsis in Healing, Ritual, and Drama*. Berkeley: University of California Press.

Scheff, T. J., and S. M. Retzinger. 1991. *Emotions and Violence: Shame and Rage in Destructive Conflicts*. Lexington, Mass.: Lexington.

Stearns, C., and P. Stearns. 1986. *Anger: The Struggle for Emotional Control in American History*. Chicago: University of Chicago Press.

Strauss, A. 1978. *Negotiations: Varieties, Contexts, Processes and Social Order*. San Francisco: Jossey-Bass.

Sullivan, H. S. 1940. *Conceptions of Modern Psychiatry*. New York: W. W. Norton.

Tannen, D. 1990. *You Just Don't Understand: Women and Men in Conversation.* New York: William Morrow.

Tavris, C. 1982. *Anger: The Misunderstood Emotion.* New York: Simon and Schuster.

Turner, S. M., K. S. Calhoun, and H. E. Adams. 1981. *Handbook of Clinical Behavior Therapy.* New York: John Wiley & Sons.

Viorst, J. 1986. *Necessary Losses.* New York: Fawcett.

Warren, N. C. 1985. *Make Anger Your Ally: Harnessing Our Most Baffling Emotion.* New York: Doubleday.

Weber, M. 1947. *The Theory of Social and Economic Organization.* New York: Free Press.

Weiss, R. S. 1975. *Marital Separation.* New York: Basic Books.

————. 1990. *Staying the Course: The Emotional and Social Lives of Men Who Do Well at Work.* New York: Free Press.

White, R. W. 1959. "Motivation Reconsidered: The Concept of Competence." *Psychological Review* 66: 297–333.

Wolpe, J. 1973. *The Practice of Behavior Therapy.* Elmsford, N.Y.: Pergamon Press.

Zajonc, R. B. 1980. "Feeling and Thinking: Preferences Need No Inferences." *American Psychologist* 35: 151–73.

Zartman, I. W. 1978. *The Negotiation Process: Theories and Applications.* Beverly Hills: Sage Publications.

Index

About the Author

MELVYN L. FEIN is Assistant Professor of Sociology at Kennesaw State College and a Certified Clinical Sociologist. He is the author of *Role Change* (Praeger, 1990) and *Analyzing Psychotherapy* (Praeger, 1992).